I Never Knew That
About
THE IRISH

I Never Knew That
About
THE IRISH

CHRISTOPHER WINN

ILLUSTRATIONS BY
Mai Osawa

Thomas Dunne Books
St. Martin's Press
New York

THOMAS DUNNE BOOKS.
An imprint of St. Martin's Press.

I NEVER KNEW THAT ABOUT THE IRISH. Copyright © 2009 by Christopher
Winn. Illustrations © 2009 by Mai Osawa. All rights reserved. Printed in the
United States of America. For information, address St. Martin's Press,
175 Fifth Avenue, New York, N.Y. 10010.

www.stmartins.com

Library of Congress Cataloging-in-Publication Data

Winn, Christopher, 1958–
    I never knew that about the Irish / Christopher Winn ; illustrations by Mai
Osawa.—1st U.S. ed.
        p. cm.
    Originally published: London : Ebury Press, 2009.
    Includes index.
    ISBN 978-0-312-66164-9
    1. National characteristics, Irish—Miscellanea. 2. Ireland—Social life and
customs—Miscellanea. 3. Ireland—Description and travel—Miscellanea.
4. Ireland—Biography—Miscellanea. I. Title.
    DA925.W56 2011
    941.5—dc22

                                                            2010044881

First published in Great Britain by Ebury Press, an imprint of
Ebury Publishing, a Random House Group Company

First U.S. Edition: February 2011

10 9 8 7 6 5 4 3 2 1

For Ros

CONTENTS

Contents

──◄ Offaly ►──

──◄ Westmeath ►──

──◄ Wexford ►──

──◄ Wicklow ►──

MUNSTER

──◄ Clare ►──

Contents

ULSTER

Contents

PREFACE

―――――◆•••◆―――――

THE IRISH are philosophical and proud, they are poetic and passionate, they are great musicians and writers, inventors and pioneers. They are hospitable, full of fun, and with a wicked and self-deprecating sense of humour that translates into the most wonderful literature and art. Irish singers and entertainers, actors and designers carry a picture of Ireland to the far corners, and while Ireland is still seen by many as predominantly rural, modern Ireland has grown rich and successful in industry with talented entrepreneurs and retailers and designers.

But who are the Irish? George Bernard Shaw, the Nobel Prize-winning playwright, described himself thus. 'I am a genuine typical Irishman of the Danish, Norman, Cromwellian and Scotch invasions.' He might have added Celtic – the Scoth, or Scotii, were a Celtic Irish tribe who crossed the sea from Ulster to Argyll and then returned. And all over Ireland there are the remnants of Neolithic civilisations that occupied Ireland even before the Celts arrived from Europe.

Hence the Irish character is a fusion of all these different peoples and cultures, forged and shaped over time into an Irish identity and personality that then spread out again from Ireland across the world – the Irish diaspora is vast and vibrant with some 80 million people worldwide claiming Irish descent, 40 million of them in the United States.

The Irish island may be small but the Irish influence is huge and this book tells the story, not just of those who created Ireland, but also of those Irish who helped create new worlds across the oceans, and imbued them with a subtle Irish flavour and a distinctive Irish philosophy.

THE PROVINCES AND
COUNTIES OF IRELAND

THE IRISH ARE fond of their counties. As well as their own distinctive physical make up, each of Ireland's 32 counties has its own characters and personalities. The different landscapes of each county imbue those born and bred there with different characteristics, pose different challenges, evoke different moods and responses.

The placid lakes of Fermanagh or Westmeath give rise to a different kind of poetry or philosophy to the mountains of Wicklow or Kerry. The wild and lonely lands of Donegal inspire a different kind of music and literature to that which comes from the picturesque meadows of Dublin or Waterford. The quiet lacustrine countryside of Longford brings forth a different type of character from the windswept bastions of Antrim.

Hence any study of the Irish people must be sensitive to the Irish landscape and that landscape is most recognisably and comfortably divided into the counties.

The counties I have grouped into the four ancient Irish provinces or kingdoms of Connacht, Leinster, Munster and Ulster, for these provinces, still much loved, define an older Ireland from which the modern land and its people developed and grew. To understand the Ireland and the Irish of today it is essential to know from where they came.

CONNACHT

County Galway

REPUBLIC OF IRELAND'S LARGEST LAKE
✦ O'FLAHERTY'S CASTLE ✦ IRELAND'S THIRD LARGEST CITY
✦ A POET AND HIS DONKEY
✦ AN ANCIENT FISHING VILLAGE ✦ FRIENDSHIP RINGS
✦ IRELAND'S LONGEST RACING FESTIVAL
✦ GALWAY OYSTERS ✦ NORA BARNACLE
✦ THE CONNEMARA BUS

*Roman Catholic Cathedral of St Nicholas,
a prominent Galway landmark.*

◄ GALWAY FOLK ►

Richard Kirwan ✦ Robert O'Hara Burke ✦ Dan O'Hara ✦ John Ford
✦ Margaret Dolan ✦ William Joyce ✦ John Huston ✦ Peter O'Toole
✦ Francis Barrett

Coounty Galway is Ireland's second largest county and contains the 7,000 acres of Connemara National Park, opened in 1980, as well as Ireland's largest Gaeltacht, or Irish-speaking area.

Lough Corrib

The county is split almost into two by Lough Corrib, which covers an area of 68 square miles (176 sq km) and is the largest lake in the Republic and second largest in all Ireland. Lough Corrib empties into Galway Bay by way of the River Corrib which, at just under 4 miles (6 km) in length is thought to be the shortest river in Europe. The river, which is popular today with whitewater rafters, flows far too powerfully to be navigable and, in the 12th century, Ireland's first canal, the Friar's Cut, was constructed to allow boats to pass between Lough Corrib and the sea.

Aughnanure Castle – Home of the O'Flahertys

Near the south shore of Lough Corrib is Aughnanure Castle, a six-storey tower house located just outside the village of Oughterard, 'Gateway to Connemara'. It was built in the 16th century by the O'Flahertys, who controlled much of the land around Lough Corrib from a series of castles, of which Aughnanure was the most powerful. In the main hall one of the flagstones was hinged as a trapdoor so that unwelcome guests could be tipped into a watery dungeon below.

The O'Flahertys were amongst the most feared of the Galway chieftains, so much so that a sign was hung over the west gate of the Norman town of Galway that read, 'From the ferocious O'Flahertys may God protect us.' In 1545 Donal O'Flaherty married the celebrated pirate queen Grace O'Malley, and today the O'Flahertys are still an influential presence in County Galway, having contributed an impressive number of mayors to the city.

Galway City

GALWAY CITY, Ireland's third largest city, lies on the banks of the River Corrib where it flows into Galway Bay. The town was once renowned for its fleet of distinctive boats called Galway Hookers (from the Dutch word *holker*, meaning a small, manoeuvrable vessel), designed to cope with the heavy seas of Galway Bay and used for fishing and trading with Holland and Spain. Galway Hookers are no longer in service, but examples still turn up to annual sailing events and races.

Galway boasts two fine churches, THE COLLEGIATE CHURCH OF ST NICHOLAS (CHURCH OF IRELAND), THE LARGEST MEDIEVAL PARISH CHURCH IN IRELAND, and the imposing Roman Catholic Cathedral of St Nicholas.

In keeping with the Irish-speaking tradition of the region, Galway is home to An Taibhdhearc, a theatre founded in 1928 that puts on plays exclusively in Irish. In 1935 a statue of Padraic O Conaire, one of Galway's most cherished Irish writers, was unveiled by Eamon de Valera in Eyre Square, which is now a memorial garden to the American president John F. Kennedy, who visited the city shortly before his assassination in 1963. O Conaire's statue has since been moved to the Galway City Museum, beside the Spanish Arch.

Padraic O Conaire
1882–1992

PADRAIC O CONAIRE was born in Galway and grew to love the Irish language when he was at school in Rosmuc, a village in the heart of the Connemara Gaeltacht. After spending some time in London working as a civil servant he returned to Galway to teach and write Irish as part of the Gaelic Revival of the early 20th century. He was one of the first to use Gaelic for journalism and he also helped run events for the Gaelic League, an organisation dedicated to the preservation of the language. He would travel around Galway and Connemara with his donkey and cart, stopping at pubs and villages to tell stories, and perhaps his most popular work is his short story about how he came to meet his little black donkey, and the fun and games they had together.

The village became renowned as a classic example of an authentic Irish community, attracting numerous writers and artists, before its pretty jumble of thatched cottages was demolished in the 1930s and replaced with modern housing, and the village was subsumed into the city of Galway.

Claddagh Rings

Claddagh

When the town of Galway was founded in the 12th century as an Anglo-Norman stronghold, it was put down alongside one of Ireland's oldest fishing villages, CLADDAGH, which dates from the 5th century and took its name from the Irish word 'cladach', meaning stony shore. The native Gaelic community of Claddagh and the Anglo-Norman merchants of the town pretty much kept themselves apart, and from medieval times right into the 20th century, Claddagh was governed by its own mayor or 'king', and kept to its own laws and customs.

Come down from the days of old Claddagh is the traditional Claddagh friendship or wedding ring, fashioned as two hands clasping a heart, surmounted by a crown. Legend tells that the ring was originally designed by a Galway man, Richard Joyce, who was captured by an Algerian corsair while sailing to the West Indies in the 17th century and sold into the service of a goldsmith in Algiers. Joyce became so adept as a goldsmith himself, that when William III came to the throne and demanded that the Moors release all their British prisoners, his goldsmith master offered half his own fortune and his daughter's hand in marriage if Joyce would stay on as a partner. The Galway man was already betrothed to a Galway lass, however, and he returned to Claddagh and gave his love the ring he had designed and made especially for her during his long exile. Today, Claddagh rings have become a cultural symbol worn by those of Irish descent all over the world.

Galway Races

They have been racing horses in County Galway since the 13th century, but the first racing festival held at BALLYBRIT, home of the present GALWAY RACES, was in August 1869, when over 40,000 people attended the two-day event. Today, the summer festival is held in the last week of July and lasts for seven days, THE ONLY WEEK-LONG RACING FESTIVAL IN IRELAND OR BRITAIN. The main race, the Galway Plate, is run on the Wednesday, while Thursday is Ladies Day and includes a 'best-dressed lady' competition.

Galway Races form the premier festival in the Irish racing calendar, and are as much a social event as a festival of horse racing, with champagne and oyster bars, jazz bands, trade stands and competitions. The original grandstand, built in the 1950s and replaced in 1999, boasted THE LONGEST BAR IN THE WORLD (now thought to be found in Düsseldorf).

Galway Oyster Festival

Founded in 1954 by Brian Collins, manager of the Great Southern Hotel, as a means of extending the tourist season, the GALWAY OYSTER FESTIVAL has become one of the world's premier oyster festivals. It is held in Claddagh over four days and nights in September, the first month of the oyster season, and attracts visitors from all over the world to sample the oysters, along with plenty of Guinness, vintage car displays, street entertainments, music and the Oyster Pearl beauty contest. The main highlight is the hotly contested World Oyster Opening Championship. Film director John Huston is said to have consumed over 3,000 oysters when he attended the festival in 1960.

Nora Barnacle
1884–1951

Nora Barnacle was born in Connemara, the daughter of a baker. She had just turned 13 when her mother threw Nora's father out for drinking too much, and mother and daughter went to live in Nora's uncle's house on Bowling Green in Galway City, now a museum in her memory. Almost immediately Nora met her first love, a 16-year-old schoolteacher called Michael Feeney, who tragically died that year of pneumonia.

Three years later, another of Nora's sweethearts, Michael Bodkin, also died of pneumonia, having stood outside Nora's window in the heavy rain, serenading her.

In 1903, after her uncle learned of an affair she was conducting with a local Protestant boy, Nora was sent away to Dublin, and it was while working as a chambermaid at Finn's Hotel that she met her future husband, the writer James Joyce.

Their first romantic encounter took place on 16 June 1904, and Joyce later chose this date as the setting for his masterpiece, the novel *Ulysses*, about an ordinary day in Dublin seen mainly through the eyes of Leopold Bloom, a Jewish advertisement canvasser.

The Connemara Bus

The Connemara Bus, driven by Hugh Ryan, is a 1949 Bedford bus that takes tourists for a four-hour drive around Connemara from Galway City, and IS THE OLDEST OPERATING BUS IN IRELAND.

The original Connemara Bus, a wooden vehicle built on to the chassis of a 1932 Bedford truck, was driven

---

Bloomsday

Since 1954, June 16th, or 'BLOOMSDAY', has been observed as a holiday in Ireland, during which Joyce's life is celebrated with readings, dramatisations and street parties. While the biggest celebrations are in Dublin, where aficionados retrace Bloom's footsteps around the city, Bloomsday is also celebrated in various places around the world that share a connection to Joyce or the novel, such as Philadelphia in the USA, where the original handwritten manuscript of *Ulysses* is kept at the Rosenbach Museum, or Hungary's oldest town, Szombathely, birthplace of Bloom's father Virag, a Jewish émigré.

by Hugh Ryan's grandfather and used to ferry the women of Connemara and their produce to market in Galway.

Connemara is famous for its green marble, and is IRELAND'S ONLY SOURCE OF TRUE MARBLE.

Well, I never *knew this*
about
GALWAY FOLK

Richard Kirwan

———◄ 1733–1812 ►———

RICHARD KIRWAN, scientist and eccentric, was born in CLOUGH-BALLYMORE, near Kinvara. In 1787 he published his most famous work, 'Essay on Phlogiston', which held that phlogiston was the substance given off by combustion – a theory that was later disproved when it was discovered that combustion involved burning oxygen from the

atmosphere. He was also a colourful figure in the fields of chemistry, geology and meteorology and is credited with introducing the study of mineralogy to Ireland in his 'Elements of Mineralogy' – the first essay on the subject in English. In 1799 he became President of the Royal Irish Academy.

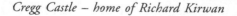

Cregg Castle – home of Richard Kirwan

Richard Kirwan's family were one of the 14 'Tribes of Galway', powerful merchant families made wealthy from trade with the Continent, who dominated Galway politics from the 12th century until the late 18th century. Unlike most of the tribes, who were of Anglo-Norman origin, the Kirwans had Irish roots.

In 1754 Richard Kirwan inherited CREGG CASTLE, near the village of Corandulla north of Galway City, when his older brother was killed in a duel. Cregg Castle was built by the Kirwans in 1648 on the site of a 13th-century castle and was one of the last fortified houses to be constructed in Ireland. Richard put up a laboratory in the grounds, the remains of which can still be seen. Cregg Castle is now a hotel.

ROBERT O'HARA BURKE (1821–61) THE FIRST MAN TO CROSS AUSTRALIA FROM SOUTH TO NORTH, was born near Craughwell. Burke became an army officer and then a policeman, and emigrated to Australia in 1853. He was chosen to lead an expedition, which became known as the Burke and Wills expedition (along with English surveyor William Wills), whose aim was to travel from Melbourne to the Gulf of Carpentaria, on Australia's northern coast. They succeeded in reaching the Gulf, but both Burke and Wills died on the return journey at a place called Cooper's Creek, from where their bodies were eventually recovered and laid to rest in Melbourne.

Sure it's poor I am today,
For God gave and took away,
And left without a home poor Dan
  O'Hara
With these matches in my hand,
In the frost and snow I stand
So it's here I am today your broken
  hearted . . .
Dan O'Hara's Song

DAN O'HARA was a tenant farmer who lived with his wife and seven children in a small stone cottage in the shadow of the Twelve Bens in Connemara. Theirs was a simple but happy life, typical of rural 19th-century Ireland, full of storytelling and singing round the turf fire of an evening. Unfortunately, most of Dan's land was given over to potatoes, and in 1845, at the start of the Great Famine, the crop failed,

leaving Dan with no income and unable to pay the rent. He and his family were evicted and had no choice but to emigrate to America. Dan's wife, and three of their children, died on the voyage, and the survivors arrived in New York destitute. The children were taken into care and Dan was reduced to selling matches on the streets. His story has been made famous in song.

Film director JOHN FORD (1894–1973) was born John Martin Feeney (sometimes Sean Aloysius O'Feeny) in Cape Elizabeth, Maine, to Irish parents from County Galway. Remembered especially for his classic western *Stagecoach* (1939) which began his cinematic partnership with John Wayne, Ford is THE ONLY DIRECTOR EVER TO HAVE WON FOUR BEST DIRECTOR OSCARS, for *The*

Informer in 1935, *The Grapes of Wrath* in 1940, *How Green Was My Valley* in 1941 and *The Quiet Man*, which was filmed entirely in Ireland, in 1952. He had a five-year affair with Katharine Hepburn who, with four wins, has won more Best Actress Oscars than anyone. In later life Ford was famous for wearing a trademark black eye-patch.

MARGARET DOLAN (1893–2004), THE OLDEST WOMAN IN IRELAND when she died aged 111, was born in TUAM.

Buried in Bohermore Cemetery in Galway City is WILLIAM JOYCE (1906–46), founder of the National Socialist League and broadcaster of Nazi propaganda in the Second World War. Joyce had an Irish father and, although born in New York, he grew up in Galway. Fanatically anti-Jewish and anti-Communist, Joyce was unwilling to fight against Hitler and at the start of the war he fled to Germany, where he got work as an English language broadcaster. Accused by the *Daily Express* of using 'English of the haw-haw, "dammit-get-out-of-my-way" variety', Joyce became known as Lord Haw-Haw. He was executed for high treason at Wandsworth prison in London in 1946, and his remains were reinterred at Bohermore in 1976.

John Huston
◄ 1906–87 ►

St Clerans in Craughwell, a small village about 10 miles (16 km) east of Galway. His daughter, the actress Anjelica Huston, went to school for a while at Kylemore Abbey in Connemara. In 1948 Huston won two Oscars for *The Treasure of the Sierra Madre* (for Best Director and Best Screenplay), and in 1985, at the age of 79, he became THE OLDEST PERSON EVER TO BE NOMINATED FOR THE BEST DIRECTOR OSCAR, for *Prizzi's Honor*. Huston was also an artist and in 1982 was asked to design that year's label for Château Mouton Rothschild. St Clerans is now a hotel.

The American-born actor and film director JOHN HUSTON (*The Maltese Falcon, The African Queen*) was of Scots-Irish descent. In the 1950s he became an Irish citizen and bought and restored a Georgian house called

Film actor PETER O'TOOLE is thought to have been born in Connemara in 1932, although he also has a birth certificate from a hospital in Leeds, Yorkshire. He is best known for his role as T.E. Lawrence in the

Kylemore Abbey

1962 film *Lawrence of Arabia* and is also THE MOST NOMINATED ACTOR NEVER TO ACTUALLY WIN AN OSCAR – with a grand total of eight nominations. In 2003 he accepted an Academy Honorary Award for his lifetime contribution to film. In honour of his Irish ancestry he always wears one item of green clothing, usually a sock.

FRANCIS BARRETT was born in 1977 into a family of Galway Travellers, and at age 19 he was chosen to represent Ireland at boxing in the 1996 Atlanta Olympics, becoming the FIRST TRAVELLER TO REPRESENT IRELAND IN ANY SPORT AT OLYMPIC LEVEL and THE FIRST TRAVELLER TO CARRY THE NATIONAL FLAG AT THE OPENING CEREMONY.

County Leitrim

CRUISING CAPITAL OF THE SHANNON ✦ FATHER OF
INDUSTRIAL GERMANY ✦ HARPISTS AND PRESIDENTS
✦ A BENEVOLENT DESPOT ✦ A FINE MODERN WRITER

*Carrick-on-Shannon,
'the cruising capital of the Shannon'.*

◄ LEITRIM FOLK ►

Bishop Patrick O'Healy ✦ Robert Strawbridge ✦ Revd Joseph Digges

COUNTY LEITRIM is the most sparsely populated county in the Republic of Ireland. Much of the county is covered in water and it is often remarked that land in Co. Leitrim is sold not by the acre but by the gallon.

Carrick-on-Shannon

The county town, CARRICK-ON-SHANNON, is described as 'the cruising capital of the Shannon'. It is a popular base for boats using the Shannon Erne Waterway, which links Ireland's two greatest rivers and forms part of THE LONGEST NAVIGABLE INLAND WATERWAY IN EUROPE, stretching for 250 miles (400 km) from Lough Erne in Co. Fermanagh to the mouth of the River Shannon at Limerick.

Irish Father of Industrial Germany

The Shannon Erne Waterway, opened in 1994, is actually the restored Ballinamore and Ballyconnell Navigation, which was constructed in 1860 as part of the Ulster Canal, meant to link Limerick with Belfast. The Navigation was designed and executed by the Dublin-born engineer WILLIAM

THOMAS MULVANY (1806–85), who also established numerous other building and irrigation projects to help as job creation schemes during the Great Famine.

On a trip to London, Mulvany met Michael Corr, an Irish businessman born in Slane in Co. Meath, and brought up in Brussels where his family had fled after the uprising led by Robert Emmet in 1803. After establishing that Mulvany was an experienced surveyor, Corr asked him to have a look at some coal deposits he owned in the Ruhr valley in Germany, near the village of Gelsenkirchen.

At that time Germany had very little mining expertise and imported most of its coal from England, but Mulvany recognised that there was considerable potential here for development. And so, with backing from some wealthy Irish investors, and using the experience he had gained draining rivers and bog-land in the west of Ireland, Mulvany set to work exploiting the rich coal seams of the Ruhr valley. He brought over skilled English miners from Durham, who settled in Düsseldorf, and in 1856, on St Patrick's Day, he opened the Ruhr's first deep coal-mine, which he named HIBERNIA.

Two more mines followed in quick succession, SHAMROCK and ERIN, and at the same time Mulvany built up the area's industrial infrastructure with a transport network of railways and canals, thus creating the beginnings of Germany's mighty Ruhr valley industrial complex. Mulvany, the 'FATHER OF INDUSTRIAL GERMANY', is commemorated in Düsseldorf with his own street, Mulvanystrasse.

An interesting side note to the development of coal-mining in the Ruhr valley region was the discovery in 1856 of the well-preserved skeleton of a primitive man, the first recognised human fossil. The remote and little-known valley west of Düsseldorf where he was found is called NEANDERTAL, or 'Neander valley', and this name has since become the generally accepted term for an ancient or prehistoric man.

Mohill

MOHILL is a pleasant small town set on a gentle slope in peaceful lacustrine country in the south of Co. Leitrim. TURLOUGH O'CAROLAN (1670–1738), Ireland's National Composer, and the last of the traditional Irish harpist composers, married Mary Maguire in Mohill and they had their home in the town for many years. In 1986 a bronze statue of the harpist was unveiled by President Patrick Hillery in the town centre.

One of the main cross streets in Mohill is called Hyde Street in memory of Ireland's first president, DOUGLAS HYDE, who spent much of his childhood on this street, where his father and grandfather lived. A keen champion of the Gaelic Revival, Hyde wrote the first play performed in the Irish language, *Casadh an tSugain,* or *The Twisting of the Rope,* presented in 1901.

Lough Rynn Castle

Just to the south of Mohill is LOUGH RYNN CASTLE, built in 1832 for the Earl of Leitrim, and the most famous 'big house' in the county. During the Great Famine of 1845–9, the landlord, WILLIAM SYDNEY CLEMENTS, LORD LEITRIM (1806–78), gained a reputation for running the estate with 'benevolent paternalism'. However, after he became the 3rd Earl on the death of his father in 1854, he apparently turned into a ruthless despot, evicting both Protestant and Catholic tenants without mercy and, according to Shane Leslie in his play *Lord Mulroy's Ghost,* despoiling the virgin daughters of his tenants.

Whether Lord Leitrim deserved such calumny is open to debate. In 1860 he narrowly escaped an assassination attempt while walking down the main street in Mohill when a local man, James Murphy, took a shot at him with a blunderbuss for refusing a duel to 'take satisfaction for your ruffianly conduct towards my wife'. It turned out that Murphy took exception to anyone who even talked to his wife, but the attack, and further similar incidents, for which the perpetrators were not punished very heavily, convinced the Earl that he was being persecuted and this no doubt contributed to his isolation and strange behaviour. He was finally the victim of a successful assassination in Milford, Co. Donegal in 1878 by three men, one of whom was said to be the father of a girl badly treated by the Earl.

Lough Rynn Castle is now a hotel. The hotel library was dedicated to the writer JOHN McGAHERN (1934–2006), not long after his death. McGahern had lived

for the last 30 years of his life in the village of Fenagh, near Mohill, where he worked a small farm and wrote his most celebrated novel *Amongst Women,* which tells the story of an embittered ex-IRA man and his family, and is set largely in Co. Leitrim. Former Taoiseach Bertie Ahern, who performed the dedication ceremony, called John McGahern 'one of Ireland's finest modern writers'.

John McGahern

Well, I never knew this
about
LEITRIM FOLK

THE FIRST IRISH BISHOP TO DIE FOR HIS FAITH, BISHOP PATRICK O'HEALY (1545–79) was born in DROMAHAIR. He became a Franciscan as a boy and studied in Spain at the new University of Alcala, near Madrid. In 1576 he travelled to Rome and was made Bishop of Mayo. On his return to Mayo, O'Healy was arrested on suspicion of colluding with the Pope and King Philip of Spain to invade Ireland, and was eventually executed at Kilmallock in Co. Limerick for failing to swear the Oath of Supremacy acknowledging Elizabeth I as Head of the Church.

THE FIRST METHODIST PREACHER IN AMERICA, ROBERT STRAWBRIDGE (1734–81), was born in DRUMSNA into the only Protestant family at that time in the south of Co. Leitrim. Converted to Methodism by John Wesley, he preached widely throughout Ireland until he received the call to 'go to the New World and take the Gospel to the frontier'. In 1760, at the age of 26, he sailed to America and settled at Sam's Creek, in Maryland, where he rented a two-storey log house which he opened for Bible study and preaching. Here he held the first Methodist classes in America and baptised the first American Methodists. In 1764 he built the

Log Meeting House nearby, where the first Methodist Society of America was formed and which became known as the Mother Church of American Methodism. The Meeting House was demolished in 1844, but Robert Strawbridge's own house still stands and is now an American Landmark.

The 'Father of Irish Beekeeping', the REVD JOSEPH DIGGES (1858–1933), lived for most of his life in MOHILL. In 1883 he came to Mohill as curate, and two years later became private chaplain to the Clement family (Earls of Leitrim) of Lough Rynn Castle, which is when he took up beekeeping.

For over 30 years between 1901 and his death in 1933 he edited *The Irish Bee Journal*, later *The Beekeeper's Gazette*. He was a conscientious editor and only ever failed to produce four issues including, much to his chagrin, the May 1916 issue, which was blown up *en route* to the printers during the Easter Rising. In 1904 he published *The Irish Bee Guide*, or *The Practical Bee Guide, a Manual of Modern Beekeeping*, which became, and has remained, Ireland's standard work on beekeeping. Although he is buried in Dublin, there is a stained-glass memorial window to him in his church at Clooncahir, just outside Mohill.

County Mayo

A Saxon Abbey ✦ Only Mosque Outside Dublin
✦ Ireland's Largest National Park
✦ Castlebar Races ✦ Museum of Country Life
✦ The Abbey That Wouldn't Die ✦ Cross of Cong
✦ Browne Country

Ballintubber Abbey, 'the abbey that wouldn't die'.

◄ MAYO FOLK ►

Ulick Bourke ✦ Michael Davitt ✦ Margaret Burke Sheridan
✦ Charles Haughey ✦ Mary Robinson

Mhaigh Eo

Castlebar

The name Mayo – Mhaigh Eo, or 'plain of the yew trees' – first appears with MAYO ABBEY, the remains of which can be found in flat lands some 12 miles (19 km) south of Castlebar. Founded in 668 by St Colman of Lindisfarne, Mayo Abbey is THE ONLY ABBEY IN IRELAND ESTABLISHED FOR SAXON MONKS, and it became a great centre of learning. Among the Saxon scholars who studied there, it is said, was Alfred the Great, one of whose sons is buried here.

Opened in 1998, BALLYCROY NATIONAL PARK in the north-west of County Mayo is Ireland's sixth and newest national park. Covering nearly 46 square miles (119 sq km), it is also IRELAND'S LARGEST NATIONAL PARK, and one of the largest areas of blanket bog left in Europe.

THE FIRST-EVER HURLING MATCHES took place on the great plains of Moytura.

IRELAND'S FIRST PURPOSE-BUILT MOSQUE, and the only mosque outside Dublin, was opened in Ballyhaunis in 1987. It is also THE MOST WESTERLY MOSQUE IN EUROPE.

Mayo's county town was founded in 1613 by John Bingham, ancestor of the Earls of Lucan, on the site of the 12th-century castle of the de Barrys, hence Castlebar, or 'castle of the Barrys'.

During the rebellion of 1798, on 27 August, a combined force of French troops and Irish rebels under the command of the French General Humbert attacked the British garrison at Castlebar and inflicted a crushing defeat. The British soldiers fled in such a panic that the battle became known as the 'Castlebar Races'.

After his victory General Humbert set up a provisional government in Castlebar and declared a Republic of Connacht, as a prelude to a Republic of Ireland. A member of a local landowning family, John Moore, was appointed as its president. The Republic, however, was never formally recognised by France and suffered a fatal blow when Humbert's French troops surrendered to the British at the Battle of Ballinamuck on 8 September.

On 21 October 1879, the Irish National Land League was founded at the Imperial Hotel in Castlebar. The League was formed to help tenant farmers gain ownership of the land on which they worked and, in pursuance of this goal, instigated various peaceful forms of civil unrest during what became known as the Land War. The most effective type of protest the League employed was the 'boycott', named after a particularly intransigent land agent called Captain Charles Boycott, whereby tenants, tradespeople and the local community would refuse to deal with or engage with an unpopular landlord.

Lord Lucan

The most infamous member of the Bingham family who founded Castlebar was RICHARD BINGHAM, 7TH EARL OF LUCAN, born in the town in 1934. In November 1974 he disappeared after his children's nanny Sandra Rivett was found murdered in the basement of his estranged wife's home in Lower Belgrave Street in London. The alarm was raised when Lady Lucan ran into a nearby pub, the Plumber's Arms, covered in blood, shouting 'Murder! Murder!' She later claimed that Lord Lucan had killed Rivett by mistake, thinking it was her, his wife.

Later that night Lord Lucan turned up at the house of his friend Susan Maxwell-Scott at Uckfield, in Sussex, where he made several phone calls and then left. She was the last person known to have set eyes on him. Three days later the police found his Ford Corsair abandoned near the docks at Newhaven, covered with bloodstains, and in the boot a piece of lead-piping similar to one found at the crime scene. Lord Lucan has never been seen since, although there have been numerous 'sightings' over the years, the most recent being in Australia in 2000.

In 1999 Lord Lucan was ruled officially dead, but his son George is still not able to claim the title because no body has been found to provide 'definite proof' that the 7th Earl is deceased.

Turlough Park House

Set in the grounds of TURLOUGH PARK HOUSE, a massive Victorian pile just east of Castlebar, is the Museum of Country Life, where various displays illustrate aspects of

Turlough Park House

Irish rural life from between 1850 and 1950. It is the first branch of the National Museum of Ireland to be located outside of Dublin.

Ballintubber Abbey

BALLINTUBBER ABBEY, 7 miles (11 km) south of Castlebar, sits on the

Tochar Phadraig, the ancient pilgrim path taken by St Patrick on his way to Croagh Patrick, the Holy Mountain. The abbey was founded in 1216 by Cathal O'Conor, King of Connacht, and has become known as 'The Abbey that Wouldn't Die'. Although suppressed by Henry VIII and left roofless by Oliver Cromwell, Ballintubber Abbey can boast THE LONGEST UNBROKEN ATTENDANCE RECORD IN IRELAND, with mass being celebrated here every day for nearly 800 years.

Louisburgh

LOUISBURGH, a smart, breezy little town of four Georgian streets on the southern shores of Clew Bay, was

Cathal O'Conor was the last High King of Ireland before the Anglo-Norman invasion. His father, Turlough O'Conor, ordered the making of Mayo's greatest medieval treasure, the ornate CROSS OF CONG, behind which the monks of the monastery at Cong used to process. Made of oak and covered in gilt bronze, the cross stands 30 inches (76 cm) high and is said to contain a fragment of the True Cross – there is an inscription which reads: 'In this cross is preserved the cross on which suffered the Founder of the World,' and another 'Pray for Turlough O'Conor, King of Ireland.' The Cross of Cong is now in the National Museum in Dublin.

founded in 1795 by John Browne, the
3rd Lord Altamont. In 1758 Browne's
nephew had taken part in the capture
of Louisburgh in Nova Scotia, and
Co. Mayo's Louisburgh was named in
honour of this feat.

CLEW BAY, which is studded with
365 islands, one for each day of the
year, was the domain of the pirate
queen GRACE O'MALLEY (1530–
1603), ancestor of Lord Altamont –
the present Lord Altamont, Jeremy
Browne, is her only remaining direct
descendant. Grace O'Malley's life is
remembered in the Grainne ni
Mhaille Centre in Church Street,
Louisburgh.

Not far from Louisburgh, at
Bunlahinch near Roonagh Lough, is
IRELAND'S OLDEST BRIDGE, a rare
'clapper' bridge thought to date from
the 12th century. Made from 30 big
limestone slabs that rest on rough
stone piers about 3 ft (1 m) above the
water, it is 50 ft (15 m) long and has
37 arches, MORE ARCHES THAN ANY
OTHER BRIDGE IN IRELAND.

The Brownes of Westport House

WESTPORT HOUSE, which sits above
the River Carrowbeg near where it
runs into Clew Bay, is the ancestral
home of the BROWNE FAMILY, THE

FIRST ENGLISH FAMILY TO SETTLE
IN THE WEST OF IRELAND and the
last direct descendants of the pirate
queen Grace O'Malley. The Brownes
arrived in County Mayo in 1580 when
landowner John Browne, the first
person to accurately map Connacht,
settled in the tiny village of The
Neale, near Kilmaine. His great-
grandson, Colonel John Browne,
married Maud Bourke, daughter of
Theobald Bourke, 3rd Viscount
Mayo, who was Grace O'Malley's
grandson.

Browne acquired many of the
estates of his in-laws, including
the ruined castle of Cathair-na-Mart,
the 'stone fort of the bees', which
had been destroyed in 1588. Using
the foundations of the castle, the
dungeons of which can still be seen
inside the house today, Browne began
to build a fortified house on the site
in about 1685, but construction
stopped when Browne, as a Catholic,
took the side of James II against
William of Orange and almost lost
the estate, despite being involved in

drafting the Treaty of Limerick in 1691.

John Browne's son Peter managed to hold on to Cathair-na-Mart and changed the name to Westport. Then his son John, who was educated at Oxford and became a Protestant, commissioned the German architect Richard Cassels, who was living in Ireland, to design a classical house incorporating the core of the original begun by his grandfather. John, who became the 1st Earl of Altamont in 1771, also started to lay out the new town of Westport, to replace the old village, which he considered to be too close to the house.

John's grandson, the 3rd Earl of Altamont, brought in the English architect James Wyatt to complete the house, and the sumptuous dining-room at Westport House is considered to be amongst James Wyatt's finest work. Wyatt was also asked to oversee the design the new town of Westport.

In 1800 John Browne, the 3rd Earl of Altamont, was created Marquess of Sligo, and the family have continued to live at Westport House ever since, the present owner being the 10th Marquess.

In 1960 the house was opened to the public for the first time, and the grounds now include a small zoo and teashop.

Westport

The town of Westport, laid out to the designs of James Wyatt at the end of the 18th century, is one of Ireland's few planned towns and is considered to be County Mayo's most elegant show town. Particularly picturesque are the tree-lined Mall, which runs along the River Carrowbeg, and Bridge Street, where colourful pubs and shops jostle for attention. One such establishment, which specialises in musical evenings is Matt Molloy's, owned by The Chieftains' flautist, MATT MOLLOY.

Irish Republican JOHN MACBRIDE (1865–1916) was born in Westport. In 1903 he married the revolutionary Irish nationalist Maud Gonne, the object of poet W.B. Yeats's long unrequited love, and they had a child Sean MacBride, who would go on to be chairman of Amnesty International and win a Nobel Peace Prize in 1974. John MacBride was executed for his part in the Easter Rising in 1916.

Well, I never knew this
about
MAYO FOLK

ULICK BOURKE (1829–87) founder of the Gaelic Union, was born in Linnenhall Street in CASTLEBAR, where there is a plaque marking his birthplace. The Gaelic Union was the forerunner of the Gaelic League founded by Douglas Hyde in 1893, and was dedicated to promoting the use of the Irish language.

Michael Davitt
—◄ 1846–1906 ►—

MICHAEL DAVITT was born in the village of STRAIDE, situated between Foxford and Castlebar. His parents were evicted for rent arrears during the Great Famine, and the family decided to take their chances in England rather than suffer the workhouse. At the age of 11, Davitt lost an arm while operating a spinning wheel in a Lancashire cotton mill.

As a young man Davitt became interested in Irish history and joined the Irish Republican Brotherhood to agitate for Irish independence. He was the leading figure behind the founding of the Irish Land League in Castlebar in 1879. The success of the League's campaign of peaceful protest, as devised by Davitt, is said to have inspired Mahatma Gandhi to employ similar methods in his own struggle against the British Empire.

In 1887 Davitt, by now a prominent political figure, performed the opening ceremony of the Michael Davitt swing bridge linking the mainland to Ireland's biggest island, Achill Island. This bridge was replaced in 1947 by a new Michael Davitt Bridge, which itself was widened in 2007.

Michael Davitt is buried near the ruined friary in his home town of Straide.

Margaret Burke Sheridan
—◄ 1889–1958 ►—

IRELAND'S FIRST PRIMA DONNA, MARGARET BURKE SHERIDAN, was born in CASTLEBAR. Orphaned at four years old, Margaret was raised in a Dublin orphanage, where her talent was soon recognised by the nuns, and she was sent to London for voice training. The radio pioneer Guglielmo Marconi got to hear about her while he was staying in the west

The paternal grandparents of former US First Lady PAT NIXON (1912–93) emigrated to America from County Mayo. Pat was born Thelma Catherine Ryan on the eve of St Patrick's Day, so her father called her his 'St Patrick's babe in the morn' – and the name 'Pat' stuck. Her husband Richard Milhous Nixon also had Irish roots, his ancestors hailing from County Antrim.

CHARLES HAUGHEY (1925–2006), fourth leader of Fianna Fail and sixth Taoiseach, was born in CASTLEBAR.

of Ireland, working on his transatlantic radio station in Galway, and he arranged for her to perform at La Scala in Milan. There 'La Sheridan', as she became known, enjoyed a tempestuous professional relationship with Toscanini, who described her as the 'Empress from Ireland' – in contrast to the name she used for herself, which was 'Maggie from Mayo'. She became particularly known for performing the works of Puccini, by whom she was coached personally.

Fiery and spirited, she exhibited all the expected characteristics of a true prima donna, but underneath she was shy and vulnerable. She retired suddenly in 1935 and returned to Dublin, where she lived quietly for the rest of her life. Surprisingly, she never sang professionally in Ireland, her home country.

MARY ROBINSON, THE FIRST FEMALE PRESIDENT OF IRELAND, was born in BALLINA in 1944.

County Roscommon

LAST LARGE-SCALE COAL-MINE
✦ ANCIENT CAPITAL OF CONNACHT
✦ UNIQUE RAILWAY STATION ✦ THATCHED WINDMILL
✦ A MEDIEVAL ABBEY AND A HOLLYWOOD STAR
✦ ISLANDS IN THE LOUGH ✦ HARP FESTIVAL

*Boyle Abbey, noted for its exquisite
carvings of beasts and foliage.*

◀ ROSCOMMON FOLK ▶

Arthur Murphy ✦ James Curley ✦ John Blake Dillon ✦ Roderic O'Conor
✦ Thomas Flynn ✦ Matt Molloy

COUNTY ROSCOMMON is the only inland county in Connacht and the longest shoreline with the River Shannon of any Irish county.

Arigna

The ARIGNA coalfield, in the north of the county near Lough Allen, was closed in 1990, having been THE LAST LARGE-SCALE COAL-MINE IN IRELAND. Coal had been mined there since the end of the 18th century, and it was coal from the Arigna mine that was used at Ireland's first coal-fired iron foundry, set up at Arigna by the O'Reilly brothers in 1788. Today the Arigna Mining Experience allows visitors to tour the mine and experience conditions at the coalface.

Cruachan

TULSK, in the middle of the county, stands close to Rathcroghan, THE LARGEST CELTIC ROYAL SITE IN EUROPE, where a low, flat-topped mound is thought to be all that is left of CRUACHAN, ancient capital of Connacht and palace home of the legendary Queen Maeve. It was here that the two bulls fought to the death at the end of the tale of The Tain, or 'The Cattle Raid of Cooley.'

Castlerea

The HELL'S KITCHEN RAILWAY MUSEUM, created by Sean Browne in Castlerea, is the first railway museum of its kind in Ireland and is housed in a pub in the main street. The museum, which includes an A55 diesel engine, along with station boards, lamps, signalling equipment and timetables, possesses THE LARGEST COLLECTION OF RAILWAY MEMORABILIA IN THE REPUBLIC.

Elphin

The village of ELPHIN, where Oliver Goldsmith and Oscar Wilde's father William went to school, boasts the only working windmill in the west of Ireland. Built around 1730, the windmill has an unusual revolving roof made of thatch, and the sails are turned into the wind by using cart-wheels on a circular track. After being in use for over 100 years, grinding meal for the local population, the mill was left derelict until its restoration by local community enterprise in 1992. It is now open to the public.

Boyle

Sitting prettily on the banks of its own river, with the Curlew Hills as a picturesque backdrop, BOYLE is Co. Roscommon's show town. It boasts Connacht's most important medieval abbey, a Cistercian house founded in 1161 and now one of Ireland's largest and best-preserved ruins. The church, which was consecrated in 1218, is a splendid example of the transition from Norman to Gothic and is particularly noted for the exquisite carvings of beasts and foliage on the capitals of the arcade pillars.

Boyle also has some fine Georgian houses, the noblest of which is King House, built in 1730 by Sir Henry King. When the King family moved to Rockingham House (*see* page 34), King House was taken over by the Connaught Rangers and later the Irish army. It is now a tourist centre and houses interactive exhibitions of Roscommon history. The Boyle Arts Festival is held here in July.

Boyle is the birthplace of Hollywood actress MAUREEN O'SULLIVAN (1911–98), whose father was an officer in the Connaught Rangers based at King House. One of MGM's biggest stars in the 1930s, she is best remembered for playing Jane opposite Johnny Weissmuller's Tarzan, and has a star on the Hollywood Walk of Fame at 6541 Hollywood Boulevard.

She had seven children by her first husband, Australian writer John Farrow, including actress MIA FARROW, who was married at 21 to Frank Sinatra, 30 years her senior, and at 24 to conductor André Previn. In the 1980s she starred in many of the best films produced by her then partner Woody Allen.

Lough Key

The almost circular LOUGH KEY sits in beautiful wooded country to the north of Boyle, and is thought by many to be the loveliest lake in

Ireland, quite a claim in a country renowned for its glorious lacustrine scenery. Lough Key contains 30 islands, including Castle Island, where there are the remains of a castle that belonged to the MacDermots, Kings of Moylurg. The MacDermots, once a prominent Connacht family, were patrons and abbots of Boyle Abbey, where many of them are buried.

The *Annals of Lough Key*, part of the celebrated *Chronicles of Ireland*, were compiled on Castle Island, and the *Annals of Boyle* were put together on Trinity Island. They now reside in the Library at Trinity College, Dublin.

Buried on Trinity Island is the headless body of Sir Clifford Conyers, commander of the English forces defeated by Hugh Roe O'Donnell at the Battle of Curlew Pass in 1599, during the Nine Years' War (1594–1603).

Local folklore tells of Una Bhan, a daughter of a MacDermot chief, who fell in love with the son of a rival family. Her enraged father confined Una to Castle Island, where she pined away and died. Every day Una's heartbroken lover, Thomas McCostello, swam out to the island to lie beside her grave, until one day he caught pneumonia and died. Una's distraught father buried Thomas next to his daughter, beneath a rose tree that grew up and became entwined over the grave in a lover's knot.

Rockingham

South of the lough is the Lough Key Forest Park, formed from part of the Rockingham estate, owned until 1957 by the King family who built King House in Boyle. At the heart of the estate once stood Rockingham House, a rather severe pile designed by John Nash. It burnt down in 1957, but the impressive grounds survive and a viewing tower stands in its place.

Rockingham House

Harp Festival

The O'Carolan Harp Festival, held in August in Keadue, commemorates Ireland's National Composer Turlough O'Carolan, who spent his last years in the village and is buried in the old church at Kilronan nearby. The festival attracts harpists and traditional musicians from around the world for competitions and concerts.

*Well, I never knew this
about*
ROSCOMMON FOLK

Writer ARTHUR MURPHY (1727–1805) was born in CLOMQUIN. Educated in France, he entered the law as a clerk in Cork and then practised as a barrister at Lincoln's Inn in London, while also writing plays and working as a journalist. Murphy is best remembered for his biographies of Samuel Johnson, Henry Fielding and the actor David Garrick.

Astronomer JAMES CURLEY (1796–1889) was born in ATHLEAGUE. At the age of 21 he emigrated to Philadelphia and ended up at the oldest Roman Catholic university in the United States, Georgetown University in Washington, DC, where he taught natural philosophy and mathematics for 48 years. A keen astronomer, he became the first director of the Georgetown Observatory, which he planned and built, and won fame by accurately calculating the longitude of Washington DC.

Writer and politician JOHN BLAKE DILLON (1814–66) was born in BALLAGHADERREEN. In 1842, along with Thomas Davis and Charles Duffy (*see* Monaghan), he founded the nationalist newspaper *The Nation*, and later, the Young Ireland movement. This was a romantic and idealistic organisation which grew out of Daniel O'Connell's Repeal Association and was designed to promote a non-sectarian Irish cultural nationalism. He was also the father of John Dillon, the last leader of the Irish Parliamentary Party, and grandfather of James Dillon, sometime leader of Fine Gael.

Post-Impressionist painter RODERIC O'CONOR (1860–1940), born in MILTON, was a member of the celebrated O'Conor clan, descendants of the High Kings of Ireland and one of the oldest families in Europe. Sometimes called an 'Irish Expressionist', he studied at the Metropolitan School of Art in Dublin and the Royal Hibernian Academy, before moving to France, where he spent the rest of his life. Shy, and always striving for greater excellence, O'Conor joined the group of artists living and painting at Pont-Aven in Brittany, a Celtic part of France where he felt at home with his Irish roots. He became great friends with Paul Gauguin who, like O'Conor, was descended from an ancient royal line. Because he had a private income and didn't need to make money from his art, O'Conor kept most of his paintings for himself and since his death they have become highly sought after.

THOMAS FLYNN, Bishop of Achonry, was born in BALLAGHADERREEN in 1931. Appointed in 1976, he served for

31 years before retiring in 2007 as THE LONGEST SERVING BISHOP IN IRELAND.

MATT MOLLOY, flautist with the Chieftains since 1979, was born in BALLAGHADERREEN in 1947. He is also owner of Matt Molloy's pub in Westport, Co. Mayo. Chieftain is the English translation of the Irish word *Taoiseach*.

County Sligo

*W.B. Yeats — 'the place that has really
influenced my life most is Sligo.'*

◄ SLIGO FOLK ►

Brother Walfrid ✦ Leo Milligan ✦ Neil Jordan ✦ Shane Filan
✦ Kian Egan ✦ Mark Feehily

Yeats Country

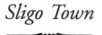

COUNTY SLIGO is as dominated by W.B. YEATS as it is by Ben Bulben, and every year students come from around the world to attend the Yeats International Summer School, to celebrate the Yeats Festivals, and to take tours of Yeats country. Innisfree, a tiny island in Lough Gill, close to Sligo town, was the inspiration for one of Yeats's most popular poems, 'The Lake Isle of Innisfree', written in 1893.

Sligo Town

SLIGO is north-west Ireland's most important town and the second largest town in Connacht. Maurice FitzGerald, ancestor of the Earls of Kildare, built a castle here in 1245, now gone, and founded the beautiful Dominican Friary of the Holy Cross, of which some fairly impressive fragments survive, including a section of cloister arcading with fine carved pillars and an early 16th-century carved stone tomb surmounted by a glorious traceried canopy. The 15th-century High Altar is the only sculptured example of its kind still to be found in any medieval Irish church.

The Model Arts Centre and Niland Gallery in Sligo displays a selection of the work of W.B. Yeats's brother Jack Yeats (1871–1957), the best-known Irish artist of the 20th century. Born in London, Jack grew up in Sligo, and the scenery of the west of Ireland strongly influenced his emergence as an 'Irish Expressionist'. He also wrote novels and designed the sets for J.M. Synge's *The Playboy of the Western World*.

Coney Island, out in the bay beyond Rosses Point, is accessible by foot at low tide and gets its name from the profusion of rabbits who have made their home there, 'coney' being the old name for a rabbit. They

Sligo Town Hall

say it was a Sligo sea captain who named New York's Coney Island, which was also overrun with rabbits, after the island off Co. Sligo – although the Coney Island in Lough Neagh makes the same claim.

Rock of the Spaniards

Grange is a pretty village lying between Ben Bulben and the sea. To the west is a beach protected by a long narrow spit of land called Streedagh Point, and some way out to sea stands a rock known as CARRICKNASPANIA, or Carraig na Spainneach, 'Rock of the Spaniards', recalling the time in 1588 when three ships from the Spanish Armada were wrecked in Donegal Bay, and the bodies of Spanish seamen were washed ashore in their hundreds. One observer, Sir Geoffrey Fenton, remarked, 'I numbered in one strand less than five miles in length eleven hundred dead corpses.'

Lola Montez
1821–1861

Grange has another 'Spanish' connection, albeit tenuous, for this is where 'LOLA MONTEZ, THE SPANISH DANCER' was born in 1821. Lola

Montez was, in fact, Elizabeth Gilbert, daughter of a young English officer and a very young mother, 15-year-old Eliza Oliver from Castle Oliver in County Limerick. When Elizabeth was two years old, the family were sent to India, and not long afterwards her father died of cholera and her mother remarried. Elizabeth was what might be described as a 'spirited' girl, something of a handful, and she was soon sent back to her stepfather's family in Scotland to be taught how to behave as a lady.

It didn't work. As hot-tempered and headstrong as she was beautiful, Elizabeth was passed from school to school until at the age of 16 she eloped with an army lieutenant called Thomas James. The marriage didn't last and Elizabeth, who had always been keen to appear on the stage, reinvented herself as a Spanish dancer called 'Lola

Montez' – her first performance almost ending in disaster when she was recognised and exposed, by a most annoying acquaintance, as Mrs James.

Despite inventing an exotic flamenco-style dance called the 'Tarantula Dance' (which involved searching for a spider amongst her clothing and hence the removal of most of that clothing), Lola wasn't much of a dancer, and her tour through Europe had to be financed by a series of wealthy lovers including, it is commonly accepted, the novelist Alexander Dumas and the composer Franz Liszt. She apparently carried a whip with her everywhere, which she used, not just to ward off unwanted attention, but also to lambast anyone who criticised her performance on stage, and to punish any of her lovers whose performance in the boudoir fell short of her exacting standards.

Her greatest conquest was the aging King Ludwig of Bavaria, who became besotted with her when she allowed him to examine her bosoms after he complimented her figure. He built her a palace full of fountains that ran with perfume, made her the Countess of Landsfeld, and gave her a huge allowance from the public purse, until she eventually decided to relieve him of the burden of running Bavaria. Her own imperious rule, however, did not go down well with the good citizens of Bavaria, and they rose up in protest, causing the previously popular King Ludwig to abdicate and Lola to flee.

Some time afterwards she reappeared in California, where she performed to great acclaim for the miners of the Gold Rush, and later toured Australia, where she was not so well received, upsetting many Outback wives by lifting her dress during her act to reveal that she was wearing no underwear.

Returning, perhaps in dudgeon, to California, and with her health deteriorating, she took up lecturing. In 1861, while staying in New York, she died from pneumonia, aged just 39.

Inishmurray

Lying about 4 miles (6.4 km) out to sea off Mullahgmore is the deserted island of INISHMURRAY, uninhabited since 1947. One of Ireland's very first monasteries was founded here by St Molaise in the 6th century, and the remains of this early church are remarkably well preserved. There are three beehive chapels, almost intact, and a huge variety of carved crosses and tombstones, all surrounded by a high cashel, or dry-stone wall.

Older still is a collection of rounded stones known as Cursing Stones, which are placed on top of one of the stone altars. It is impossible to say how many stones there are, since each time they are counted the number arrived at is different. To lay a successful curse you must turn one of the stones anti-clockwise as you speak your imprecation – if you turn the stone the other way, the curse comes back on to you.

It is believed that Inishmurray is THE SOUTHERNMOST BREEDING GROUND OF THE EIDER DUCK.

Ballymote

BALLYMOTE'S powerful castle is a square, keepless structure, almost symmetrical, with round towers at each corner, not dissimilar to Beaumaris Castle on Anglesey. Put up in the early 14th century by Richard de Burgo, Earl of Ulster, known as the Red Earl, it was the last of the Norman castles to be built in Connacht.

Just outside the town are the rather more scant remains of a Franciscan friary where the celebrated *Book of Ballymote* was put together, towards

the end of the 14th century, for Tonnaltagh McDonagh of Ballymote Castle. The book is a compilation of old manuscripts and ancient documents from the McDonagh family's collection, and includes a life of St Patrick, Irish history and legends, and an important key for deciphering the old Irish Ogham script. Ogham is to be found carved on 4th- and 5th-century standing stones, consists of 20 letters, and is read clockwise, starting upwards from the bottom left-hand corner.

Michael Corcoran
1827–63

MICHAEL CORCORAN, who was born in Carrowkeel, Ballymote, in 1827, commanded the 'Fighting 69th' infantry regiment for the Union during the American Civil War. At the time the 'Fighting 69th', which traces its roots back to the American Revolution, was formed almost entirely from Irish Americans, as Corcoran, a close confidant of Abraham Lincoln, was inspirational in attracting his fellow Irishmen to join the regiment. Alas, he died in the Civil War, tragically young at 36, when his horse rolled on top of him and fractured his skull.

In 2006 New York's mayor, Michael Bloomberg, came to Ballymote to unveil Ireland's National Monument to the Fighting 69th. Around the top of the monument is written 'Michael Corcoran 1827–1863', and underneath is a piece of the World Trade Center, donated by the family of Michael Lynch, who died when the towers were brought down on 11 September 2001, and whose family hail from County Sligo.

Well, I never knew this about
SLIGO FOLK

Brother Walfrid
◄ 1840–1915 ►

BALLYMOTE was the birthplace of Andrew Kerins, a crofter's son who somehow survived the deprivations of the Great Famine and joined the Marist Brothers, a Catholic religious order dedicated to the spiritual well-being and education of young people throughout the world. Kerins studied in France, took the name BROTHER WALFRID, and in 1870 was sent to live amongst the poor in Glasgow, where he was soon appointed headmaster of the Sacred Heart School. Poverty and malnutrition were rampant in Glasgow at that time, especially among the immigrant Irish, and Brother Walfrid set up soup kitchens to provide people with at least one hot meal a day. He also harnessed the popularity of a new craze called football, organising local teams and matches as a way of keeping young people out of the alehouses. Football, he quickly realised, was a good way of raising money to finance the soup kitchens.

In 1887 Hibernian, a football team established by the Irish in Edinburgh, won the Scottish Cup, and such was the joy and celebration amongst the

Irish population in both Edinburgh and Glasgow that Brother Walfrid decided to form a similar team in Glasgow. On 6 November 1887, at a meeting in St Mary's church hall in Calton, Glasgow, Brother Walfrid founded Celtic Football Club, with the aim of 'alleviating poverty in Glasgow's east end parishes'. He chose the name Celtic to reflect the club's Irish and Scottish roots.

Drawing its support mainly from Catholic fans, Celtic Football Club, founded by a crofter's son from County Sligo, has grown into one of the world's biggest football clubs, with more supporters' organisations across the globe than almost any other. In 1967 Celtic became THE FIRST-EVER BRITISH CLUB TO WIN THE EUROPEAN CUP.

A statue of Brother Walfrid was unveiled outside Celtic's home ground at Celtic Park in 2006, while in his birthplace of Ballymote a small park and memorial bust commemorate the town's most famous son.

LEO MILLIGAN, father of comedian Spike Milligan, was born in 1890 at No. 5, Holborn Street, SLIGO TOWN, where there is now a plaque commemorating Spike's connection with the town.

NEIL JORDAN, film director (*The Company of Wolves, Mona Lisa, The Crying Game, Interview with a Vampire*), was born in SLIGO TOWN in 1950.

Three members of the boyband WESTLIFE were born in SLIGO TOWN, SHANE FILAN in 1979, and KIAN EGAN and MARK FEEHILY in 1980.

LEINSTER

Dublin City

*The Four Courts, one of Dublin's
most distinctive riverside landmarks.*

◄ DUBLIN CITY FOLK ►

Jonathan Swift ✦ John Field ✦ George Bernard Shaw ✦ Oscar Wilde
✦ Sean O'Casey ✦ Barry Fitzgerald ✦ Cedric Gibbons ✦ Samuel Beckett
✦ Francis Bacon ✦ Brendan Behan ✦ Gay Byrne ✦ Bono
✦ Sir George Downing ✦ Henry Archer ✦ George Francis FitzGerald
✦ Lucien Bull ✦ Fredrick Boland

The city of DUBLIN is the very heart of Ireland. It has been the biggest city in Ireland throughout most of its history, except for two short periods when Drogheda and then Belfast briefly held that honour. One quarter of the population of the Republic of Ireland live within the Dublin conurbation, and it is among the fastest-growing cities in Europe.

Black Pool

Although the site has been occupied since prehistoric times, the first record of the city we now know as Dublin comes from Ptolemy's famous map of Ireland drawn in AD 140, where it appears as Eblana. The Celts who lived there knew it as the Dubh Linn, or 'Black Pool', which was formed where the River Poddle ran into the Liffey and is now hidden beneath the gardens of Dublin Castle.

The source of the Liffey in the Wicklow mountains is only 12 miles (19 km) away from where it enters the Irish Sea in Dublin Bay, but the river's meandering course leads it for an actual distance of nearly 80 miles (129 km) through the counties of Wicklow, Kildare and Dublin.

Politics and Power

Dublin is the political capital of Ireland, and has been since the Vikings took it over in 841. They built a wooden stronghold above the Black Pool, and within a century the town had become the capital of the Norse kingdom, making it THE OLDEST NORSE CAPITAL CITY IN EXISTENCE, predating Reykjavik in Iceland by about 30 years.

The Celts under Brian Boru regained Dublin at the Battle of Clontarf in 1014, and then the Normans arrived in 1169 and the town became the centre of English rule, based in Dublin Castle, until the establishment of the Irish Free State in 1921. Today the Irish Parliament, the Dail, sits at Leinster House, which was on the city outskirts when it was built in 1744 and was then the largest private house in Dublin.

During the Anglo-Irish Ascendancy of the later 18th century, Ireland for a while had its own Parliament, which sat in EUROPE'S FIRST PURPOSE-BUILT PARLIAMENT HOUSE, completed in 1739 and now occupied by the Bank of Ireland. This period ushered in a golden age of building in Dublin, which endowed the city with the glorious Georgian streets and squares for which it is renowned, and saw the construction of the noble Customs House by James Gandon, the Four Courts, built in 1786, where Ireland's High and Supreme Courts sit, City Hall, now the Royal Exchange, and many of the buildings of Trinity College.

Dublin Firsts

In 1759 Arthur Guinness opened his brewery at St James's Gate to the south-west of the city centre. By 1838 it was the biggest brewery in Ireland, and by 1914 the biggest in the world.

It remains THE WORLD'S LARGEST BREWER OF STOUT and is still THE BIGGEST BREWERY IN EUROPE. In 1904 a storehouse building was attached to the main brewery, THE FIRST STEEL-FRAMED BUILDING IN IRELAND AND BRITAIN, predating the Ritz Hotel in London by two years. Originally a fully operational fermentation plant, it now houses several floors of exhibitions that tell the story of Guinness, its history and how it is made. At the top is DUBLIN'S HIGHEST BAR, THE GRAVITY BAR, which provides a 360-degree view of the whole of Dublin.

In January 1878 IRELAND'S FIRST TELEPHONE LINE connected the Gresham Hotel in O'Connell Street – today Europe's widest city thoroughfare – with Maguire's hardware store in Dawson Street. Two years later, in 1880, IRELAND'S FIRST TELEPHONE EXCHANGE was opened by the United Telephone Company on the top floor of Commercial Buildings in Dame Street. There were five subscribers and initially a small boy was employed to operate the switchboard, but he got bored and went off to play marbles, so the company trained up a young Dublin woman, MISS AGNES DUGGAN, to be IRELAND'S FIRST PROFESSIONAL TELEPHONE OPERATOR.

Medical Dublin

TRINITY COLLEGE, Dublin, Ireland's oldest university, was founded in 1592 by Elizabeth I, and attracted artists and scientists from across Ireland. TCD, as it became known, established a reputation for scientific research, particularly mathematics, chemistry and medicine, and by the 18th century Dublin was at the forefront of medical innovation and discovery.

THE FIRST VOLUNTARY HOSPITAL IN BRITAIN AND IRELAND, THE DR STEEVENS HOSPITAL, was opened in Dublin in 1733, funded from the will of RICHARD STEEVENS, Professor of Medicine at TCD, who died in 1710.

THE FIRST MATERNITY HOSPITAL IN THE WORLD, THE ROTUNDA, was founded by Portlaoise's DR BARTHOLOMEW MOSSE (1712–59) in 1745. Here, in the 20th century, Dublin-born DR ROBERT COLLIS (1900–75) developed a practical incubator for premature children and pioneered the technique of feeding such babies via a tube through the nose, which overcame the problem of feeding them by mouth before they had learnt how to suck.

Dublin doctor ROBERT ADAMS (1796–1875), surgeon to Queen Victoria, performed IRELAND'S FIRST OPERATION UNDER ANAESTHETIC, and was the first doctor to recognise that blackouts were caused by a lack of oxygen to the brain.

Dr Robert Graves (1796–1853), of Dublin's Meath Hospital, was a leading pioneer of what became known the Dublin School of Medicine. He introduced the timing of the pulse by watch, and first advocated 'feeding a fever' instead of trying to starve it out. The hypodermic syringe was invented at Meath Hospital in 1844, by Dr Francis Rynd (1801–61).

In 1865 Francis Cruise (1834–1912) invented the first practical endoscope for seeing inside a patient's body, using mirrors and a paraffin lamp. In the same year Dr Robert McDonnell performed Ireland's first blood transfusion on a young girl who had caught her hand in a roller at the paper mill, and he went on to develop and improve the technique over the next decade. One Dublin surgeon, having followed the experiments closely, subsequently described them in detail to his brother, who used the idea of blood transfusions in a novel. The brother's name was Bram Stoker, and the novel was *Dracula*.

A Question from Dublin

In 1780 a Dublin theatre manager named James Daly invented a new concept and a new word by scrawling the word 'quiz' on walls and pavements across the city until people wondered what was going on. Nearly 100 years earlier, however, a Dublin man had already got the world scratching its head with a poser of his own . . .

William Molyneux
1656–98

William Molyneux, founder in 1683 of the Dublin Philosophical Society, was one of Ireland's earliest and most influential natural philosophers, which is what they used to call seekers after knowledge before 1833, when neologist William Wherwell came up with the term 'scientist' at the request of the poet Samuel Taylor Coleridge.

Molyneux wore many hats. Educated at Trinity College, Dublin, he was a barrister, an engineer, the inventor of a telescope mounted on a sundial and a meteorologist – his weather records, which included readings of barometric pressure, were the first-ever scientific observations of the Irish weather. He was also an author and politician who wrote a book called *The Case of Ireland's being Bound by Acts of Parliament in England, Stated*, arguing that England had no right to legislate for Ireland. The book was used subsequently as a manual by independence movements not just in Ireland, but also in France and the American colonies.

It is not for these achievements, magnificent though they were, that William Molyneux is chiefly remembered, but for posing a problem that has had the greatest philosophers, teachers, thinkers and men of science arguing to this day. 'Molyneux's Problem', as it became known, occurred to him when his wife became blind shortly after their marriage, and he wrestled with it for 20 years without being able to come up with a definitive answer. Finally, in 1693, he wrote to one of the finest minds of the day, the philosopher John

Locke, and put the question to him: 'If a man who is born blind is taught how to recognise the shape of a globe and a cube by feel, could he distinguish them by sight alone if he were then given the ability to see?'

Molyneux was inclined to think that the man would not be able to recognize the objects by sight and Locke agreed with him, asserting that this would be the view of the 'acute and judicious proposer'.

The answer has defined philosophers ever since: those answering 'no', because they think that man's knowledge of the external world can only come from real experience and scientific observation, are called Empiricists, and those answering 'yes', because they believe man is born capable of reason, independent of the senses, are called Rationalists.

Having foxed the finest minds in the world for generations to come, William Molyneux, no doubt satisfied his work was done, was laid to rest in Dublin's oldest church, St Audoen's, in 1698.

Well, I never knew this
about
DUBLIN FOLK

Artistic Folk Born in Dublin

JONATHAN SWIFT (1667–1745), Dean of St Patrick's and author of the classic satire *Gulliver's Travels*, which has never been out of print since it was first published in 1726.

JOHN FIELD (1782–1837), THE FIRST COMPOSER TO WRITE NOCTURNES, a form of musical composition evocative of the night, later made famous by Chopin.

Playwright GEORGE BERNARD SHAW (1845–1950), the only man to have been awarded a Nobel Prize for Literature (for contributions to writing in 1925) and an Oscar (for Best Adapted Screenplay for *Pygmalion* in 1938).

I often quote myself. It adds spice to my conversation.

I'm an atheist and I thank God for it.

Life contains but two tragedies. One is not to get your heart's desire; the other is to get it.

Youth is wasted on the young.

George Bernard Shaw quotes

OSCAR WILDE (1854–1900), playwright, novelist and poet, who is thought to be the most quoted writer in history after Shakespeare.

A cynic is a man who knows the price of everything but the value of nothing.

I can resist everything except temptation.

Oscar Wilde quotes

SEAN O'CASEY (1880–1964), play-wright noted particularly for *Juno and the Paycock* and *The Plough and the Stars*.

Actor BARRY FITZGERALD (1888–1961), room-mate of Sean O'Casey while working at the Abbey Theatre, who starred in classic films such as *How Green Was My Valley* in 1941 and *The Quiet Man* in 1952. In 1944 he was nominated for Oscars for both Best Actor and Best Supporting Actor, in his role as Father Fitzgibbon in *Going My Way* – the only person in the history of the Academy Awards to have been nominated for two different Oscars in the same performance.

Art director CEDRIC GIBBONS (1893–1960), one of the 36 founders of the Academy of Motion Picture Arts and Sciences and regarded as the most influential and important art director in the history of motion pictures. He designed the Oscar statuette in 1929 and was nominated for

the Oscar for Best Art Director 39 times, winning 11 times – second only to Walt Disney, who won 26 times. While Gibbons always claimed to be born in Dublin, some believe that he was actually born in New York.

SAMUEL BECKETT (1906–89), playwright and novelist, who won the Nobel Prize for Literature in 1969. Best remembered for his play *Waiting for Godot*.

FRANCIS BACON (1909–92), figurative painter and descendant of Elizabethan philosopher Francis Bacon.

BRENDAN BEHAN (1923–64), the archetypal Irish writer, a famous figure on the Dublin literary and pub scene, who was imprisoned in his youth for IRA activity. Loud, boisterous, companionable, brilliant, witty and

drunken, he described himself as 'a drinker with a writing problem'. He died in Meath Hospital at the young age of 41 after collapsing at the Harbour Lights Bar from a drink-related seizure.

I have never seen a situation so dismal that a policeman couldn't make it worse.

If it was raining soup, the Irish would go out with forks.

Brendan Behan quotes

GAY BYRNE, born 1934, presenter from 1962 to 1999 of *The Late Late Show*, which was credited with initi-

ating the modernisation of Irish society in the 1960s and went on to become the WORLD'S LONGEST-RUNNING TELEVISION CHAT SHOW.

BONO, born Paul David Hewson in 1960, Ireland's most famous pop star and philanthropist.

Other Native Dublin Folk

SIR GEORGE DOWNING (1623–84), the second man to graduate from Harvard University, and the man who built Downing Street, home of the British Prime Minister.

HENRY ARCHER (1806–63), originator of the Ffestiniog Railway which opened in North Wales in 1836, and inventor of the perforated stamp in 1848.

GEORGE FRANCIS FITZGERALD (1851–1901), physicist and professor of physics at TCD, who was the first person to suggest the possibility of radio waves, laying down the basis for wireless telegraphy. He was also the first to put forward the theory that nothing could travel faster than light and formulated an early idea of relativity, which greatly contributed to Einstein's own Theory of Relativity.

LUCIEN BULL (1876–1972), the inventor of high-speed photography and, hence, slow-motion. Educated in France, Bull went to work for a French biologist called Etienne Marey who was experimenting with high-speed photography to study human and animal movement. Marey's camera could only shoot one frame every 15 minutes because the film had to be stopped in order to be exposed, so Bull devised a camera in which the film could run continuously while the subject was illuminated many times per second. In 1904 he could record 1,200 images per second, and by 1952 he had achieved one million images per second. On the way he became the first person to obtain photographs of insects in flight, a drop of water falling, and a bullet breaking through glass.

FREDERICK BOLAND (1904–85), first Irish ambassador to Britain and the United Nations. Boland was President of the General Assembly in 1960 on the famous occasion when First Secretary of the USSR Nikita Kruschev took off his shoe and pounded the desk with it.

County Carlow

FIRST ROMAN CATHOLIC BISHOP IN AMERICA
✦ MISSION TO AUSTRALIA ✦ FIRST IRISH CARDINAL
✦ IRELAND'S SMALLEST CATHEDRAL
✦ SHEEPSHEARING CAR MAKER

*Doorway at Killeshin, one of the finest remaining
Romanesque doorways in Ireland.*

◄ CARLOW FOLK ►

Walt Disney Ancestors ✦ Pierce Butler ✦ Brian Mulroney

Carlow College

CARLOW COLLEGE, known locally as St Patrick's, was founded in 1782 for the education of both the priesthood and the laity in philosophy, theology and social studies. It is one of Ireland's oldest educational institutions and boasts a number of distinguished past students.

John England
1786–1842

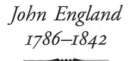

One of the first, if not the first, Roman Catholic bishop to be appointed in the United States, JOHN ENGLAND was born in Co. Cork and educated at St Patrick's. He was consecrated Bishop of Charleston in South Carolina on 21 September 1820 and took up the post in December that year. Bishop England was hugely influential in the organisation and integration of Roman Catholics and the Roman Catholic faith into the new republic, at a time when there was great debate about the relationship between religion and the State. Thomas Jefferson, the greatest of the great minds behind the American Constitution, while espousing religious freedom, preferred 'a wall of separation between Church and State', a principle with which Bishop England heartily agreed.

On 8 January 1826, Bishop John England became THE FIRST CATHOLIC CLERGYMAN TO PREACH IN THE US HOUSE OF REPRESENTATIVES, and in his sermon he rebutted the claim of ex-President John Quincy Adams that the Roman Catholic Church was intolerant of other religions and therefore incompatible with republican institutions. 'We do not believe that God gave to the church any power to interfere with our civil rights, or our civil concerns,' said Bishop England. 'I would not allow to the Pope, or to any bishop of our church, the smallest interference with the humblest vote at our most insignificant balloting box.'

John Therry
1790–1864

JOHN THERRY was born in Cork, attended St Patrick's and was ordained in 1815. When he learnt that there were no priests in Australia to minister to convicts who were Catholic, he volunteered to go there as a missionary and sailed from Cork on the *Janus*, along with over 100 prisoners, arriving in Sydney in May 1820. He devoted the next 44 years to helping Catholics in Australia adapt to the challenging

conditions and pressures of a newly emerging country and to overseeing their moral and religious welfare. On the day of his arrival Father John Therry had dreamt of building in Sydney 'a mighty church of golden stone dedicated to the Virgin Mary'. For this purpose he was allocated a piece of barren land in the east of the town, which has since become the prime location in modern Sydney. The foundation stone of St Mary's Cathedral was laid by Governor Macquarie on 29 October 1821. Twice the church was burned down, the original building in 1865, the year after Father Therry died, and then the temporary structure that replaced it in 1869. The present sandstone building was begun in 1868 and is THE LARGEST CHURCH IN AUSTRALIA.

St Mary's Cathedral, Sydney

Paul Cullen
1803–78

PAUL CULLEN, THE FIRST IRISH CARDINAL, was born in Co. Kildare and attended St Patrick's from 1816 to 1820. In 1832 he was made Rector of the Irish College in Rome, which brought him to the attention of Pope Gregory XVI. In 1849 he became Archbishop of Armagh and Catholic Primate of Ireland, and in 1850 he presided over the Synod of Thurles, the first national synod held in Ireland for hundreds of years. In 1852 he became Archbishop of Dublin, and in 1866 he was appointed Cardinal Priest of San Pietro in Montorio.

Cardinal Cullen is credited with restoring the position of the Roman Catholic Church in Ireland and with bringing unity to the divided church in Ireland. At the First Vatican Council in 1870 he was responsible for composing the final definition of papal infallibility by which the church allows the office of the Pope to be the ruling and final agent in deciding what will be accepted as the formal beliefs of the church.

St Laserian's Cathedral

ST LASERIAN'S CATHEDRAL in Old Leighlin is one of Ireland's undiscovered treasures, a gloriously rugged 12th-century church that was medieval Ireland's smallest cathedral. It stands on the site of a monastery founded by St Gobban in the early 7th century, where a synod was held in AD 630 at which it was decided that the Irish church should follow the Roman rather than the Celtic procedure for setting the date of Easter. The wooden monastery, in which St Gobban was buried, was destroyed by fire in 1060, and the

present stone church was begun around 1152. Despite alterations over the centuries much of the Norman structure survives, and there is an 11th-century font and a beautiful canopied sedilia that is unique in Ireland – it has four bays rather than the usual three.

Tullow

TULLOW, a pleasant farming town on the River Slaney between Carlow and the Wicklow Mountains, is known as the 'granite town' because of its magnificent granite public buildings. From 1725 until 1925, luxurious MOUNT WOLSELEY, just outside the town, was the family home of FREDERICK YORK WOLSELEY (1837–99),

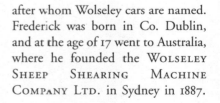

after whom Wolseley cars are named. Frederick was born in Co. Dublin, and at the age of 17 went to Australia, where he founded the WOLSELEY SHEEP SHEARING MACHINE COMPANY LTD. in Sydney in 1887.

This became THE FIRST COMPANY IN THE WORLD TO PRODUCE A SHEEPSHEARING MACHINE.

In 1889 Wolseley returned to England and set up in Birmingham. After he retired in 1894, the company was run by Herbert Austin, an engineer who had joined the company in Australia. Under Austin the company began making Wolseley bicycles and cars to keep the workers busy outside the shearing season.

In 1901 Wolseley Cars were bought by Vickers and eventually became part of the British Motor Corporation, with the Wolseley name being used for luxury versions of the standard BMC models. The last use of the Wolseley name was in 1975. The Wolseley Sheep Shearing Machine Company developed into Wolseley plc, a builder's merchant whose best-known brand today is Plumb Center.

Well, I never knew this about
CARLOW FOLK

A number of ancestors of WALT DISNEY are buried in the graveyard of Clonmelsh Church in TINRYLAND. Also lying here are members of the Butler family.

Pierce Butler
◄ 1744–1822 ►

PIERCE BUTLER, one of the Founding Fathers of America, was born at GARRYHUNDON in Co. Carlow, a younger son of Sir Richard Butler MP, the 5th Baronet of Cloughgrenan. Being a younger son, and so unable to inherit the family fortune, Butler joined the British army and was sent to America. There his regiment, the 29th Regiment of Foot, were involved in the Boston Massacre of 1770, when troops opened fire on a rioting crowd, killing five of them.

Butler took some leave and travelled to Charleston, in South Carolina, where he met and married Mary Polly Middleton, the daughter of Henry Middleton, a wealthy plantation owner and second President of the Continental Congress. Butler sold his army commission, bought some land, and when the Revolutionary War broke out in 1775, took the side of the Americans, organising South Carolina's military defences and becoming South Carolina's representative to the Continental Congress.

In 1787 he was chosen to represent South Carolina at the Constitutional Convention in Philadelphia, where America's constitution was being formulated. Pierce Butler is credited with having been instrumental in devising the Electoral College system, whereby voters elect Electors to the Electoral College and these Electors then elect the President and Vice-President. Occasionally this system can give rise to a situation where a presidential candidate succeeds by winning the electoral vote while losing the popular vote, as happened in 2000, when the Democrat Al Gore gained half a million votes more than Republican George W. Bush but had five fewer electoral votes.

'The Weeping Times'

While favouring strong federal government, Pierce Butler, as a plantation owner, was also a leading proponent of the controversial Fugitive Slaves Clause, found in the early Constitution, whereby slaves who escaped to another state could be reclaimed by their 'owner' in the state from which they had escaped. This was one of the elements that contributed to the American Civil War.

Just before that conflict, in 1859, Pierce Butler's grandson, another Pierce Butler, ran into financial difficulties and sold off every one of his slaves in Georgia, in THE BIGGEST SINGLE SALE OF HUMAN BEINGS IN US HISTORY. Because of all the painful separations that ensued as families were torn apart, the event became known as 'the weeping times'.

The family of BRIAN MULRONEY, 1984 to 1993, came originally from 18th Prime Minister of Canada from LEIGHLINBRIDGE.

County Dublin

FATHER OF THE MODERN GHOST STORY
✦ THE OVAL DINING ROOM ✦ TIME AND PLACE
✦ QUARTERNIONS ✦ ROYAL CASTLE
✦ FATHER OF SEISMOLOGY

*The Casino in Marino, the finest
Neo-Classical building in Ireland.*

◄ DUBLIN FOLK ►

Colonel Molesworth Phillips ✦ Sir William Orpen ✦ Paddy Moloney
✦ Colm Meaney ✦ Stephen Roche ✦ Ken Doherty ✦ Padraig Harrington
✦ Ivan Beshoff ✦ Jim Fitzpatrick

COUNTY DUBLIN is dominated by the city of Dublin but retains its own identity with a number of historic and distinctive villages and communities, particularly to the north and west, as well as a thin coastal strip.

The county can claim THE HIGHEST PUB IN IRELAND, Johnny Fox's, in the little hilltop village of Glencullen, 906 ft (276 m) up in the Wicklow Mountains. It is also one of Ireland's oldest pubs, established in the same year as the Irish Rebellion, 1798.

Chapelizod

The oldest of Co. Dublin's villages, CHAPELIZOD, on the River Liffey west of Dublin, is reputed to be the burial place of Iseult of Ireland, Isolde from *Tristan and Isolde*. It has a famous bridge across the river, which use to be called Chapelizod Bridge but in 1982 was renamed the Anna Livia Bridge to mark the centenary of the birth of author James Joyce. Anna Livia was the name he gave to the River Liffey in his novel *Finnegan's Wake*.

The 'Father of the Modern Ghost Story', SHERIDAN LE FANU (1814–73), great-nephew of playwright Richard Brinsley Sheridan, and pre-eminent author of Gothic tales of suspense, horror and mystery, lived in Chapelizod. His novel *The House by the Churchyard* was inspired by a house that still stands beside the village church. Le Fanu's best-known work is the dark psychological novel *Uncle Silas*, while his vampire story *Carmilla* inspired Bram Stoker, and with its lesbian undertones spawned a number of films exploring the theme by Hammer Films and, most famously, by Roger Vadim.

Sheridan Le Fanu

Lucan House

LUCAN HOUSE was built in 1770 on the site of Lucan Castle, the home of Patrick Sarsfield, 1st Earl of Lucan, the Jacobite commander at the Siege of Limerick. It is one of the finest Palladian houses in Ireland and its Oval Dining Room inspired the Oval Office of the White House in Washington. The house is now the Italian Ambassador's residence.

Lucan House

CASTLEKNOCK gets its name from the ruined Norman castle which sits atop one of two small hills rising from the plain west of Phoenix Park. The site was once second in importance only to the Hill of Tara.

Today, Castleknock's fame lies in its claim to have THE LARGEST TENNIS FACILITY IN IRELAND and as the birthplace of Hollywood actor COLIN FARRELL, who played Alexander the Great in Oliver Stone's 2004 film *Alexander*, and Captain John Smith in the 2005 film *The New World.*

Dunsink

The Observatory at DUNSINK, built on top of a hill to the north-west of Phoenix Park, was founded in 1783 for the first Andrews Professor of Astronomy at Trinity College Dublin, and is THE OLDEST SCIENTIFIC INSTITUTION IN IRELAND. The location of the observatory was adopted as Dublin's meridian, the

Dunsink Meridian, and later Dunsink Mean Time held sway in Ireland until 1916, when Greenwich Mean Time was adopted. From 1865 until 1937 Dunsink provided Dublin with a time signal, linking a master clock in the observatory by telegraph to a series of clocks positioned around the city.

Sir William Rowan Hamilton
1805–65

The greatest mathematician of his age, Dublin-born WILLIAM ROWAN HAMILTON was perhaps the most famous Director of Dunsink Observatory. Something of a child prodigy he could work out mathematical calculations by the age of three, speak Greek, Latin and Hebrew by five, and a further ten languages by 13. He studied maths at Trinity College Dublin and was made director of the Observatory at the age of 22 in 1827. He lived there for the rest of his life.

It was in 1843 that he had the revelation that would make his name a byword in the world of mathematics. On a fine autumn morning on 16 October he took himself off for a walk beside the Royal Canal below the Observatory to ponder a problem that had been niggling at him. As he was leaning on the parapet of an old stone bridge across the canal he experienced a 'Eureka!' moment when the answer came to him, and he quickly took out his pocket knife and carved his newly discovered formula on the stonework.

$$i2 = j2 = k2 = ijk = -1$$

Rowan Hamilton had invented QUARTERNIONS, a type of complex number where -1 can have three different square roots – mathematics would never be the same again.

> Here as he walked by
> on the 16th of October 1843
> Sir William Rowan Hamilton
> in a flash of genius discovered
> the fundamental formula for
> Quarternion multiplication
> $$i^2 = j^2 = k^2 = ijk = -1$$
> & cut it on a stone of this bridge

The original Quaternions inscription has long since been worn away, but in 1954 a plaque was placed on the bridge where this momentous happening occurred which was unveiled by Eamon de Valera. Today, every year on 16 October, in one of Dublin's more riotous events, mathematicians from all over the world gather at Dunsink and walk from the Observatory along the canal to the bridge, recreating Rowan Hamilton's Walk.

Luttrellstown Castle

The glorious 15th-century LUTTRELLS-TOWN CASTLE, built by the Luttrell family around 1420 and owned by, among others, the Guinness family, was visited twice by Queen Victoria, in 1844 and 1900. In 1999 'royalty' graced Luttrellstown once more, when David Beckham and Victoria 'Posh Spice' Adams were married there seated upon golden thrones. The castle now forms the heart of the Luttrellstown Golf Resort and Country Club.

Robert Mallet
1810–1881

For much of the 19th and 20th centuries County Dublin, which has never experienced an earthquake of any note, was nonetheless a centre of seismology. In 1846 Dublin-born engineer and geologist ROBERT MALLET, who would become known as the Father of Seismology, presented a paper to the Royal Irish Academy entitled 'The Dynamics of Earthquakes', THE FIRST SEISMOLOGICAL STUDY IN THE WORLD, in which he first introduced the very word 'seismology'.

Later, in between building the lighthouse on Fastnet Rock and designing and manufacturing the iron railings round Trinity College, he went down to Killiney and detonated huge gunpowder explosions on the beach there, measuring the time taken for the shock waves to travel through the sand, and analysing the different speeds of the shock waves as they passed through the various rock strata. To help with doing this he invented the world's first self-registering mercury seismometer.

He made further explosive tests in Dalkey Quarry, and then hurried off to Naples, after it was rocked by a huge quake in December 1857, to make the first scientific analysis of an actual earthquake site. Eleven thousand people died in what was then the third largest earthquake ever known, and which has since been estimated at 6.9 on the Richter scale. Mallet observed the way in which the buildings collapsed and how objects were thrown about, and deduced for the first time that the quake must have a focus, for which he came up with the term 'epicentre'.

Mallet's work was carried on in Co. Dublin during the 20th century by one of the Jesuit priests at RATH-FARNHAM CASTLE, Father O'Leary, who constructed his own seismograph, the 'Big O'Leary', in a shed in the grounds. This could monitor tremors and earthquakes anywhere in the world, and between 1917 and 1967 Rathfarnham Castle became a valuable international source of seismological information.

Well, I never knew this about
COUNTY DUBLIN FOLK

COLONEL MOLESWORTH PHILLIPS (1755–1832), who sailed on Captain Cook's last voyage, as commander of his ship's marine detachment, was born in SWORDS. Phillips accompanied Cook on shore when they arrived at Kealakakua Bay in Hawaii and was by his side when they were attacked by natives. In the scuffle, Cook was killed and Phillips badly injured, but he managed to get his men back to the safety of the boats lying offshore, and he even swam back to rescue one of his marines who was struggling in the water and about to be overwhelmed by the natives.

Phillips later married Susan Burney, the sister of novelist Fanny

Burney, and in 1795 he inherited his uncle's estate in Belcotton, Co. Louth, where he lived out his retirement.

SIR WILLIAM ORPEN (1878–1931), portrait painter, whose work is considered to be the most authentic visual expression of the Celtic Revival, was born in STILLORGAN.

PADDY MOLONEY, chief architect of the iconic musical group the Chieftains, was born in DONNYCARNEY in 1938.

Actor COLM MEANEY, who acted in 216 *Star Trek* episodes, more than any other actor except Michael Dorn (who played the Klingon Worf 281 times), was born in FINGLAS in 1953. Trained at the Abbey Theatre School of Acting in Dublin, he first appeared as engineer Miles O'Brien in the pilot episode of *Star Trek: The Next Generation* in 1987 and stayed with the show

until 1993. He then transferred as the same character to the spin-off series *Deep Space Nine*, remaining there until the last episode in 1999.

1987 Tour de France winner STEPHEN ROCHE was born in DUNDRUM in 1959.

KEN DOHERTY, THE ONLY SNOOKER PLAYER TO BE BOTH WORLD AMATEUR CHAMPION (1989) AND WORLD PROFESSIONAL CHAMPION (1997), was born in RANELAGH IN 1969.

THE FIRST GOLFER FROM THE REPUBLIC OF IRELAND EVER TO WIN A GOLF MAJOR, 2007 Open champion PADRAIG HARRINGTON was born in BALLYROAN in 1971. He was also THE FIRST EUROPEAN TO WIN A MAJOR GOLF TOURNAMENT IN THE NEW MILLENNIUM.

IVAN BESHOFF (1883–1987), who arrived in Ireland from Odessa in 1913 and founded Beshoff's Fishmongers in Howth, as well as the Ivan Beshoff Fish and Chip shops. He lived to be 104 and was the last survivor of the 1905 mutiny on the battleship *Potemkin*, the first sizeable expression of discontent against the Russian Tsar, and a prelude to the Russian Revolution.

Celtic artist JIM FITZPATRICK, whose iconic 1968 poster of Che Guevara became such a powerful image of anti-Vietnam war protest, and was published just before the Cuban revolutionary died in Bolivia, was born in Co. Dublin. A close friend of Phil Lynott, he was also responsible for many of the memorable sleeve designs for Thin Lizzy's records.

County Kildare

SPORTING KILDARE ✦ EARLIEST IRISH PARLIAMENT
✦ FIRST IRISH-BORN ARCHBISHOP OF DUBLIN
✦ FERME ORNÉE ✦ FIRST RED-BRICK HOUSE
✦ LARGEST ONE-STREET TOWN ✦ A DUEL
✦ A FAMOUS CAVALRY CHARGE

Castledermot, home of the earliest Irish Parliament.

◄ KILDARE FOLK ►

Sir Richard Griffith ✦ John Edward Kelly ✦ Dame Kathleen Lonsdale
✦ Josef Locke ✦ Christy Moore

[73]

COUNTY KILDARE has more miles of canal than any other Irish county, some 93 miles (150 km) of waterway. Monasterevin, located where the Grand Canal crosses the River Barrow, is famed for its numerous bridges and is known as the 'Venice of Ireland'. The Grand Canal is partially fed from IRELAND'S LARGEST AQUIFER, or underground reservoir, which lies beneath the Curragh.

Sporting Kildare

Motor sport

In 1903 one of the earliest international motor races, the Gordon Bennett auto race, was held on the roads around Athy. Since an English driver had won the previous year the race should have been run in England, but motor racing was banned there and so Ireland was chosen instead. In recognition of Ireland's generosity in hosting the event, the British decided to adopt green as their national racing colour – and British racing teams continued to use British Racing Green until the 1970s, when sponsorship rules were relaxed and teams began to run cars in the colours of their sponsors.

Golf

THE CURRAGH is home to IRELAND'S FIRST GOLF COURSE, which was laid out in 1852 by Scotsman David Ritchie of the Musselburgh Golf Club.

Horse-racing

Ireland is celebrated worldwide for breeding and training successful race-horses, and Co. Kildare is the head-quarters of Irish racing, home to the National Stud and to Ireland's two leading racecourses, THE CURRAGH, near Newbridge, and PUNCHESTOWN, near Naas.

The Curragh races were the destination for THE WORLD'S FIRST-EVER RAILWAY EXCURSION ORGANISED FOR A SPORTING EVENT, in 1846.

THE TETRARCH (1911–35), known as the 'Spotted Wonder' and variously described as 'probably the greatest two-year-old of all time' and 'possibly the greatest runner ever', was foaled at the Straffan stud near Ardclough. In 1913 The Tetrarch won all seven of his races and in 1919 he was voted leading sire in Great Britain and Ireland. A race at the Curragh is named after him, the Tetrarch Stakes.

Both 2000 Grand National winners, PAPILLON (Grand National) and COMMANCHE COURT (Irish Grand National), were trained by Ted Walsh at Kill.

Cheltenham Gold Cup winners CAPTAIN CHRISTY (1974) and KICKING KING (2005) were trained by father and son team Pat and Tom Taaffe at Alasty.

SHERGAR (1978–83?), the Aga Khan's racehorse and winner of the 1981 Epsom Derby by an all-time record ten lengths, was kidnapped from the Ballymany stud near the Curragh in 1983. He was never found. It is generally believed that he was abducted by the IRA and held for a ransom of £2 million, but was killed when he became troublesome during the drawn-out negotiations.

Cycling

PADDY FLANAGAN (1941–2000), THE FIRST CYCLIST TO WIN THE RAS TAILTEAN TWICE, in 1960 and 1964, was born in KILDANGAN. The Ras Tailtean is an eight-day cycle race run through Ireland in May.

Sir Laurence O'Toole
1128–80

The first native-born Irish archbishop of Dublin, SIR LAURENCE O'TOOLE, was born in Castledermot. The son of a Leinster chieftain, he was taken hostage by the MacMurroughs, but was subsequently given into the care of the abbot of Glendalough, a position he himself later attained before taking on the see of Dublin. Laurence's sister was given in marriage to Diarmait MacMurrough as a sign of peace between the O'Tooles and the MacMurroughs, but Diarmait treated her abominably and eventually eloped with Devorgilla, wife of Tiernan O'Rourke, Prince of Breffni, the event which gave rise to the Norman invasion of 1170 led by the Earl of Pembroke, otherwise known as 'Strongbow'. For the rest of his life Archbishop O'Toole was occupied in trying to keep the peace between the Norman invaders and the native Irish Dubliners.

North Cross and the South Cross. Amongst the exquisite carvings on the crosses are representations of Adam and Eve, the Apostles, Daniel in the Lion's Den and two rare portraits of David and his harp, THE EARLIEST KNOWN PICTURES OF AN IRISH HARP.

In 1181, during the Norman invasion, a castle was built by Walter de Riddlesford, and Castledermot developed into a walled market town.

THE EARLIEST RECORDED IRISH PARLIAMENT MET AT CASTLEDERMOT on 18 June 1264.

Castledermot

The quiet village of CASTLEDERMOT, originally Diseart Diarmad, meaning 'Dermot's hermitage', takes its name from St Diarmad, who founded a monastic cell here in around AD 500. The much revered Archbishop of Cashel and King of Munster, Cormac Mac Cuillenan, was educated at the monastery and was buried beneath the ruins in AD 938.

Remaining from this time is a truncated round tower built in 919, now 66 ft (20 m) high, attached to the old church and unusual in having medieval battlements at the top in place of a cap roof. Also two of Ireland's finest high crosses, the

Larchill Arcadian Gardens

A few miles to the north of Naas, by the village of Kilcock, lies 'the most fashionable garden in all Ireland', according to the Ordnance Survey of 1830. LARCHILL ARCADIAN GARDEN is THE ONLY SURVIVING *ferme ornée,* OR ORNAMENTAL FARM, IN EUROPE. Laid out in the 18th century, the gardens were rediscovered and rescued from decay in the 1990s by the de Las Casas family. *Ferme ornée* gardens were an invention of the 18th-century Romantic Movement, and sought for the first time to reflect the Greek concept of

Arcadia, or man in harmony with nature, by including natural features and landscape in their design.

At Larchill, a farmyard for rare pigs and goats sits at the heart of 65 acres (26 ha) of ornamental gardens complete with peacocks, woodland trails, a dovecot, a lake, ten Gothic castellated follies, a walled garden, pastureland for llamas, emus and rare breeds of cattle and sheep, and the extraordinary 'Foxes Earth' – put there on the instructions of a previous owner, fanatical foxhunter ROBERT WATSON, who was convinced he would be reincarnated as a fox and wanted a safe place to hide from the hounds.

Jigginstown House

Located just south of the county town of Naas are the extensive remains of THE FIRST RED-BRICK HOUSE IN IRELAND, JIGGINSTOWN HOUSE, begun in 1633 by the Earl of Strafford, later Lord Lieutenant of Ireland, as a place to entertain Charles I. Strafford was executed in 1641 and the house was never completed, but with a frontage nearly 450 ft (137 m) in length it would have been the largest house in Ireland.

Celbridge

CELBRIDGE is celebrated as THE LARGEST TOWN IN IRELAND TO HAVE ONLY ONE COMMERCIAL STREET.

James Carberry's brewery, now Norris's Bar, in Celbridge, was possibly the first place ever to serve a Guinness brew – in 1722 it was taken over by Dr Arthur Price, the owner of Oakley Park, whose land steward was Richard Guinness, renowned for his skill in making a 'brew of a very palatable nature'. Richard's son Arthur, founder of the Guinness brewery at St James's Gate in Dublin, was born in Celbridge in 1725.

In the grounds of CELBRIDGE ABBEY is the Rock Bridge, the oldest stone bridge across the River Liffey. Overlooking it is Vanessa's Bower, where the author of *Gulliver's Travels*, Dean Jonathan Swift, would often walk with his love Esther 'Vanessa' Van Homrigh. Her father, who had built Celbridge Abbey in 1660, was Lord Mayor of Dublin, and it was he who was presented by William of Orange with the chain of office still worn by the Lord Mayor today.

In 1780, one of Ireland's greatest orators, HENRY GRATTAN (1746–1820), composed his most famous speech, 'The Declaration of Rights', while at contemplation in Vanessa's Bower. The speech, allied to Grattan's

powerful oratory, achieved legislative independence for the Irish parliament in 1782.

Grattan's grandfather had owned Celbridge Abbey, and his mother was born there. Grattan was a regular visitor to what became his uncle's house, and here he could relax from the rigours of fighting for Catholic emancipation and work on his speeches.

Lyons

In 1796 the LYONS estate came into the hands of NICHOLAS LAWLESS, 1ST BARON CLONCURRY, a wool merchant and banker. In 1797 he began building the present stone house, which was completed by his son VALENTINE LAWLESS (1773–1853), a prominent member of the United Irishmen and supporter of

both Henry Grattan and Daniel O'Connell, 'The Liberator'.

In 1815 O'Connell fought a pistol duel on the Lyons estate against John D'Esterre, a member of the Dublin Corporation who objected to a speech in which O'Connell had referred to the 'Corpo' as a 'beggarly corporation'. D'Esterre was mortally wounded, and O'Connell was haunted by the memory of the affair for the rest of his life – until his death 30 years later he paid an allowance to D'Esterre's daughter and wore a black glove on his right hand whenever he went to church.

Lyons Castle

Valentine Lawless's granddaughter, the poet EMILY LAWLESS (1845–1913), was born at Lyons House. Much associated with the Irish Revival, her poetry gives an authentic feminine view of Irish folk tradition and history, such as was made popular in the middle of the 19th century by the Young Ireland poets. Her most celebrated work is 'Wild Geese', a realistic and unromanticised look at the Gaelic soldiers who fled Ireland after the Battle of Aughrin in 1691 and fought in the French army. In the poem we hear the voice of Mother Ireland:

> She said, 'They gave me of their best,
> They lived, they gave their lives for me;
> I tossed them to the howling waste,
> And flung them to the foaming sea.'

Lyons was later the home of TONY RYAN, creator of Ryanair, who died in 2007.

Bishopscourt

Another great supporter of Catholic emancipation was WILLIAM PONSONBY, 1ST BARON PONSONBY OF IMOKILLY (1744–1806), whose family seat was BISHOPSCOURT, near Kill. The Ponsonbys were one of Ireland's leading political families. William's father had been Speaker of the Irish House of Commons and William himself was a member of the Irish Commons and also Postmaster-General.

In 1769 William married Louisa Molesworth, and they had five sons and one daughter. Their second son, Major-General Sir William Ponsonby, commanded the Union Brigade of cavalry at the Battle of Waterloo. It was named the Union because it included regiments from England, Scotland and Ireland. After an initial effective charge the Brigade lost their heads and continued to gallop into the enemy lines, with the result that their ranks were decimated by the French artillery, Ponsonby being one of those killed.

The heroic but undisciplined charge of the Union Brigade at Waterloo is frequently cited by military historians as a classic example of a flawed military manoeuvre.

The Major-General's sister Mary married the British Prime Minister Earl Grey, after whom the tea is named.

Well, I never knew this
about
KILDARE FOLK

Sir Richard Griffith
— 1784–1878 —

The 'Father of Irish Geology', SIR RICHARD GRIFFITH grew up on his father's estate at Millicent, near CLANE. After studying engineering, mining and geology in London he returned to Ireland to serve as a bog commissioner and inspector of mines. He engineered many of Ireland's early roads and railways, and in 1825 was put in charge of the Boundary Commission for the Ordnance Survey of Ireland which had responsibility for compiling land valuations and mapping the boundaries of every town in Ireland. During this work he privately collected material for THE FIRST GEOLOGICAL MAP OF IRELAND, which he published in 1839.

Jack 'Nonpareil' Dempsey
— 1862–96 —

Middleweight boxer JACK 'NONPAREIL' DEMPSEY was born John Edward Kelly, in CURRAN. He was called 'Nonpareil', meaning 'without equal', because almost no one could defeat him, and he won 62 of his 65 fights. Such was Dempsey's fame that his name was replicated by a famous early 20th-century heavyweight champion, William Harrison Dempsey, who also fought under the name 'Jack' Dempsey.

Dame Kathleen Lonsdale
◄ 1903–71 ►

DAME KATHLEEN LONSDALE, THE
FIRST WOMAN TO BE ELECTED A
FELLOW OF THE ROYAL SOCIETY,
was born in NEWBRIDGE. She was
the first female professor at University College London, and a pioneer
of the use of X-rays to study crystals.
Her achievements included the
discovery of the structure of benzene,
and the first accurate measurements
of the structure of diamond. In 1968
she became THE FIRST FEMALE
PRESIDENT OF THE BRITISH ASSO-
CIATION FOR THE ADVANCEMENT
OF SCIENCE.

Josef Locke
◄ 1917–99 ►

World-renowned tenor JOSEF
LOCKE, born Joseph McLaughlin in
Derry, lived for many years in semi-
retirement at the beautiful Georgian
KINGSWOOD HOUSE in Kingswood
village, after a long dispute with the
British tax authorities.

In 1992 Josef Locke was introduced
to a new audience in a film by Peter
Chisolm called *Hear My Song*. It
tells the story of the manager of a
London music hall who tries to lure
the tenor out of his retirement in Co.
Kildare.

Iconic folk musician, songwriter and
guitarist CHRISTY MOORE was born
in NEWBRIDGE in 1945. His first
album, *Paddy on the Road*, was
released in 1969 and was recorded with
Dominic Behan, brother of the writer
Brendan Behan. He named his second
album *Prosperous*, after the town
where it was recorded, Prosperous in
Co. Kildare, which was founded in
1780 by Robert Brook as a cotton-
manufacturing centre.

County Kilkenny

HISTORIC BUILDINGS ✦ KILKENNY CATS
✦ OLDEST IRISH ALE
✦ A MAGNIFICENT FLYING MACHINE ✦ MINING TOWN
✦ CULM CRUSHERS ✦ LARGEST RUIN ✦ CONKERS
✦ WAR OF THE ROSES

Kilkenny Castle guards Ireland's smallest city.

◄ KILKENNY FOLK ►

Kitty Clive ✦ Edmund Ignatius Rice ✦ John O'Donovan ✦ Nora Sands

Kilkenny

Although it is IRELAND'S SMALLEST CITY, KILKENNY can boast of possessing more historic buildings than almost any Irish town outside Dublin. Situated in the town centre, between the castle and the cathedral, is one of Ireland's few surviving Tudor almshouses, the SHEE ALMSHOUSE, built in 1582 by Sir Richard Shee, a wealthy merchant, to accommodate 'twelve poor persons'.

toll, meaning tax, and *sae,* meaning hall. Hence, this is the place where tolls were collected, but since being erected in 1761 it has also served as a courthouse, custom house and guildhall. The Tholsel straddles the pavement above an open arcade, which is used as an exhibition space during Kilkenny's annual Arts Week and as a place for street entertainers to perform all year round.

The Tholsel

Shee Almshouse

A little to the north is the town hall, or THOLSEL, topped by a tall lantern clock tower that can be seen for miles around. The name Tholsel comes from a combination of two words,

Further north again is ROTHE HOUSE, THE ONLY EXAMPLE OF A TUDOR MERCHANT'S TOWN HOUSE IN ALL OF IRELAND. It was built between 1594 and 1610 by John Rothe Fitz Piers, father of 12, and mayor of Kilkenny, and is now run as a museum of the life and times of the Rothe family.

Rothe House

Kilkenny, which sits on the River Nore, is the only city in the Republic of Ireland that is not located either by the sea or on a tidal stretch of river.

Kilkenny Cats

There once were two cats of
   Kilkenny
Each thought there was one cat
   too many
So they fought and they hit
And they scratched and they bit
'Til instead of two cats there
   weren't any!

The inhabitants of Kilkenny are sometimes known as 'Kilkenny Cats', an expression that is also used to describe someone who fights to the death. There are many theories about the origins of this phrase, some more fanciful than others. One popular account has it that soldiers based in Kilkenny during the 1798 rebellion liked to pass the time by arranging catfights. They would tie the cats together by their tails and hang them from a beam, and then bet on which animal would survive the ensuing tussle. This practice was frowned upon by their superiors, and when on one occasion an officer came in unexpectedly, the soldiers let the cats escape by chopping off their tails, explaining away the remaining stubs by telling the officer that the felines had fought each other so fiercely all that was left were the tips of their tails!

A more likely explanation comes from medieval times when the city was divided into Englishtown and Irishtown by the Statutes of Kilkenny, and the two sides bickered for centuries, sometimes violently, to the great detriment of both.

The Kilkenny Gaelic football and hurling teams are both known as the 'Cats'.

In early summer, since 1995, Kilkenny has played host to the Smithwick's Cat Laughs Comedy festival, when for a few days Kilkenny becomes the 'Comedy Capital of the World'. Top comedians from many countries but, particularly from Ireland, Britain and America, give stand-up performances, and short, humorous films called Kitty Flicks are also shown.

Smithwick's Irish red ale is IRELAND'S OLDEST ALE and was first brewed in 1710 at the ST FRANCIS ABBEY BREWERY in Kilkenny, THE OLDEST OPERATING BREWERY IN IRELAND. It was set up by John Smithwick on the site of a Franciscan friary, where ale had been brewed by the monks since the 14th century.

The Race is to the Swift

Just outside Kilkenny is SWIFTE'S HEATH, built in 1656 by GODWIN SWIFTE and home to Dean Jonathan Swift, author of *Gulliver's Travels*, while he was studying at Kilkenny College. A more recent GODWIN SWIFT – the 'e' was dropped in the late 17th century – was a celebrated local eccentric who apparently married an Austrian baroness, von Wetslar of Schonkirchen, and called himself Viscount Carlingford, a title which had died out in 1634 with the death of his ancestor Barnham Swift. He was something of an inventor, and in 1856 he unveiled 'an air chariot to navigate the sky', shaped like a boat with wings and equipped with wheels and a screw propeller. Swift ordered a member of his staff – opinion varies on whether it was his gardener or his butler – to pilot the contraption off the roof of the house, but alas, perhaps inevitably, the unfortunate fellow plunged to earth with a sickening crunch and broke his leg. The remains of the air chariot, along with Swift's patent for it, can be seen in the Rothe House Museum.

Suitably enough, Kilkenny is home to the Irish Patents Office, established in 1927. The first Irish patent was granted to an American, Hannah Mary Smith, in 1929 for a 'portable starting cage for racing dogs'.

Castlecomer

CASTLECOMER is an attractive small town that was laid out near the original castle mound by Sir Christopher

Wandesforde in 1637, in the style of the Italian village of Alsinore. Constructed of small stone houses grouped around a market square, it WAS THE FIRST LARGE-SCALE STONE-BUILT TOWN IN IRELAND.

Castlecomer was designed as an administrative centre for the exploitation of the local anthracite deposits and to provide accommodation for the miners. The town sits right at the heart of the Leinster coalfield, home of IRELAND'S LARGEST OPEN-CAST COAL-MINES, THE DEERPARK MINES, which were worked for over 300 years until they closed in 1969. They were still mining coal near Castlecomber, in a small way and for local use, until 2000, when IRELAND'S LAST COAL-MINE was finally shut down.

THE WORLD'S FIRST UNDERGROUND CONVEYOR BELT was invented and developed at Castlecomer by RICHARD SUTCLIFFE (1849–1930), who worked there as a miner and manager between 1857 and 1885. Sutcliffe later moved to Wakefield, in England, where he set up a company, Richard Sutcliffe Ltd, to manufacture conveyor belts and another of his inventions, the world's first coal-cutting machine. Richard Sutcliffe's story is told in renowned film director Lindsay Anderson's first-ever commercial documentary, *Meet the Pioneers*, made in 1948.

In 1890, an engineer from Castle-comer, JOHN WALKER (1841–1901), invented an early type of caterpillar tread, a wide, notched belt that was wrapped around a set of wheels on both sides of the vehicle. It was described in the *Railway Supplies Journal* of 1896 as 'a remarkable novelty. The model is only a rough one yet it works nicely and easily. The moment the car moves all the wheels are instantly in motion and the pulleys lay down and take up the rails without the least friction.' Walker took the idea to the War Office in London, but they failed to spot the potential – in the First World War, when developing a method of propelling the tank across the mud of Flanders, they had to start again from scratch. Eventually, after great effort and expense, they came up with something remarkably similar to what Walker had offered them 20 years earlier.

Walker's invention did manage to attract some commercial interest in America, where his brother William was a member of the New York State Assembly. William's son Jimmy, John Walker's nephew, became a famous mayor of New York City.

In the 1940s, John Walker's caterpillar treads were manufactured at a forge in Castlecomer and put into use in the local mines.

Some poignant souvenirs from the harsh days of the 19th century can be seen lying on the ground of the coal-mining areas around Castlecomer:

small, rough grinding stones known as culm crushers. These were strapped to an upright post that was stuck in the centre of a stone platform and turned to grind down coal dust known as culm. The resulting putty was then mixed with clay, rolled into a ball and left to dry, after which it could be used as fuel by poor local farmers and their families. Castlecomer is the only place in Ireland where these culm crushers can still be found.

Kells

Kells in Co. Kilkenny is not to be confused with the Kells in Co. Meath associated with the celebrated *Book of Kells*. The Kilkenny Kells is a lovely riverside village that boasts THE LARGEST, AND SOME OF THE BEST PRESERVED MONASTIC RUINS IN IRELAND, a vast walled complex of tower houses and chapels covering some 5 acres (2 ha), the remains of an Augustinian priory dating back to 1193.

Freshford

The 52 stately horse chestnut trees that surround the glorious village green at FRESHFORD produce over 30,000 conkers every year, and provide the ammunition for the annual IRISH CONKER CHAMPIONSHIPS, which have been held in Freshford since 1999.

The glorious Romanesque portal of St Lachtain's church in Freshford is one of only two of its kind left in Ireland, the other being at Clonfert in Co. Galway. There has been a church on this spot since AD 622, but it was replaced in 1100 and the portal is all that remains from this 12th-century church – the present church dates from 1731.

Piltown

PILTOWN is the only place in Ireland where a battle associated with the English Wars of the Roses was fought. In the Battle of Piltown in 1462 the Butlers of Kilkenny, fighting for the House of Lancaster (Red Rose), were defeated by the forces of the Earl of Desmond, who was on the side of the House of York (White Rose). The Butlers lost some 400 men and according to local legend the fighting was so fierce that the streets ran red with blood – hence the Irish name for Piltown, Baile an Phuill, or 'town of the blood'.

KILDALTON COLLEGE in Piltown is IRELAND'S LARGEST AGRICULTURAL COLLEGE and occupies what was once Bessborough House, a fine Georgian mansion built in 1745.

The PILTOWN AGRICULTURAL SHOW, held in early September every year since 1825, is IRELAND'S LONGEST-RUNNING AGRICULTURAL SHOW and attracts visitors from all over Europe, especially from Wales. As well as parades of farm animals and machinery there are dog shows, competitions and stalls selling home-made produce.

Well, I never knew this
about
KILKENNY FOLK

Kitty Clive
—◄ 1711–85 ►—

WILLIAM RAFTOR, father of the actress KITTY CLIVE, was born in KILKENNY. Having fought for King James II during the Battle of the Boyne, William was deprived of his estate and had to leave Ireland. Like many exiled Irish soldiers he ended up in the French army of Louis XIV, but he was pardoned by Queen Anne and returned to Kilkenny, where his daughter Catherine (Kitty) is thought to have been born. She made her debut as actress at the Drury Lane theatre in London in 1728, and went on to become one of London's most popular comic actresses and singers, and a founding member of David Garrick's acting troupe. In 1733 she married barrister George Clive, a cousin of Clive of India. She retired to Twickenham and is buried there in St Mary's Church.

Edmund Ignatius Rice
—◄ 1762–1844 ►—

EDMUND IGNATIUS RICE, founder of the teaching order of the CHRISTIAN BROTHERS, was born in a thatched cottage in WESTCOURT, just outside Callan, the fourth of seven sons. At the age of 17 he was apprenticed to his uncle's merchant business in Waterford, at that time one of the busiest ports in Europe. In 1785 he inherited the business and got married to a local girl called Mary Elliot. A few years later tragedy struck when she was thrown from her horse while pregnant. Mary died in childbirth and their daughter was born disabled.

From that time on Edmund devoted himself to helping the poor,

Edmund Ignatius Rice's birthplace in Westcourt

eventually selling his business and using the money to build a school in a converted stable for the notorious 'quay kids' of Waterford, boys who hung around the docks thieving or waiting to be employed on errands. In 1802 two friends of Edmund's from his home town of Callan joined him and they began a second school, despite the fact that under the Penal Laws it was illegal for Catholics to set up educational establishments.

In 1808 Edmund and seven of his staff took religious vows under the Bishop of Waterford and became the Presentation Brothers, THE FIRST CONGREGATION OF MEN EVER FORMED IN IRELAND and one of the very few to be founded by a layman. Other Irish bishops began to send men to Edmund to be trained, and eventually Edmund got the approval of the Pope to run his own teaching order under Papal approval. This teaching order became known as the Christian Brothers, dedicated to

feeding, clothing, caring for and educating the poor – men and women, young and old, prison inmates, the disadvantaged and the destitute.

In 1828 Daniel O'Connell laid the foundation stone of the Christian Brothers' headquarters in Dublin, and since then the order has spread across the world, with missions in Australia,

New Zealand, Canada, the USA, India and Rome.

Edmund Ignatius Rice retired in 1838 at the age of 76 and lived out the rest of his life in Waterford. In 1996 he was beatified by Pope John Paul II, who declared him the Blessed Edmund Rice.

Many nationalists and politicians and other leading Irishmen from all walks of life were educated by the Christian Brothers, including Patrick Pearse, Eamon de Valera and Second World War flying ace Paddy Finucane, DSO, DFC and two bars, the youngest Wing Commander in the RAF.

John O'Donovan
—◄ 1806–61 ►—

JOHN O'DONOVAN, one of Ireland's pre-eminent scholars, was born at ATATEEMORE, near Slieverue, the son of a farmer. For much of his adult life he worked for the topographical department of the first Ordnance Survey of Ireland, researching the origins of Irish place-names. His greatest work was the translation of the *Annals of the Kingdom of Ireland* by the Four Masters, a compilation of records and manuscripts about the history of Ireland up until 1616, put together at a Franciscan monastery in Co. Donegal by the 'four friars' led by Michael O'Clery.

Cartoon king WALT DISNEY's ancestors, on his father's side, emigrated to Canada from Co. Kilkenny in the 19th century.

NORA SANDS, the no-nonsense dinner lady from the school that featured in the television programme *Jamie's School Dinners*, is a native of KILLEN, near Inistioge.

County Laois

*A participant in Ireland's foremost celebration
of steam, Stradbally Steam Fair.*

◀ LAOIS FOLK ▶

COUNTY LAOIS is considered to be Ireland's most land-locked county, since it is the only Irish county to be bordered entirely by other landlocked counties. The county can also boast THE ONLY FLY-FISHING MUSEUM IN IRELAND, THE IRISH FLYFISHERS AND GAME MUSEUM, opened in 1986 by Walter Phelan, in the village of ATTANAGH.

Stradbally

STRADBALLY, consisting of a single street, 1 mile (1.6 km) long, certainly lives up to its name, which in Irish means 'one street town'. Every year in August that one street is filled with hissing, belching, wheezing leviathans as vintage steam-engines, tractors and various other steaming contraptions, converge on the grounds of Stradbally Hall from all over the country, for Ireland's foremost celebration of steam, the STRADBALLY STEAM FAIR. The fair has been held here annually since 1966, attracted to the town by the Stradbally Steam Museum, which is run by the Irish Steam Preservation Society, and provides many of the working exhibits for the show. Also in the grounds IS THE LONGEST ESTABLISHED STEAM-POWERED NARROW-GAUGE RAILWAY IN IRELAND.

Since 2004 Stradbally Hall has also hosted a popular music festival called the Electric Picnic. Held in September, this has grown from a one-day event into a three-day festival.

The Cosbys of Stradbally Hall

Stradbally Hall is the ancestral home of the Cosby family, who were granted land in the area in 1563. The present hall dates from the middle of the 19th century.

Born there in 1690 was WILLIAM COSBY (1690–1736), who went on to become Royal Governor of New York from 1732 to 1736. He was at the centre of a celebrated trial that had a long-lasting influence on the freedom of the press in the English-speaking world, the Zenger Case. John Peter Zenger was the publisher of a weekly newspaper called the *New York Weekly Journal*, which published articles exposing corruption in Cosby's administration. Cosby had Zenger charged with printing 'false, malicious, seditious and scandalous libels'. At his trial, Zenger's lawyer Andrew Hamilton argued that Zenger could not be guilty of seditious libel because the criticisms printed in the *Journal* were true. In an early victory for the free press, Zenger was found 'not guilty' and released.

fought with General Wolfe at the capture of Quebec in 1759. At the moment of victory on the Plains of Abraham, Wolfe died in Cosby's arms, as shown in a famous painting by Benjamin West, *The Death of General Wolfe*, in which Philips Cosby can be seen cradling Wolfe's head in his hands.

Kevin O'Higgins
1892–1927

Sir William Cosby

William Cosby's nephew PHILIPS COSBY, also born at Stradbally Hall, in 1730, became a naval officer and

The revolutionary politician KEVIN O'HIGGINS was born in Stradbally in 1892, where his father practised as a physician. A strong supporter of the Anglo-Irish Treaty of 1921, he served as Vice President of the Executive Council and Justice Minister for the Irish Free State from 1922 to 1927. One of his first acts as Justice Minister was to order the execution of 77 Republican prisoners captured during the Irish Civil War. Amongst them was Rory O'Connor, who had been O'Higgins's best man. In 1927 O'Higgins was assassinated by three members of the anti-treaty IRA while on his way to Mass in Blackrock, Co. Dublin. A monument to the O'Higgins family stands in the Court Square in Stradbally.

Mountmellick

MOUNTMELLICK began life as a Quaker settlement around 1659, when THE FIRST QUAKER IN IRELAND, a former Cromwellian soldier called WILLIAM EDMUNDSON (1627–1712), moved into the area from Lurgan in Co. Armagh. Others soon joined him, and in 1677 IRELAND'S FIRST QUAKER SCHOOL was established in Mountmellick. Over the next 200 years the town flourished and grew, with the opening of new industries such as brewing, woollen mills, and IRELAND'S FIRST SUGAR BEET FACTORY, which opened in 1851.

In the early part of the 19th century a Mountmellick lady called JOANNA CARTER began a small cottage industry producing exquisite white-on-white embroidery, using designs inspired by the plants found growing along the banks of the River Owenass, such as dog rose, passion flowers, shamrocks and blackberries. Mountmellick Embroidery, as it became known, proved hugely popular among Victorian ladies and provided welcome employment for the women of the town during the Great Famine and afterwards. The craft was revived in the 1970s by SISTER TERESA MARGARET McCARTHY of the Presentation Convent in Mountmellick, and original examples of the art are now highly sought after.

John Shaw
1773–1823

JOHN SHAW was born in Mountmellick and emigrated to America when he was 17. He joined the merchant marine and later the US Navy, and in 1799 he was put in command of the schooner *Enterprise*.

Over the next year *Enterprise* captured eight French privateers and re-took 11 American merchant ships, becoming one of the most famous ships in the US navy.

Shaw rose to be a naval captain during the 1812 war, after which he retired to Philadelphia, where he died. Two destroyers were named in his honour, including the USS *Shaw* that blew up so spectacularly during the attack on Pearl Harbor in 1941.

Shaw Island, one of the San Juan Islands off the coast of Washington state, is also named after him. Shaw Island featured in the US television series *West Wing* as the location for a stand-off between the US Government and a group of terrorists.

The schooner *Enterprise* was the third American ship to bear that now cherished name, known worldwide thanks to the Starship *Enterprise* from the American TV series *Star Trek*. The very first *Enterprise* was a frigate called *L'Enterprise*, which was captured from the French in 1705 by the Royal Navy and re-christened HMS *Enterprise*. The present USS *Enterprise* was launched in 1961 and was the first nuclear aircraft-carrier in the world. The first Space Shuttle was named *Enterprise*, and the space tourism company Virgin Galactic have named the world's first commercial spaceship VSS *Enterprise*.

Shaw Island's 'Little Red Schoolhouse' – still in use

William Russell Grace
1832–1904

WILLIAM RUSSELL GRACE was born in GRACEFIELD LODGE, an elegant villa designed for the Grace family by John Nash in 1817, near BALLYLINAN, south-east of Portlaoise. Keen to join the navy, William ran away to sea and ended up in 1854 in Peru where, with his brother Michael, he set up a ship chandlery business, which later became Grace Brothers Ltd.

After getting married, Grace settled in New York in 1865 and set up W.R. Grace and Co. to run his shipping concerns trading between New York, South America and Europe. The company's fortunes were built on transporting guano and South American silver.

In 1880 Grace was elected as the first-ever Roman Catholic mayor of New York, and was in office to accept the gift of the Statue of Liberty from the people of France to the people of America.

William Russell Grace died in 1904, but the company continued to expand, opening the Grace National Bank in 1914. That same year a Grace ship took the honour of being the first commercial vessel to sail through the newly built Panama Canal.

As well as shipping the company was heavily involved in fertilisers and chemicals, and in the 1950s expanded by taking over two large chemical companies, the Davison Chemical Company and the Dewey & Almy Chemical Company.

In 1971 the company commissioned the construction of the 50-storey Grace Building on Sixth Avenue in New York, 630 ft (192 m) tall. W.R. Grace and Company later moved their corporate headquarters to Columbia, Maryland, and the Grace Building is today occupied by, among others, AOL Time Warner.

In 1987 W.R. Grace and Company became THE FIRST WHOLLY FOREIGN-OWNED COMPANY TO DO BUSINESS IN THE PEOPLE'S REPUBLIC OF CHINA, when they opened a can-sealing plant in Shanghai.

Meanwhile, back in Co. Laois, Gracefield Lodge is now a luxury hotel.

Well, I never knew this about
LAOIS FOLK

Thomas Prior
— 1680–1751 —

THOMAS PRIOR, founder of the ROYAL DUBLIN SOCIETY, was born in RATH-DOWNEY. His father was a farmer, and Thomas maintained a lifelong interest in agriculture and land reform. In 1731 he organised a meeting at Trinity College, in Dublin, with Dr Samuel Madden and 11 other leading pioneers, where it was decided to form a society to support and promote agriculture, science and the arts. This evolved into the Royal Dublin Society. Thomas Prior is buried in the Church of Ireland parish church in Rathdowney and there is a monument to his memory in Dublin's Christ Church Cathedral.

Castle Durrow

Nationalist politician and journalist for the *Nation* newspaper, JAMES FINTAN LALOR (1807–49) was born in Tenakill.

Robert Flower
— 1836–1919 —

Prolific inventor ROBERT FLOWER, 8th Viscount Ashbrook of Durrow, was born in CASTLE DURROW, his ancestral family home near Abbeyleix. Although Flower came up with imaginative designs for all sorts of items such as hot-water stoves and organ pipes, his real interest was in weaving, and to this end he invented an easy-to-use handloom that could be operated by the unskilled and disabled, as well as the latch-hook needle which speeded up the whole weaving process.

Flower's inventions attracted the attention of local philanthropist Ivo Vesey, the 5th Viscount de Vesci of Abbey Leix, who thought they might help to provide employment for the women of the town. In 1904 he opened a carpet factory applying Flower's techniques and utilising designs from local artists. The factory earned a reputation for producing beautiful, high-quality carpets that were sold in Harrods in London and Marshall Fields in Chicago, and found their way into such august establishments as Dublin's Mansion House and the grandstand at Ascot. Abbeyleix Carpets' greatest accolade came when they were asked to supply carpets for the White Star liner *Titanic*. Ironically, the factory was forced to close in December 1912, eight months after *Titanic* was sunk by an iceberg.

LIAM MILLER (1924–87), founder in 1951 of the Dolmen Press, which championed and published Irish poetry, was born in MOUNTRATH.

County Longford

---◆◆◆◆◆---

An Ancient Palace ✦ Floating Stones ✦ Battle of Ballinamuck

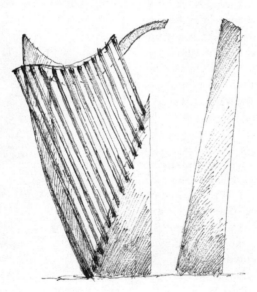

*The Harp of Granard is
home to a famous August Harp Festival.*

---◀ LONGFORD FOLK ▶---

Anne Reilly Gibson ✦ Kitty Kiernan

COUNTY LONGFORD is the third smallest county in Ireland after Co. Louth and Co. Carlow. It is quiet farming country, where the attractions are natural rather then man-made. The population is sparse, large numbers of inhabitants from Co. Longford having emigrated to Canada and America in the 18th century, partly to escape from religious persecution and partly to escape from economic poverty.

Granard

GRANARD, with its huge, high Norman motte and bailey, the highest in Ireland, is one of Co. Longford's most ancient places. In the early 5th century it was the palace residence of CAIRBRE, eldest son of Niall of the Nine Hostages, the High King of Ireland from whom descended the Ui Neill dynasties. Cairbre was a fierce opponent of St Patrick's missionary work in Ireland, and indeed tried to assassinate the saint during a royal gathering, an act that brought down St Patrick's curse on Cairbre and led to his name being expunged from the list of kings. Ironically, at the summit of the mound that marks the site of Cairbre's palace, there is a statue of his nemesis, St Patrick.

Granard is also mentioned in Irish mythology as somewhere that Queen Maeve and her army camped on their way to capture the Brown Bull of Cooley during the fabled Cattle Raid, as recounted in the Tain.

Near Granard is THE ONLY STONE CIRCLE IN THE MIDLANDS, THE DRUID CIRCLE, consisting of 24 stones, six of them still standing, the others lying on their sides.

Aughnacliffe

At AUGHNACLIFFE, about 5 miles (8 km) north-west of Granard, is Ireland's most unusual dolmen, two huge capstones balanced precariously one on top of another, both supported by a huge portal stone, 6 ft (1.8 m) high. From some angles it looks as though the capstones are floating in the air, and a single breath of wind will bring the mighty boulders crashing to the ground. It is a remarkable sight, truly one of Ireland's mystical places. The dolmen in fact

gives the village its name – Aughnacliffe in Gaelic is Achadh na Cloiche,
meaning 'field of stones'.

Battle of Ballinamuck

BALLINAMUCK today is a quiet,
attractive little town resting on peat-
land and nestling amongst gentle hills
and sparkling lakes. It seems as if the
most energetic activity that takes place
is fishing, or possibly painting.

Two hundred years ago in 1798 this
peaceful place rang to the clash of steel
and the cries of battle, as the French
and Irish forces under General
Humbert saw their dreams of an
Ireland free from British rule
destroyed. Two weeks earlier Humbert
had waded ashore at County Mayo
and secured a crushing victory over
General Lake at Castlebar, but the
expected support from various local
uprisings had not materialised and
Humbert was left isolated, with his
2,000 men facing 5,000 British under
the command of General Cornwallis.
Hugely outnumbered, the French
forces laid down their weapons and
surrendered after little more than a
brief skirmish.

The Irish forces of some 1,000 men
under Colonel Teering refused to
surrender, and after their lines were
broken up by a cavalry charge the
survivors were rounded up and taken
to the nearby village of BALLINALEE,
where many were executed in a field
now known as Bullys Acre.

The Battle of Ballinamuck was
notable for a number of reasons. It
was one of the last battles fought on
Irish soil by a foreign power, and it
was THE LAST BATTLE IN WHICH
CATHOLICS AND PROTESTANTS
FOUGHT ON THE SAME SIDE FOR A
COMMON CAUSE.

Ballinalee village saw violence
again in 1920 during the Anglo-Irish
War, when the Battle of Ballinalee saw
Sean Mac Eoin, born in Ballinalee in
1893, lead a band of some 300 local
men in a successful defence of the
town against the Black and Tans
(*see* page 104). After three days the
attackers withdrew.

The Black and Tans were a special reserve force of the Royal Ulster Constabulary, formed in 1920 to combat the IRA during the Anglo-Irish War of 1919–21. The name was derived from their black and khaki uniforms, which were similar to the colours of a well-known pack of foxhounds from Limerick, the Scarteen Black and Tans.

Well, I never knew this
about
LONGFORD FOLK

Film actor Mel Gibson's mother, ANNE REILLY GIBSON, was born in the Co. Longford parish of Colmcille, whose centre is around the village of AUGHNACLIFFE. Gibson's first name, Mel, is taken from the 5th-century Irish saint of that name, who founded the diocese of Ardagh in Co. Longford, while his second name, Colmcille, is the name of the parish where Anne Reilly was born and raised. Colmcille is another name for St Columba, who was born in Co. Donegal in AD 521, and was banished from Ireland after the Battle of the Books. He went on to found the monastery of Iona in Scotland.

Kitty Kiernan
◄ 1892–1945 ►

CATHERINE BRIDGIT KIERNAN, better known as KITTY, was born into a prosperous merchant family in Granard, one of seven children. Her family owned a number of businesses in Granard, including a timber merchant's and hardware store, a grocery shop and the Greville Arms Hotel, which is where she met MICHAEL COLLINS when he came to stay during the Co. Longford by-election campaign in May 1917. Kitty was bright, beautiful and vivacious, and Collins was something of a heroic figure, having just been released from internment for his part in the Easter Rising of the previous year. He was also a leading figure in Sinn Fein and the Irish Volunteers. Collins and Kitty fell deeply in love, Collins returned to visit Kitty in Granard many times during the next few years while his political career progressed, and they eventually became engaged.

Between 1919 and 1922, when Collins was assassinated by his own side for his part in negotiating the Anglo-Irish Treaty, Kitty and Collins wrote to each other almost every day, and their correspondence provides us with revealing insights into the man known as Ireland's 'lost leader' and the woman who knew him better than anyone.

In 1925, three years after Michael Collins's death, Kitty married Felix Cronin, an officer in the National Army of the Irish Free State. They named their second son Michael Collins Cronin.

In 1945 Kitty died of Bright's Disease, the same illness that killed all her brothers and sisters, and she was buried in Glasnevin Cemetery in Dublin, not far from Michael Collins.

County Louth

*St Peter's Catholic Church, Drogheda,
the last resting place of Oliver Plunkett's head.*

◀ LOUTH FOLK ▶

Father James Cullen ✦ Michael Scott ✦ Eamonn Campbell
✦ Des Smyth ✦ John Moore ✦ Evanna Lynch

Although COUNTY LOUTH is IRELAND'S SMALLEST COUNTY, it contains the two biggest towns in the Republic outside Dublin, Drogheda in the south of the county and Dundalk in the north.

Drogheda

————◆◆◆◆————

DROGHEDA stands on the north bank of the Boyne, a couple of miles inland, at a place where there was once a ford. The Vikings built the first Droichead Atha, or 'bridge across the ford', in AD 911 – the date 9/11 seems to have a special significance in Drogheda, for it was on 11 September in 1649 that Oliver Cromwell butchered the Royalist defenders of the town after the notorious siege of Drogheda.

The present-day Drogheda was founded by two Norman knights, Hugh de Lacy and Bertram de Verdon, who each built their own individual settlements, de Lacy on the Louth side of the river, de Verdon on the Meath side, and although Drogheda received its charter from Richard I in 1194, the two towns were not formally united until the constitution of 1415. In medieval times Drogheda expanded rapidly as a trading centre and at one time was twice the size of Dublin.

As seems fitting for a town that has a foot in two different counties, Drogheda has long been at the centre of power struggles in Ireland. In 1395

Richard II received the submission of the Ulster princes while staying at Drogheda's Dominican friary of St Mary Magdalene, of which only the striking 14th-century central bell-tower standing on the north edge of the town survives. In 1494 the Irish Parliament met in Drogheda to enact the infamous Poynings Law, which gave the English Privy Council the right of veto over every law passed by that Irish Parliament. The town was also at the centre of the struggle between Crown and Parliament during the English Civil War, and then again in 1690 when Catholic and Protestant monarchs fought the Battle of the Boyne just a few miles away.

Drogheda plays a small part in the story of Ireland's most famous international brand. In 1750, a French Huguenot brewer called JEAN PAUL ESPINASSE fell off his horse while visiting a tavern in Drogheda and died of his injuries. As a result, the lease on his brewery in Dublin became available and was taken up in 1759 by Arthur Guinness – and so began the spectacular transformation of the ST JAMES'S GATE brewery into THE BIGGEST BREWERY IN EUROPE.

The beacons installed in the River Boyne to guide ships into the port of Drogheda were designed by Captain William Bligh of 'Mutiny on the Bounty' renown, who also designed the North Bull Wall in Dublin Bay that prevents sandbars forming to

Dundalk

DUNDALK can boast IRELAND'S
FIRST ALL-WEATHER RACECOURSE,
which in September 2007 hosted
THE FIRST-EVER RACE MEETING
HELD UNDER FLOODLIGHTS IN
IRELAND.

Sir Peter Kerley
1900–78

St Mary Magdalene Bell Tower

block the mouth of the Liffey.

In Colleen McCullough's widely
read novel *The Thorn Birds*, the Irish-
owned Australian sheep station at the
centre of the story is named after the
town of Drogheda.

Clogherhead

The attractive fishing village of
CLOGHERHEAD, 8 miles (13 km)
north of Drogheda, boasts THE
ONLY BEACH-LAUNCHED LIFEBOAT IN
IRELAND. The village was used as a location in the 1997 film *The Devil's Own*,
starring Harrison Ford and Brad Pitt.

Eminent radiologist SIR PETER
KERLEY was born in Dundalk. He
studied medicine at University
College Dublin and spent the Second
World War designing a mass X-ray
screening programme for diagnosing
tuberculosis, which was introduced in
Britain in 1943 and in Ireland a couple
of years later. His other great contribution to radiology was in finding
new ways to interpret radiographs or
X-ray results. He discovered that the
horizontal lines of striped shadows
that can be seen on the lungs in radiographs, now known as Kerley A
Lines, Kerley B Lines and Kerley C
Lines, are signs of congestive heart
disease. The Royal College of Radi-
ologists gives a biennial Sir Peter
Kerley Lecture.

Thomas Coulter
1793–1843

Physician and botanist THOMAS COULTER was born in Dundalk. After studying at Trinity College Dublin he went to Mexico, where he served as a physician for the Real del Monte company, who were mining for silver in the central Hidalgo region. While he was there he undertook botanical research and collected together a selection of the local plant life, which he took with him when he returned to Ireland in 1834. In 1840, using his Mexican plant collection as the nucleus, he established the herbarium at Trinity College and became its first curator. Two of his most important finds can be seen at the herbarium today, the Coulter pine (*Pinus coulteri*) and the garden plant *Romneya coulteri*.

Carlingford Lough

CARLINGFORD LOUGH can boast THE ONLY PRIVATELY OWNED PORT IN IRELAND at GREENORE, which was constructed in 1867 to provide a rail and ferry link with Heysham and Fleetwood in Lancashire. Greenore gives its name to a brand of single malt whiskey produced by the nearby

Cooley distillery, founded in 1987 by John Teeling and THE ONLY INDEPENDENT IRISH-OWNED WHISKEY DISTILLERY IN IRELAND.

Beaulieu House

BEAULIEU HOUSE, sitting beside the church and set amongst gardens that slope down to the Boyne estuary, is Ireland's first true stately home or country house. It was begun in 1666 by Sir Henry Tichborne, on the site of an old fortified house belonging to the Plunkett family, and remodelled in the early 18th century in a Dutch style found almost nowhere else in Ireland. With no fortifications or defences, Beaulieu was designed purely as a beautiful place in which to live. The house is wonderfully preserved both outside and in, the walls hung with paintings of Tich-

borne ancestors and contemporary portraits of William III and Queen Anne. Outside, the magnificent walled garden dates from the 1730s and is the oldest of its kind in Ireland. The present owner is a direct descendant of Sir Henry Tichborne, Mrs Sydney Waddington, whose late husband Nesbit Waddington was manager of the Aga Khan's Irish stud farms. The house and gardens are open in the summer months.

Francis Leopold McClintock
1819–1907

The man who solved the mystery of Franklin's North-west Passage expedition, FRANCIS LEOPOLD MCCLINTOCK, was born in Dundalk. At the age of 12 he joined the Royal Navy as a gentleman volunteer, and in 1848

went on Sir James Clark Ross's voyage to look for the lost expedition of Sir John Franklin (*see* Co. Down). Franklin had not returned after sailing from Britain, in 1845, in search of the fabled North-West Passage to the Pacific Ocean around the Arctic coast of Canada.

This was the first of several trips to the Arctic Circle, during which McClintock discovered and mapped Prince of Wales Island and Prince Patrick Island, whose northern point is aptly named Cape Leopold

McClintock. He also perfected the skill of using sleds hauled by humans, so successfully that the technique was adopted almost universally by polar explorers until 1912, when the failure of Scott's expedition to the South Pole was blamed partly on his reluctance to use dogs.

In 1857 McClintock was asked personally by Franklin's wife to take command of the yacht *Fox* for a privately sponsored expedition to find out once and for all the truth of what had happened to her husband. In 1859 McClintock and his team reached King William Island, where they found graves and a cairn under which was hidden a journal written by Franklin's companions Captain Crozier and Captain Fitzjames. He revealed how their vessels had been trapped in the ice for two years, and

how the crews had finally abandoned ship and attempted to march across the ice to Hudson Bay. McClintock's men also came across a number of bodies, proof enough that Franklin's expedition had ended in disaster – although there was some scant comfort for Franklin's widow when McClintock was able to let her know that Franklin had discovered the North-West Passage before he perished.

As well as solving the mystery of Franklin's fate and mapping large areas of the Canadian Arctic, McClintock produced the first geological maps of the region and published accounts of his voyages, which proved hugely popular and cemented his reputation as one of the greatest Arctic explorers. McClintock retired from the navy as a rear admiral.

Well, I never knew this about
LOUTH FOLK

Mathematical genius FATHER JAMES CULLEN (1867–1933) was born in DROGHEDA. After studying maths at Trinity College Dublin, he was ordained in 1901 and began teaching at Mount St Mary's College in Derbyshire in 1905. While there he published a study of pure mathematics, which described a specific type of natural

number with particular properties that became known as a Cullen number.

Architect MICHAEL SCOTT (1905–89), who designed Dublin's controversial Busáras, or Central Bus Station, opened in 1953, and the present Abbey Theatre, opened in 1966, was born in DROGHEDA.

EAMONN CAMPBELL, producer and guitarist with the Dubliners, was born in DROGHEDA in 1946.

Professional golfer and Ryder Cup player DES SMYTH was born in DROGHEDA in 1953. In 2001, at the age of 48, he won the Madeira Island Open, becoming THE OLDEST MAN EVER TO WIN A EUROPEAN TOUR EVENT.

Film director, producer and writer JOHN MOORE (*Behind Enemy Lines, The Flight of the Phoenix*) was born in DUNDALK in 1970.

EVANNA LYNCH, the actress who plays Luna Lovegood in the Harry Potter films, was born in TERMON-FECKIN in 1991.

County Meath

IRELAND'S OLDEST HORSE-RACING VENUE
✦ IRISH GRAND NATIONAL ✦ 'NAPPER' TANDY
✦ LAYTOWN BEACH RACES ✦ AN OCTAGON SQUARE
✦ A KING'S RETREAT ✦ CROQUET WITH THE VICAR
✦ TWO TOWERS ✦ A FOX'S VIGIL

*Gormanston Castle, home to Ireland
and England's Oldest Viscountcy.*

◄ MEATH FOLK ►

Bishop John Connolly ✦ C.Y. O'Connor ✦ John Boyle O'Reilly
✦ Francis Ledwidge

County Meath is sometimes called the 'Royal County' because it was the ancient seat of the High Kings of Ireland, when they ruled from the Hill of Tara. Meath also possesses the only two areas of Gaeltacht in Leinster, where Irish is spoken as the main language, at Ráth Cairn and Báile Ghib.

Racing in Co. Meath

County Meath can boast THE OLDEST HORSE-RACING VENUE IN IRELAND at BELLEWSTOWN, a pretty village on the Hill of Crockafotha, south of Drogheda. The racecourse is on top of the hill and offers stupendous views east to the Irish Sea and north to the Mountains of Mourne. The earliest record of a race meeting on the hill comes from the August edition of the *Dublin Gazette and the Weekly Courier* in 1726, but it is believed that races have been run here in the Summer time for 200 years or more – certainly there can be no more exhilarating place for the sport of High Kings.

As befits a racecourse in the Royal County, Bellewstown has royal connections. In 1780 a former Mayor of Drogheda, George Tandy, brother of the celebrated United Irishman 'Napper' Tandy, persuaded George III to sponsor a race at Bellewstown,

valued at £100, which he called His Majesty's Plate.

Today Bellewstown holds two summer meetings, in July and August.

Irish Grand National

Co. Meath also hosts Ireland's premier steeplechase, the IRISH GRAND NATIONAL, which has been run at FAIRYHOUSE racecourse near Ratoath, traditionally on Easter Monday, since 1870. The first winner was a horse called Sir Robert Peel.

Steeple-chasing, or racing between church steeples, the most visible landmarks of the time, was invented in Co. Cork in 1752. The first steeplechase run at Fairyhouse was in 1848.

At LAYTOWN, races are run along the beach, 3 miles (5 km) of firm golden sand that provides a spectacular and unique racecourse where beating the tide is as much of a gamble as picking the winner. There has been racing at Laytown since 1867, and now this seaside town provides THE ONLY BEACH RACING UNDER JOCKEY CLUB RULES IN IRELAND OR THE BRITISH ISLES. Because of the unusual racing surface winners are hard to predict, giving the amateur punter as much chance as the professional, and this helps to make Laytown races a very popular event on the racing calendar.

James 'Napper' Tandy
◄ 1740–1803 ►

JAMES 'NAPPER' TANDY was born in Dublin and started out as a small tradesman – although he was by no means a small figure, standing 7 ft (2.1 m) tall and with a nose so big that a political rival suggested that it stand for election in its own right. He was drawn into politics by protesting against restrictions imposed on Irish commerce by the government, joined Henry Grattan's Whig Club, and assisted Theobald Wolfe Tone in setting up the Society of the United Irishmen in 1791, becoming the organisation's first secretary.

Forced to leave Ireland when his activities brought him to the notice of the authorities, Tandy travelled to America and then France, where he became deeply involved in organising the French invasion in support of the rebellion of 1798. Although he sailed to Co. Donegal ready to join the fight, when Tandy heard that the French forces under General Humbert had surrendered, he tried to make his way back to France, but was caught in Hamburg and extradited to Dublin. After a brief period of imprisonment he returned to France as part of a prisoner exchange and lived out the rest of his life in exile there.

He is sometimes known as the 'Forgotten Patriot', but his name has entered Irish folklore with a mention in the Irish ballad 'The Wearing of the Green', a song about repression written around the time of the 1798 rebellion. Tandy, as an Irish exile in France, is referred to by the singer thus:

> *I met wid Napper Tandy and he took me by the hand*
> *And he said 'How's dear ould Ireland, and how does she stand?'*

Also at Laytown is the National Ecology Centre known as SONAIRTE, the only establishment of its kind in Ireland. Serving schools and businesses, the centre promotes ecological education and awareness of conservation and sustainable living. It offers an interactive renewable energy park and organic gardens, along with exhibits showing various forms of solar, wind and water power.

Slane

The smart and tidy village of SLANE, which sits on the River Boyne, is a fine example of Georgian town planning and was laid out in the early 18th century by Viscount Conyngham. In 1766 a flour mill was built in Slane, the biggest in Ireland at the time, to process corn from all over the country. In the 20th century the mill was changed to cotton production, and by the 1970s had become the only surviving factory in Ireland that still worked on the complete process of cotton production, from raw cotton to the finished sheeting.

Across the road from the mill are the gates of Slane Castle, seat of the Conyngham family, and nearby is Slane's unique town

square, THE ONLY SQUARE IN IRELAND IN THE FORM OF AN OCTAGON. Surrounding the square are four identical houses built, according to local lore, by four spinster Conyngham sisters who were not on speaking terms but wanted to keep an eye on each other.

The road to Slane from Dublin is perhaps the nearest thing there is in Ireland to a Roman road, being unusually straight. At one time access to the village had been along roads that were 'narrow and full of bends, making travel difficult and slow'. In 1815, however, an Act of Parliament decreed that 'the road from Dublin to Slane be straightened, repaired and kept in good repair', at a cost to the Treasury of over £7,000.

The reason behind all this effort and expense was nothing to do with Slane being a vital communications hub, or the need for rapid movement of troops or goods between the capital and this tiny backwoods village; it was rather because the Prince Regent, later King

Slane Rectory

George IV, had made known that he might want to make the journey to Slane in great haste – to discuss important matters of state with his mistress the Marchioness Conyngham, who was eagerly awaiting him at Slane Castle.

Croquet

One of Ireland's first croquet lawns was laid out in the gardens of the fine old Rectory at Slane. Croquet, which is French for 'crooked stick', was brought to Ireland from France in the 1830s. It had been developed from the old game of 'paille maille' by a French doctor as a means of gentle exercise for his patients, and quickly became popular in Ireland. An article about County Meath which appeared in 1858 features the first-ever mention of the word 'croquet' in the English language,

stating that 'there is no game which has made such rapid strides in this country within a few years as croquet'. The game spread from Co. Meath to England and the rest of Britain in 1851.

Mornington

MORNINGTON, a small village on the south bank of the Boyne estuary, once known as Marinestown, is notable for two stone beacon towers set on the level strand of the beach, which mark the mouth of the Boyne and act as landmarks for ships out in the Irish Sea. The more substantial square beacon, 60 ft (18 m) high, is called MAIDEN TOWER, while the smaller round tower, which is about 40 ft (12 m) high, is known as the LADY'S FINGER.

They were both built in the days of Elizabeth I, and the Maiden Tower is thought to have been named as a compliment to the Queen, although local legend tells a different tale, of a young maiden who flung herself from the top of the Maiden Tower believing her lover had been lost at sea. Her gesture was rendered less than effective due to the softness of the sand which broke her fall, but she did succeed in dislocating her finger, which from that day on was left sticking upwards, providing a most distinctive name for the second beacon.

In the 18th century the Mornington estate belonged to the Wellesley family. The 1st Earl of Mornington was father to Arthur Wellesley, born in Dublin, who went on to become the Chief Secretary of Ireland, Duke of Wellington, victor of the Battle of Waterloo, champion of Catholic emancipation and twice Prime Minister.

Gormanston Castle

Where Mornington marks the northern boundary of Co. Meath's short coastline, Gormanston marks the southern boundary. It is set on the north bank of the River Devlin, which forms the boundary between Co. Meath and Co. Dublin, and provides a title for the premier Viscount of Ireland, Viscount Gormanston. Created in 1478, the Viscountcy is the oldest in either Ireland or Britain. A strange event, apparently witnessed at GORMANSTON CASTLE several times during the last century, concerns a tradition whereby, when the head of the family is on his deathbed, all the foxes of Meath gather at the door of the castle and keep watch until the Viscount has passed away. This tribute is said to be given in thanks for a previous Viscount Gormanston who hid and protected a desperate vixen and her cubs from the hunt.

Gormanston Castle now forms the centrepiece of a boys' school run by the Franciscan Order.

Well, I never knew this about
MEATH FOLK

The second Roman Catholic bishop of New York, BISHOP JOHN CONNOLLY (1750–1825), was born in SLANE.

C.Y. O'Connor
◄ 1843–1902 ►

CHARLES YELVERTON O'CONNOR, one of the world's great engineers, was born in CASTLETOWN, near Navan, the youngest son of a landowner called John O'Connor. Educated at Waterford, he gained experience working on the Waterford to Kilkenny railway line, and when he emigrated to New Zealand in 1865 he was put in charge of numerous rail and water management projects. In 1891 he was invited by the first premier of Western Australia, John Forrest, to become chief engineer of the rapidly expanding Australian west.

His first major project was the building of a harbour at Fremantle, 12 miles (19 km) south of Perth at the mouth of the Swan River. Many engineers had regarded the project as impossible, owing to sand shoals and a limestone bar that blocked the river mouth, but O'Connor overcame both problems and created a magnificent harbour for commercial shipping that still serves today as Western Australia's main port.

O'Connor's greatest achievement was the design and construction of THE WORLD'S LONGEST WATER

PIPELINE to deliver fresh water over 350 miles (563 km), uphill, from Mundaring Weir in the hills near Perth to the goldfields of Kalgoorlie. The pipeline took five years to build, was opened in 1903, and still provides Western Australia's sheep farms and goldfields with a regular supply of water today.

O'Connor never saw his masterpiece in operation. In 1902, driven to despair by false allegations of corruption and incompetence, he rode his horse into the sea south of Fremantle and shot himself. The horse then returned to the shore with O'Connor's body on its back. The brilliant Irish engineer who had transformed the face of Western Australia was dead at just 59. The beach where he committed suicide is known as C.Y. O'Connor Beach, and a statue standing permanently in the water just offshore serves as a memorial to him.

There is a bronze statue commemorating O'Connor at the harbour entrance in Fremantle, and the lake created by Mundaring Weir, the highest overflow dam in the world when it was built, is now called Lake O'Connor.

John Boyle O'Reilly
◄ 1844–90 ►

And I long for the dear old river,
Where I dreamed my youth away;
For a dreamer lives forever,
And a toiler dies in a day.

These are lines from the poetry of JOHN BOYLE O'REILLY, said to be President Kennedy's favourite poet. The river referred to is the Boyne, for O'Reilly was born on its banks, in DOWTH CASTLE, not far from Drogheda. After an early career in journalism, O'Reilly enlisted in the British army, eventually joining the 10th Hussars, but found himself becoming more sympathetic to the Irish Nationalist cause, and secretly became a member of the Irish Republican Brotherhood, or Fenians. He then began recruiting more Fenians from within the regiment, but was caught, arrested and deported to Australia. From here he escaped to America, ending up in Boston, where he worked his way up to the editorship of the *Boston Pilot* and set about giving a voice to the Catholic Irish of the city. He built up the readership of the *Pilot* until it became one of the most widely read newspapers in America. Despite his fervent nationalism O'Reilly rejected violence, and his poetry retained a lyrical and romantic style that reflected the Irish Revival happening back in his homeland.

Francis Ledwidge
◄—— 1891–1917 ——►

And wondrous impudently sweet,
Half of him passion, half conceit,
The blackbird calls adown the street
Like the piper of Hamelin.

These words were written by FRANCIS LEDWIDGE (1891–1917), after hearing a blackbird sing 'while walking at evening through the village of Slane in summer'. Sometimes known as 'the blackbird poet', Ledwidge was one of those young poets of such promise whose life was cruelly cut short on the killing fields of Belgium during the Great War. He was born in SLANE, the eighth of nine children in an impoverished family, and was forced to leave school at 12 to seek work as a farm hand, road builder and copper miner – and trade union activist. All the while he wrote poetry, inspired by the glorious scenery of the Boyne valley, much of which was published in the *Drogheda Independent*.

Ledwidge's work caught the attention of local writer Lord Dunsany, who lived in IRELAND'S LONGEST CONTINUOUSLY OCCUPIED HOME, DUNSANY CASTLE, not far from Trim. Lord Dunsany was an established writer and dramatist, well known in Dublin literary circles, and he was able to publicise the young poet's work and even introduced Ledwidge to W.B. Yeats.

Despite being a member of the Irish Volunteers, many of whom opposed supporting the British in the First World War, Ledwidge enlisted in Lord Dunsany's regiment, the Royal Inniskilling Fusiliers, possibly in despair at losing his great love, Ellie Vaughey, to another man.

Ledwidge's first book, *Songs of the Field*, came out in 1915, at the time when he was fighting at Gallipoli. His second, *Songs of Peace*, appeared in 1916 while Ledwidge was on leave in England. He then returned to fight at the Somme and was killed by a random shell at Boesinghe village, in Belgium, on 31 July 1917.

County Offaly

At the Heart of Ireland
✦ Ireland's Spookiest Castle ✦ The Hawthorn
✦ Oldest Decorated Gospel ✦ Pyramid of Kinnitty
✦ A Leap in the Dark ✦ Stoney Brothers

Cloghan Castle near Banaghe, was built by the O'Maddens in the 14th century, and is one of Ireland's oldest inhabited private dwellings.

◄ OFFALY FOLK ►

Joseph Stirling Coyne ✦ Barack Obama ✦ John Joly

COUNTY OFFALY, once known as King's County after King Philip of Spain, husband of Mary I of England (whose own Queen's County is now Co. Laois), can boast IRELAND'S OLDEST INHABITED CASTLE at CLOGHAN, built in 1239 and now a wedding venue, and THE OLDEST HORSE FAIR IN IRELAND, held every September in BANAGHER.

Birr

The handsome Georgian heritage town of BIRR revolves busily round its ancient market square, EMMETT SQUARE, the geographical heart of Ireland. In the centre of the square is a column erected in 1747 to carry a statue of the Duke of Cumberland, victor of the Battle of Culloden in 1746, known to the Scots as 'Butcher Cumberland'. The statue was removed in 1915, ostensibly because it was in danger of falling down, more probably to avoid upsetting the sensibilities of the Highland troops who were garrisoned in the town. Along one side of the square, also dating from 1747, is one of

Ireland's oldest coaching inns, the DOOLEY ARMS, which went up in flames one night in 1809 after a merry evening of celebration by the members of the Galway Hunt – known ever since as the Galway Blazers.

Birr is known for its hurling team, four times winners of the All-Ireland hurling championships. Indeed, the first-ever All-Ireland hurling final was played in Birr, in 1888, between Tipperary and Galway. The match was won by Tipperary.

Charleville Forest

The flamboyant, faintly sinister Gothic appearance of CHARLEVILLE FOREST CASTLE, south-west of Tullamore, built in the early 19th century by Francis Johnston for Charles Bury, Earl of Charleville, enhances its reputation as 'Ireland's spookiest castle'. Bury's young daughter met a tragic early death there while sliding down the banisters, and guests, who have included Lord Byron,

have reported seeing apparitions and hearing strange noises during the night. The castle has appeared on numerous television programmes including *Scariest Places on Earth* and Living TV's *Most Haunted*, and is frequently used as an atmospheric film location.

The trees surrounding the castle are the remnants of Ireland's oldest primordial oak wood, where Druids once hunted and performed their mysterious rituals, and include the ancient Charleville Oak, reputed to be THE BIGGEST OAK TREE IN EUROPE.

Charleville has many times been left empty and almost derelict but today it is run and maintained by a Trust and its future seems assured.

IRELAND'S LARGEST ONE-DAY SHOW, the annual TULLAMORE LIVESTOCK SHOW, is held in the castle grounds in August.

The Hawthorn Tree

Drivers are sometimes nonplussed by an unexpected bend in the road leading west from Birr towards a small village called Clareen, the site of a monastery founded in the 6th century by St Ciaran. The bend was put there to avoid St Ciaran's Bush, an old and twisted hawthorn tree that local people decided it would be unwise to cut down. Hawthorns are common in Ireland, cheering up hedgerows across the land, flowering brightly in white and pink in May – hence its other name, May tree. A lone hawthorn, however, is often associated with sacred places, and it is thought that Christ's crown of thorns was made from a hawthorn. For these reasons it is considered unlucky to move or cut down a hawthorn – when a hawthorn was felled to make way for the DeLorean car factory in Co. Antrim in the 1980s, many people forecast disaster and, sure enough, DeLorean closed after less than a year with huge losses.

Durrow

A fine Georgian mansion, a medieval church and a 10th-century cross mark the site of DURROW ABBEY, founded by St Columba in the 6th century. Almost at the dead centre of Ireland, Durrow seems to be at some sort of hub, and the whole area is criss-crossed with an unusually high number of ley lines. A line of oak trees, descendants of the oldest oaks in Ireland, mark the route of one of Ireland's most ancient highways, which seems to emerge from a misty past. Come down to us from that misty past, and now in Trinity College Library in Dublin, is the famous illuminated *Book of Durrow*, THE EARLIEST KNOWN DECORATED GOSPEL MANUSCRIPT, said to date from the 7th century, which was compiled at the abbey. When the abbey was dissolved in the 16th century the book disappeared, but it was found 100 years later in the possession of a local farmer who had been reading it to his cows every night in the hope of increasing their milk yield.

Kinnitty

The pretty village of Kinnitty, lying at the head of Forelacka Glen, in the shadow of the Slieve Bloom Mountains, can boast of its very own pyramid. Standing 30 ft (9 m) high, the KINNITTY PYRAMID is an exact replica of the pyramid of Cheops in Egypt, and was built in 1830 by Lt.-Col. Richard Wesley Bernard, on his return from working in Egypt, as his family crypt. The only tomb of its kind in Ireland, the pyramid can be found in the graveyard behind the Church of Ireland and contains the remains of four members of the Bernard family. The first to be buried inside was Mary Bernard, who died in 1842 after being bitten by a dog, and the last person to be interred behind the thick iron entrance door was Ellen Georgina Bernard, who died in 1907.

The Bernards' family home, KINNITTY CASTLE, is now a luxury hotel. JACK OSBOURNE, son of Black

Sabbath lead vocalist Ozzy Osbourne, was married at Kinnitty Castle in 2005.

Leap Castle

Nearby LEAP CASTLE, a 15th-century Irish tower house, vies with Charleville Forest Castle as the most haunted house in Ireland, and is said to possess an 'elemental', or ghost with an unpleasant smell – of course the smell could emanate from the nearby oubliette, a type of dungeon where prisoners were locked up and forgotten about, and from which three wagonloads of bones were removed in the 19th century.

George Johnstone Stoney
1826–1911

GEORGE JOHNSTONE STONEY, the physicist who introduced the term 'electron' for the basic unit of elec-

tricity, was born at Oakley Park in Clareen, west of Birr. After graduating from Trinity College Dublin, Stoney became an astronomical assistant to William Parsons, 3rd Earl of Rosse, at Birr Castle, just down the road from where Stoney had grown up, where Parsons had built what was then the largest telescope in the world, the Leviathan. Stoney went on to become the first science professor at the newly established Queen's College, Galway, where he was appointed Professor of Natural Philosophy. He was a practical scientist as

well as a theoretical genius and invented a novel kind of heliostat, a clockwork instrument that controls a mirror to follow the sun in order to reflect a steady beam of sunlight for use in scientific experiments.

It was Stoney's love of simplicity and standard terms that could be easily understood which led him to coin the term 'electron', and it likewise made him a great supporter of the metric system, which he found far less complicated for scientific expression than the imperial system. He was a firm opponent of Home Rule, which he believed would dissipate collective scientific knowledge and was against the spirit of science. Stoney also championed the cause of women in higher education, with the result that women were able to earn medical qualifications far earlier in Ireland than they were in Britain.

George Johnstone Stoney is buried in Dundrum, Dublin, where the road in which he lived is named Stoney Road in his honour.

Bindon Blood Stoney
1828–1909

BINDON BLOOD STONEY, the 'Father of Irish Concrete', was, like his older brother George Johnstone Stoney, born in Oakley Park, Clareen. Again like his brother, he became an astronomical assistant working on the great telescope at Birr Castle, but whereas George became a scientist, Bindon qualified as an engineer. His first major achievement was the iron latticework Boyne Bridge at Drogheda, where his technique for testing new design concepts helped John Benjamin MacNeill to construct what was at the time the longest cast-iron structure in the world. Stoney's account of the lessons learnt during the construction of this pioneering structure formed the basis of his seminal work *The Theory of Strains in Girders and Similar Structures*, which is still considered a standard reference work for structural engineers today.

Bindon Stoney's next major project was the development of Dublin docks, for which he devised a brilliant new building method using huge, pre-cast concrete blocks instead of stone and rubble to create the dock walls. He also designed a metal diving bell in which six men could be lowered to the river bed to excavate the soil where the concrete blocks were to be placed. The diving bell, which was fed with air from a barge moored on the surface, can still be seen on the quayside in Blood Stoney Road on Sir John Rogerson's Quay. It was in use right up until the 1960s, over 100 years after Stoney had invented it in 1860.

Stoney's docks resulted in berths that were unaffected by the tide and were the deepest yet known, and civil engineers from all over the world came to Dublin to study his revolutionary methods.

Science and invention run through the veins of the Stoney family – a distant relation was Alan Turing, inventor of the early computer mechanism at Bletchley Park in England that helped break the German Enigma code.

Well, I never knew this about
OFFALY FOLK

The playwright and author of *The Scenery and Antiquities of Ireland*, JOSEPH STIRLING COYNE (1803–68), was born in BIRR. He is also remembered as one of the contributors to the first edition of *Punch* magazine, which he helped to found.

During the famine years of the mid 19th century the tiny Offaly village of MONEYGALL was blessed with a popular and well-considered shoemaker called JOSEPH KEARNEY. In 1850 his son Fulmuth, then aged 19, emigrated to New York, where he prospered. Over 100 years later, in Hawaii in 1961, Joseph's great-great-granddaughter Ann gave birth to a son. His name? BARACK OBAMA.

John Joly
◄ 1857–1933 ►

JOHN JOLY, one of Ireland's most prolific and fertile minds, was born in Hollywood House, the Church of Ireland rectory in BRACKNAGH. He graduated in engineering at Trinity College Dublin and spent the rest of his working life there as Professor of Geology and Minerology.

In the early years of his career Joly came up with a number of useful scientific inventions, including a meldometer for detecting the melting point of various minerals, a steam calorimeter to measure specific heat energy, and a photometer, made from a sheet of tinfoil between two pieces of wax, that measures the intensity of light from different sources.

In 1894 he was one of the first to devise a technique for colour photography, which became known as the 'Joly process' and produced colour slides that could be viewed on an ordinary projector – many of his slides survive, and can be seen at the National Library of Ireland.

Another first that Joly came up with, in conjunction with fellow Trinity professor Henry Horatio Dixon, was the 'cohesion-tension theory' to explain how the sap rises in plants through the evaporation of water from leaves – this was much ridiculed by experts at first but has long since been proved correct.

John Joly is best known for his contribution to the debate stirred up by Charles Darwin between creationists and evolutionists. A predecessor of Joly's at Trinity College, Archbishop James Ussher, using the chronology of the Bible, had calculated that the Earth was about 6,000 years old, a figure adhered to by modern-day creationists. In 1913 Joly measured the radioactive decay of minerals to estimate the age of the earth to be 4.5 billion years, a figure much more in line with believers in the theory of evolution.

Joly's interest in radioactivity led him to study the use of radium for the treatment of cancer, and after some successful trials he persuaded the Royal Dublin Society to set up the ground-breaking Radium Institute to provide treatment for cancerous tumours.

John Joly died in Dublin and is buried in Mount Jerome Cemetery.

County Westmeath

CATHEDRAL OF CHRIST THE KING
✦ REPUBLIC'S OLDEST DISTILLERY
✦ THE ARCH OF CTESIPHON

Cathedral of Christ the King, Mullingar.

◄ WESTMEATH FOLK ►

Adolphus Cooke ✦ T.P. O'Connor ✦ Brinsley MacNamara
✦ Michael O'Leary

COUNTY WESTMEATH can boast of having, in LOUGH LENE, THE FIRST INLAND AND FRESHWATER LAKE TO OBTAIN A EUROPEAN BLUE FLAG, awarded for its unpolluted, crystal-clear water.

Mullingar

MULLINGAR'S most distinctive feature is the vast Renaissance-style cathedral, with its green dome and twin west towers 180 ft (55 m) high, which loom over the town centre. It WAS THE FIRST CATHEDRAL IN EUROPE TO BE DEDICATED TO CHRIST THE KING.

Kilbeggan

KILBEGGAN, 'the church of St Becan', is the home of Locke's Distillery, THE OLDEST LICENSED WHISKEY DISTILLERY IN THE REPUBLIC OF IRELAND, and the second oldest in the world after Bushmills in Co. Antrim. It was established in 1757 and granted a licence two years later in 1759. The pure water of the Brusna River, on which Kilbeggan stands, contains special minerals from its bogs and limestone catchment areas, and these added a distinctive flavour to the whiskey.

In 1843 the distillery was taken over by the first John Locke, and it remained in the Locke family until it closed down in 1957.

In the 1920s the lucrative American market was closed to Irish whiskey because of Prohibition. During that time an illegal 'bootleg' concoction of inferior quality, that had nothing to do with the Irish company, was sold in America under the Locke's label, and this gave Locke's whiskey a bad reputation, making it difficult for the brand to re-establish itself after Prohibition was abandoned in 1933.

In 1982, 25 years after the distillery finally closed its doors, the local community took over the deserted buildings, which had been left virtually untouched, and restored them into a museum complete with a fully working water-wheel. In 1988 the Cooley Distillery bought the old Kilbeggan distillery and over the next few years began to produce, in their own distillery in Co. Louth, the brands once associated with Locke's – Kilbeggan, Locke's Blend and

Locke's Malt. The finished product is then stored in the original old warehouse at Kilbeggan.

In 2007, on the 250th anniversary of the opening of the Kilbeggan distillery, whiskey production began there once again.

Ctesiphon

The whiskey warehouse at Kilbeggan is something of a rarity itself, in being Ireland's only perfectly preserved 'Ctesiphon' structure. The Ctesiphon technique was devised by Irish engineer JIM WALLER (1884–1968), whose family hailed from Co. Tipperary. During the First World War, Waller had been shown how soldiers daubed their tents with concrete to camouflage and strengthen them, and he reckoned that this idea might usefully be applied to constructing relatively inexpensive buildings.

The method was simplicity itself. A heavy sackcloth was draped over a wooden frame of timber arches, and then multiple layers of concrete were laid on to the structure, which would settle into a corrugated shape as the concrete caused the sackcloth to sag between the wooden ribs. Once the concrete was set, the timber was removed and a spacious, self-supporting arch, which needed no centre pillar, was left behind.

The shape of the arch, greater in height than width so that the weight was evenly distributed, was inspired by the extraordinary Taq-i Kisra arch of the imperial palace at Ctesiphon, 20 miles (32 km) south of modern Baghdad in Iraq, where Waller had worked as a surveyor between the wars.

In the 1st century BC, Ctesiphon was the biggest city in the world, part of the mighty Parthian empire, and in the 3rd century the Sassasian Persians built a vast imperial palace there. They covered the throne room with the largest vault ever constructed in Persia, the Taq-i Kisra, built of crude brick, 110 ft (34 m) high and 80 ft (24 m) wide. The unsupported arch is still standing, after over 1700 years.

Well, I never knew this
about
WESTMEATH FOLK

Adolphus Cooke
◄─── 1792–1876 ──►

ADOLPHUS COOKE of COOKES-BOROUGH, a hamlet a few miles east of Mullingar, is buried in the grounds of Cookesborough's St John the Baptist's Church of Ireland church, in a mausoleum shaped like a beehive. Cooke built the mausoleum for his father Robert, and thoughtfully had it shaped like a beehive so that should his father have the misfortune to be reincarnated as a bee he would at least wake up in familiar surroundings. Adolphus had good cause to be concerned about his father, who seemed unable to make up his mind as to his true identity, having a few years earlier returned to Cookesborough as a turkey.

Adolphus himself was perfectly certain that he was going to come back as a fox, in common with his fellow Leinster squire, Robert Watson of Ballydarton in Co. Carlow. Like Watson, Cooke had a number of huge foxholes dug on his Cookesborough estate where he wanted to be laid to rest, just in case.

Alas, while Watson was fortunate enough to be buried in his foxhole to cries of 'Gone Away!', Cooke suffered at the hands of the hidebound and reactionary rector of Killucan, who insisted that Cooke be buried in the churchyard, alongside his father.

T.P. O'Connor
◄─── 1848–1929 ──►

Journalist and politician THOMAS POWER O'CONNOR was born in ATHLONE, the son of a shopkeeper. He studied history and modern languages at Queen's College, Galway, entered journalism as a junior reporter in Dublin, and then, in 1870, moved to London, where his ability to speak French and German got him a job on the *Daily Telegraph,* reporting on the Franco-Prussian War.

In 1880 he entered Parliament as Member for Galway, sitting for Charles Stewart Parnell's Home Rule League, and in 1885, sitting for the same party, he was elected Member for Liverpool, home to a large Irish population. LIVERPOOL IS THE ONLY CONSTITUENCY OUTSIDE IRELAND EVER TO RETURN AN MP FROM AN IRISH NATIONALIST PARTY, and although his party ceased to exist in 1918, O'Connor continued as an independent under the same nationalist banner. He remained Liverpool's MP through five general elections until his death in 1929, by which time he had become 'Father of the House of Commons', having served for over 49 years.

In 1917 T.P. O'Connor was appointed THE FIRST-EVER PRESIDENT OF THE BOARD OF FILM CENSORS.

BRINSLEY MACNAMARA (1890–1963), author of the controversial novel *Valley of the Squinting Windows,* was born near DEVLIN, a small town that is believed to have been the model for Garradrimna, the fictional town in his book. The story takes a look at rural life and the role of gossip in small communities, and the people of

Devlin were so upset that there were court cases and the book was publicly burnt. MacNamara's father, a schoolteacher, was forced to emigrate, and MacNamara himself never felt able to return to his birthplace. He died in Dublin.

MICHAEL O'LEARY, chief executive of Europe's largest low-cost airline, Ryanair, was born near MULLINGAR in 1961. He studied business at Trinity College, Dublin, and at the age of 26 became financial adviser to Tony Ryan, then head of Guinness Peat Aviation, a leasing company. O'Leary helped Ryan set up Ryanair, and he is credited with introducing the idea of ancillary revenue, whereby the airline sells seat tickets for almost nothing, and derives its profits from the sale of on-board entertainment, food and drink, hotel bookings, car hire and other related activities. This

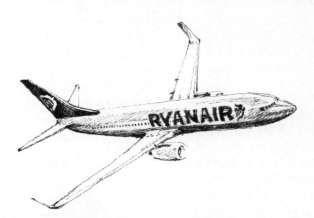

business acumen has made O'Leary into one of Ireland's super-rich – amongst his proudest possessions is his stud at Gigginstown, outside Mullingar, where he now lives, which provided him with a Cheltenham Gold Cup winner in 2006, War of Attrition.

County Wexford

THE WORLD'S ONLY CLIMBABLE CORINTHIAN COLUMN
✦ THE LONGEST CHURCH IN IRELAND
✦ ORIGINS OF A RECORD ✦ AMNESTY INTERNATIONAL

*Duncannon Lighthouse, on the Hook Peninsula, dates
from 1774 and is the oldest of its kind in Ireland.*

◄ WEXFORD FOLK ►

James Pierce ✦ Jim Bolger ✦ Eoin Colfer ✦ Aidan O'Brien

Being IRELAND'S SUNNIEST
COUNTY, COUNTY WEXFORD is
known as 'Ireland's sunny south-east'.
Curracloe, a few miles north of
Wexford, boasts THE LONGEST BEACH
IN THE REPUBLIC OF IRELAND, at
just over 5 miles (8 km) long. In 1997–
8 the beach was used as the location
for the filming of the D-Day landing
scenes in Steven Spielberg's film
Saving Private Ryan – partly because
Curracloe looked similar to Omaha
Beach in Normandy and partly
because it was close to the Ardmore
film studios where many of the interior scenes were being shot.

Browne Clayton Monument

A few miles to the east of New Ross,
on Carrigadaggan Hill, stands THE
ONLY CORINTHIAN COLUMN IN
THE WORLD THAT YOU CAN CLIMB
UP INSIDE, the 94 ft (29 m) high
BROWNE CLAYTON MONUMENT.
Built of granite from Mount Leinster,
the monument was completed in 1841
and is a replica of Pompey's Pillar at
Alexandria, in Egypt. It was erected
by local resident General Robert
Browne Clayton to commemorate his
commanding officer Sir Ralph Aber-
crombie, who was mortally wounded
fighting against Napoleon in Egypt
in 1801. The architect was Thomas

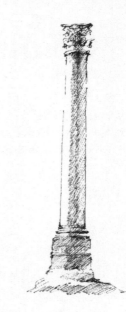

Cobden, who built the exotic
Duckett's Grove in Co. Carlow.

Dunbrody Abbey

DUNBRODY ABBEY, on the outskirts
of Campile, south-east of New Ross,
is considered the most beautiful
ruin in Co. Wexford. Built in the
early 13th century as a Cistercian
monastery, it became known as the
Abbey of St Mary of Refuge, as it
was one of the few places in Ireland
where outlaws could claim sanc-
tuary. At nearly 200 ft (60 m) in
length it is ONE OF THE LONGEST

CHURCHES IN IRELAND. Nearby is a full-size yew hedge maze, one of only two in Ireland.

The name Dunbrody was given to a cargo vessel built in Quebec in 1845 by an Irish emigrant boat-builder, and commissioned by the Graves family of New Ross to carry cargo between Canada and Ireland. It became one of the notorious 'famine ships' that carried up to 300 emigrants to the New World on each voyage west. A replica of the *Dunbrody* is moored on the quay in New Ross and offers visitors the chance to experience the

sights and sounds of life aboard a famine ship. Adjacent is the 'Wall of Honour', dedicated to all Irish emigrants.

Castlebridge

THE NORTH SLOBS, an area of marshy mud-flats near CASTLE-BRIDGE, just north of Wexford Harbour, is not only THE MOST IMPORTANT AREA FOR WILDFOWL IN IRELAND but THE BIRTHPLACE OF THE WORLD'S BESTSELLING COPYRIGHTED BOOK, *The Guinness Book of Records*.

It all began one grey, cold November day in 1951, when SIR HUGH BEAVER, managing director of the Guinness Brewery, went shooting on the North Slobs with a group of friends. The hunt proved fruitless, and while they were crouching in the reeds waiting for some birds to come along, Beaver got into an animated discussion about which was the fastest game bird in Europe – the golden plover or the grouse?

The argument continued into the evening over dinner at Castlebridge House, and Beaver realised that there was actually no reference source they could consult to give them the answer to their question. He was sure that there must be other similar debates going on all the time in pubs and bars all over the country, and a book that could supply the answers to such matters could prove very popular.

The idea took shape when fellow Guinness executive Christopher Chataway, who would set a world record himself in 1954, running the

5,000 metres in 13 minutes and 51.6 seconds, suggested to Beaver that his old university friends Ross and Norris McWhirter, who ran a fact-finding agency in London, might be good editors of such a book. In 1954 the brothers compiled the first collection, and Beaver had 1,000 copies printed, which he gave away to pubs for people to talk about over a pint of Guinness. It was such a success that the Guinness Book of World Records publishing company was set up at 107 Fleet Street in London, and the first copy of *The Guinness Book of Records* went on sale on 27 August 1955.

Sean MacBride
1904–88

Castlebridge is very proud of a tree planted on the village green by SEAN MacBRIDE on a visit there in the 1970s. Sean MacBride was the son of W.B. Yeats's muse Maud Gonne and Irish Republican John MacBride, executed for his leading role in the 1916 Easter Rising. He was born in Paris but went to school at Gorey in Co. Wexford and retained a great affection for the part of Ireland where he grew up.

As well as being active in Irish politics, MacBride played an influential role in international politics, working for human rights worldwide. He was a founding member of Amnesty International, assistant secretary-general of the United Nations, president of the controversial MacBride Report on Communications and the Media, chairman of UNESCO and winner of the Nobel Peace Prize in 1974. He spent his later years in his mother's house in Dublin, Roebuck House, where he died at the age of 83. He is buried in Glasnevin Cemetery.

Well, I never knew this
about
WEXFORD FOLK

In the 19th century Wexford was home to a number of firms making farm machinery. They were attracted into the area by the numerous ironworks and foundries established there to take advantage of the oak woods of Shillelagh and water power from the River Slaney. One of the most successful of these farm equipment manufacturing firms was founded in 1847 by a Wexford mill owner and inventor called JAMES PIERCE (1813–68), who had already won renown with his Pierce Fire Machine, a fan used to replace bellows in the domestic fireplace. Pierce designed a range of cast-iron implements from threshers to ploughs, and Pierce & Company prospered, by 1914 becoming the largest manufacturer of farm machinery in Ireland and exporting their products across the world.

Unfortunately, the First World War closed off many of those international markets and Pierce & Company had to adjust to once more supplying just the Irish market. The company remained an important manufacturer until the 1980s, when competition from larger foreign firms forced its closure.

Jim Bolger

The parents of JIM BOLGER, Prime Minister of New Zealand 1990–7, grew up in Co. Wexford, from where they emigrated to New Zealand in 1930. His mother's childhood home was at Knockbrandon, Monaseed.

EOIN COLFER, author of the *Artemis Fowl* children's book series, was born in WEXFORD in 1965.

AIDAN O'BRIEN, perhaps the most successful Irish racehorse trainer of all time, was born in WEXFORD in 1969. He became Ireland's Amateur Champion Jockey in 1993–94 and then applied for a trainer's licence. He won the National Hunt jumps title in his first season, and in his second year as a trainer be broke the record for the number of wins in one year.

In 1995 he took over from the legendary Vincent O'Brien, voted the greatest trainer of all time by the *Racing Post*, at the training establishment backed by John Magnier and the Coolmore Stud at the Ballydoyle stables in Co. Tipperary. Since then he has won numerous major prizes in Ireland, the UK, France and America and has been British champion trainer three times, in 2001, 2002 and 2007.

County Wicklow

WICKLOW TREES ✦ CORK OAK
✦ AVONDALE FOREST PARK ✦ DUBLIN 'SETTS'
✦ ARKLOW ✦ WIND FARMS

*Wicklow Head, easternmost point on the
Republic of Ireland mainland.*

◀ WICKLOW FOLK ▶

Kate Tyrell ✦ Richard Crosbie

With its mixture of golden sandy beaches, glorious mountain scenery and sparkling lakes, all within easy reach of Dublin, COUNTY WICKLOW is known as the Garden of Ireland. Carved out of parts of Co. Dublin and Co. Carlow in 1606, Co. Wicklow was the last of the present-day counties to be established. WICKLOW HEAD, 2 miles (32 km) from Wicklow town centre IS THE EASTERNMOST POINT ON THE REPUBLIC OF IRELAND MAINLAND.

The Wicklow Mountains form THE LARGEST UPLAND AREA IN IRELAND, and THE LARGEST AREA OF GRANITE UPLAND IN IRELAND OR BRITAIN, while the Wicklow Way is THE OLDEST LONG-DISTANCE WALKING TRAIL IN IRELAND.

Handweavers, is THE ONLY EXAMPLE IN THE WORLD OF A MATURE WEEPING MONTEREY CYPRESS.

Wicklow Trees

Nearly 20 per cent of Co. Wicklow is covered in trees, making it IRELAND'S MOST HEAVILY FORESTED COUNTY. Amongst its trees are some very unusual specimens, such as a CORK OAK, found in the great oak woods of Shillelagh, that is one of only two in Ireland.

At KILMACANOGUE, a couple of miles south of Bray, in gardens created in the early 1870s by James Jameson, a member of the famous whiskey family, and now owned by the Avoca

Avondale Forest Park

Examples of every kind of Irish tree can be found in the AVONDALE FOREST PARK, near Rathdrum. Avondale is celebrated as the birthplace of the 'Uncrowned King of Ireland' Charles Stewart Parnell (1846–91), and it was Parnell's ancestor SAMUEL HAYES (1743–95) who built Avondale House and planted the magnificent woods on the estate.

Hayes was a barrister, MP for Wicklow in the Irish House of Commons, and a member of the agricultural committee of the Royal Dublin Society. His great concern was the frightening rate at which the woodlands of Ireland were disappearing from the landscape. He wrote THE FIRST BOOK ON PLANTING

Professor Augustine Henry
1857–1930

TREES IN IRELAND, and in 1788 presented a bill to Parliament 'for encouraging the cultivation and better presentation of trees'. He was also THE FIRST PERSON IN IRELAND TO WIN A PRESERVATION ORDER FOR A TREE, an achievement that paid off handsomely, for many of the trees he planted himself at Avondale were preserved and are still growing there today, amongst the oldest trees in Ireland.

Charles Stewart Parnell himself, despite his preoccupation with politics, ran the Avondale estate very efficiently and imaginatively when it came into his possession. He helped to develop the port at Arklow, from where he could ship out lead and timber from the estate, designed and built his own water-powered sawmill, and collected enough gold out of the River Avonmore to make a wedding ring for his mistress Kitty O'Shea. He also opened a granite quarry producing 'setts', or square block cobbles, which were much used in the 18th and 19th centuries for paving the streets of Irish towns and cities – some of Avondale's setts can still be seen in Dublin, around the castle, at Smithfield and near the Guinness brewery.

In 1904 the Avondale estate was acquired by the Irish State, and a number of experimental 1-acre (0.4-ha) plots were planted with different types of tree to see which flourished best in the Irish climate. It was discovered that the kinds of tree found in the USA and Canada, especially the Sitka spruce, did better than the Scandinavian varieties.

These experiments were carried out by PROFESSOR AUGUSTINE HENRY, who was the first to realise that the Irish climate was actually more like that of Canada and the north-west states of America than that of Scandinavia. Professor Henry, born in Scotland of Irish parents, studied at Queen's College, Galway and Queen's College Belfast, and then went to live in China, where he spent 20 years working for the Imperial Customs Service as a doctor. During his spare time Henry indulged in his favourite hobby, which was studying and collecting plants, and would send the seeds or bulbs of any new and interesting species back to the Botanical Gardens at Kew. Over the years he sent back more than 150,000 specimens, many of which have become popular in Irish gardens, such as buddleia, camellia, the orange-flowered Henry lily and, for the fruit bowl, the Chinese gooseberry, or kiwi fruit. Botanist Ernest Wilson said of Henry, 'No one in any age has contributed more to the knowledge of Chinese plants than this scholarly Irishman.'

On his return from China, Henry went to study forestry in France, and in 1913 was appointed the first Professor of Forestry at the Royal College of Science in Dublin. With his tree-planting experiments, and the introduction of so many favourites into Irish gardens, Professor Augustine Henry in no small way influenced how Ireland looks today.

Arklow

ARKLOW, which sits at the mouth of the River Avoca, has been a port since Roman days, and a settlement here appeared on Ptolemy's map of Britannia, which was drawn up in the 2nd century. The sandy estuary was always shifting, and this made Arklow unsuitable for any large-scale maritime activity other than fishing, although there were a number of small shipbuilding yards engaged in producing the distinctive Arklow 'nobby', a type of fishing vessel useful for catching shoal fish off the shallow sandbars. In the early 1800s the port was improved to handle ore from the mines at Avoca, and the number of shipbuilding businesses grew to supply vessels for Arklow's expanding merchant fleet.

In 1826 IRELAND'S FIRST ROYAL NATIONAL LIFEBOAT INSTITUTION RESCUE STATION was located at Arklow, and it is still in operation there today.

One of the most renowned of Arklow's shipyards was established by JOHN TYRELL in 1864. IRELAND'S FIRST MOTOR-POWERED FISHING BOAT was launched from here in 1908, while *Gypsy Moth III*, with which Sir Francis Chichester won the first single-handed transatlantic yacht race in 1960, was designed and built at the yard. The last timber boat to come out of Tyrell's was the Irish navy's sail-training vessel *Asgard II*, in 1981.

Six miles (9.6 km) from Arklow out in the Irish Sea is Ireland's first offshore wind farm, the ARKLOW BANK WIND PARK, inaugurated in 2004 and THE FIRST IN THE WORLD TO DEPLOY WIND TURBINES IN EXCESS OF 3 MEGAWATTS.

The Oldhams

For a while in the 19th century, thanks to Dublin-born geologist THOMAS OLDHAM (1816–78), Bray was famous as the site of THE OLDEST FOSSILS IN THE WORLD, about half a billion years old. Numerous small, round and frond-like marks on the rocks at the foot of Bray Head, they were discovered in 1840 by Oldham and given the name Oldhamia. Although fossils of algae, thought to be over a billion years old, were found in Australia in the 20th

century, the Bray specimens remain the oldest in Ireland and made an important contribution to the study and understanding of geology and timelines.

Thomas Oldham went on to become the first superintendent of the Geological Survey of India, and the first of many Irish geologists to work on that project. He was followed to India by his son, RICHARD DIXON OLDHAM (1858–1936), also born in Dublin, whose studies of the great Assam earthquake in 1906 produced evidence that the earth must have a molten core.

Well, I never *knew this* *about* **WICKLOW FOLK**

Kate Tyrell
➤ 1863–1921 ➤

Mariner KATE TYRELL was a member of the Tyrell shipping family from ARKLOW, and owner of the *Denbighshire Lass*, which in the 1920s became THE FIRST SCHOONER TO FLY THE IRISH TRICOLOUR.

One of the first successful Irish female mariners, Kate Tyrell was also one of the first Irishwomen to keep her maiden name after getting married, an outrage that horrified Irish society at that time.

Richard Crosbie
➤ 1755–1800 ➤

At 2.43 p.m. on 19 January 1785, in Ranelagh Gardens, Dublin, RICHARD CROSBIE doffed his hat to the watching crowds, climbed into the flimsy basket suspended beneath the tall, rubberised silk hydrogen balloon, beautifully embellished with the arms of Ireland, and ordered the

guy ropes to be cut. After a brief, heart-stopping pause the balloon ascended majestically into the sky and Richard Crosbie had joined the gods as THE FIRST IRISHMAN TO FLY.

Richard Crosbie had been born 30 years earlier at Crosbie Park, near Baltinglass. He inherited his father's interest in mechanical matters and carried out numerous experiments while at Trinity College, Dublin. In November 1783 the Montgolfier Brothers sent two brave colleagues aloft in a balloon from Versailles, achieving the world's first manned

flight, and this triumph inspired Crosbie to plan his own attempt. To make things a bit more spectacular he planned to cross the Irish Sea to Britain, thus becoming the first man to make a sea crossing. To this end he designed and built a prototype balloon and launched it into the sky from Ranelagh with his pet cat on board. It was with mixed feelings that he watched as the balloon floated away on the breeze north-west towards Scotland. The following day, having been sighted over Gatehouse of Fleet, the balloon descended into the sea near the Isle of Man, and was fortunately recovered, along with its feline passenger, by a passing Manx fisherman.

When his own turn came, Crosbie didn't get the chance to emulate his cat, because bad light forced him to abandon the idea of crossing the sea, but his short flight from Ranelagh to Clontarf on that January day was nonetheless historic and put Ireland at the forefront of the aviation race, where it would remain for over 150 years, as the destination for the first transatlantic flights.

MUNSTER

County Clare

CAPITAL OF IRISH MUSIC ✦ WHISTLING AMBASSADOR
✦ MATCHMAKING ✦ DROMOLAND CASTLE
✦ A YOUNG IRELANDER ✦ THE LITTLE ARK
✦ SUMMER SCHOOL ✦ THE FIRST CO-OP
✦ A POPULAR LANDLORD

*O'Brien Tower, on the highest point
of the Cliffs of Moher.*

◄ CLARE FOLK ►

Brian Merriman ✦ Biddy Early ✦ Eugene O'Curry
✦ Sir Frederick William Burton ✦ Michael Cusack ✦ Abe Grady
✦ Des Lynam

The Singing County

The little village of DOOLIN, near Lisdoonvarna, is considered one of Ireland's top venues for Irish music, and is sometimes called the traditional music capital of Ireland, giving credence to COUNTY CLARE's nickname of the 'Singing County'. The village has three well-known pubs that feature live traditional music every night, O'Connor's bar, McDermott's pub and McGann's.

Micho Russell
1915–94

MICHO RUSSELL, Ireland's Whistling Ambassador, lived all his life in Doolin, where he was born into a musical family who entertained in the village pubs and organised music festivals. He taught himself to play the tin whistle by the time he was 11, and became an avid collector and performer of traditional Irish music and folk songs. When the revival of the genre began in the 1960s, Micho was at the forefront, and would introduce his songs with stories from Irish folklore and legend.

He wrote a number of books about the music of western Ireland, and Co. Clare in particular, and made several recordings of traditional songs he had adapted and added to. One of his best-known songs was 'John Phillip Holland', written in honour of the inventor of the submarine, who was born in nearby Liscannor.

In 1994 Micho Russell died as a result of a car crash, and the following year the folk of Doolin organised the Micho Russell Festival Weekend in his honour. It has been held on the last full weekend in February every year since and is now one of the premier festivals of the traditional music calendar. In 2006 the festival was renamed the Russell Memorial Weekend in memory of all three musical Russell brothers, Micho, Packie and Gussie.

Summer School

Ireland's largest traditional Irish music summer school, THE WILLIE CLANCY SUMMER SCHOOL, has been held at Milltown Malbay every July since 1979. Students come from all over the world to learn about Irish music and dance, or ceilidh.

WILLIE CLANCY was born in MILL-TOWN MALBAY in 1918.
His parents were both musical, singing and playing the concertina and flute at local gatherings, and Willie learned the tin whistle before he was five. He soon added the flute, but found worldwide fame as one of Ireland's best uilleann pipers. The uilleann pipes are not dissimilar to Scottish bagpipes but are distinctive of Ireland.

Irish drum played like a tambourine, only using a short wooden stick called a 'tipper', or tick, rather than a hand.

Singer MAURA O'CONNELL, known for her blend of Celtic folk music and American country music, was born in Ennis in 1958. She now lives in the country music capital of the world, Nashville, Tennessee.

Lisdoonvarna Matchmaking Festival

MICHAEL TUBRIDY, a founding member of the traditional Irish music group THE CHIEFTAINS, was born in KILRUSH in 1935. The Chieftains were put together in 1962 with Tubridy playing flute, concertina, bombarde and bodhrán, a kind of

As well as being Ireland's only active spa town, LISDOONVARNA is home to EUROPE'S BIGGEST MATCHMAKING FESTIVAL. For over 150 years, in September and October, unattached men and women have flocked to the town to find a partner – and possibly to enjoy a Guinness or two and a dance to the tune of an Irish jig. The tradition stems from the days when farming families from the area would gather in the town after the crops had been harvested and, with time to relax, they would take the waters and let their sons and daughters become acquainted. What began as a local event has today blossomed into an international festival, with singles descending on Lisdoonvarna from all over the world. The serious matchmaking tends to happen over the weekend, while during the week there are such colourful excitements as horse racing, barbecues, dance nights and marching bands. On the last weekend there is a Grand Finale at which the best-matched new couple are crowned 'Mr Lisdoonvarna' and the 'Queen of the Burren'.

Dromoland Castle

In the 11th century, DROMOLAND was a defensive stronghold under the control of Donough O'Brien, a son of Brian Boru, High King of Ireland, born not far away at Killaloe. The estate remained in the O'Brien family for the next 900 years until it was sold in 1962 to an American industrialist with Irish roots, Bernard McDonough. He transformed the castle into a luxury hotel, which is now run by a consortium of Irish-American investors.

Dromoland was nearly lost to the family in the 18th century, during the time of the 2nd Baronet Sir Edward O'Brien, a passionate racehorse owner and trainer who gambled the entire estate on a horse race. Fortunately for Sir Edward, his horse Sean Buis won, and he not only kept Dromoland, but added considerably to the family fortune and was able to finance the

rebuilding of the castle in Georgian style. Sean Buis was buried with honour beneath the Temple, close to the old castle entrance. In addition to the castle Sir Edward built the Turret, an observation tower on the hill opposite to the estate entrance from where he could watch his horses training and racing. The settlement that grew up around the new castle he called Newmarket after the famous horse-racing centre in England.

The present Dromoland Castle, as we see it today, is extravagantly Gothic and was built for the 4th Baronet in the early 19th century by James and George Paine, pupils of the architect John Nash.

William Smith O'Brien
1803–64

Irish nationalist WILLIAM SMITH O'BRIEN was born into the O'Brien family of Dromoland Castle, direct descendants of 11th-century High King Brian Boru. His mother, Charlotte Smith, was a founder member of the Church Missionary Society and worked tirelessly to alleviate the distress of local people affected by the Great Famine. O'Brien inherited both her concern for the poor and her Limerick properties, and added his mother's maiden name to

his own to express his admiration for her.

Although a staunch Protestant, he was a champion of Catholic emancipation and a believer in non-sectarian protest. As MP for Co. Clare and then Co. Limerick, Smith O'Brien became increasingly disillusioned with the Union, of which he had originally been a supporter, and he became close to Daniel O'Connell, joining the Repeal Association in 1843. In 1846, however, he broke away to join the Young Irelanders and in 1848, when the government suspended habeas corpus during the Great Famine, he led the Young Irelanders in a rebellion, which culminated in the Battle of Widow McCormack's Cabbage Patch (*see* Co. Tipperary). For this he was transported to Tasmania, although he eventually received a full pardon and returned to Ireland in 1856.

The Little Ark

An unexpected sight for visitors who venture inside the tiny Moneen church near Kilbaha, is a small wooden hut, something between a bathing hut and a wheelbarrow, propped up on wooden blocks beside the font. This is the famous 'LITTLE ARK OF KILBAHA', the brainchild in 1852 of a local priest called FATHER MICHAEL MEEHAN, who wanted somewhere to celebrate mass but was denied permission to build a church in Kilbaha by the fiercely Protestant landlord.

Undeterred, Father Meehan commissioned Owen Collins, a carpenter in Carrigaholt, to build a portable box on wheels, which could be taken down to the beach and placed between the high and low water marks, traditionally considered no-man's-land. He put a small altar at one end, and for the next four years his congregation gathered at the foreshore on Sundays and knelt around the ark to worship. The Little Ark soon began to attract attention far beyond Kilbaha and huge numbers would turn up in all weathers to attend services. Eventually, the landlord was shamed into finding a site for a Catholic church, and the foundation stone for the church of Our Lady, Star of the Sea, was laid there in July 1857.

Ralahine

Not far from Newmarket-on-Fergus are the slightly desolate remains of RALAHINE CASTLE, built in the 16th century by the MacNamaras and later at the centre of an innovative social experiment in the 19th century. In 1831, JOHN SCOTT VANDELEUR, the man who owned the castle and estate, handed over 620 acres (250 ha) of land to his tenants to set up IRELAND'S FIRST CO-OPERATIVE COMMUNE, THE RALAHINE AGRICULTURAL AND MANUFACTURING CO-OPERATIVE ASSOCIATION. He was inspired by a meeting with the Welsh socialist,

Robert Owen, founder of a successful workers' community at New Lanark in Scotland.

By pooling their resources, the 53 men, women and children of the Ralahine Co-operative were able to purchase expensive farm machinery that they could never have afforded as individuals, and they soon became the proud owners of IRELAND'S FIRST MOWING MACHINE and a splendid horse-drawn muckspreader. For two years the commune operated very successfully, but alas, in 1833 John Scott Vandeleur lost all his money at gambling and had to flee Ireland, leaving the estate and the co-operative's land to be sold off to pay his debts.

Cornelius O'Brien
1782–1857

Standing beside the road, on a hill overlooking the sea, not far from the Holy Well of St Brigid at Liscannor,

there is a grand column commemorating CORNELIUS O'BRIEN, Member of Parliament for Clare for 20 years from 1832 until 1852. The inscription on the memorial mysteriously states that O'Brien died in 1853 and that the column was paid for with donations from 'grateful tenants'. While the date is most probably the result of a mistake by the stonecutter (O'Brien died in 1857), some people speculate that O'Brien erected the column himself while he was still alive, and paid for it through a clause in his tenancy agreements that required his tenants to contribute to his memorial fund.

In fact, Cornelius O'Brien, who, like the O'Briens of Dromoland, was descended from Brian Boru, was a conscientious and popular landlord who took his duties very seriously. He was born on the family estate at Birchfield, near Ennistymon, became a solicitor and magistrate, and as an MP fought for repeal of the Union and for tenants' rights – he was one of the few landlords not to evict a single one of his tenants during the Great Famine. It would appear that he was much more effective as a landlord than an MP – Lord Palmerston described him as 'the best Irish MP we ever had. He didn't open his mouth in twenty years'.

It was Cornelius O'Brien who began to develop the CLIFFS OF MOHER as a tourist attraction,

providing employment and invest-
ment for the local population. He
built a series of low walls made out
of the unique local stone and an observation tower at the highest point on
the cliffs, now known as O'Brien's

Tower. He also laid on a piper to sere-
nade visitors, but unfortunately the
poor fellow got drunk and toppled
over the cliff. Today, the Cliffs of
Moher are one of the top three most
visited attractions in Ireland.

Well, I never knew this
about
CLARE FOLK

Brian Merriman
◄— 1747–1805 —►

BRIAN MERRIMAN, author of Irish literature's most famous comic masterpiece
Cuirt An Mhean Oiche (The Midnight
Court), was born the illegitimate
son of a country gentleman in
ENNISTYMON. His epic poem, an
allegory of Ireland's struggle against

tyrannical overlords, relates the tale of
a narrator who falls asleep beside Lough
Graney, near Feakle, and finds himself
before a court of women presided over
by a great matriarch, or Queen of the
Fairies. The women have put the men
of Ireland on trial for their failings as
husbands and lovers, and for their reluctance to marry, and when they spot the
unmarried narrator lying on the shore
they decide that he should be the first
man to be punished for his shortcom-
ings. As they begin to advance on him
with menace, the narrator wakes up in
a cold sweat . . .

Merriman told the story in the
Irish language, and although he never
wrote it down himself, some of his
audience did and some of their manuscripts survive today and form the
basis of the many translations. The
language is earthy, direct and richly
comic, and the tale became immensely
popular, particularly as publications

of the original were banned by the Irish Censorship Board until as recently as the mid 1940s.

Not much else is known of Merriman's life other than that he was a teacher, married with two daughters, and is buried in an unmarked grave somewhere in the churchyard at Feakle.

Biddy Early
— 1798–*c*1850 —

Another celebrated Co. Clare storyteller was BIDDY EARLY, born near KILBARRON in 1798. She collected herbs for healing recipes, communicated with the animals and was known as a wise woman who could foresee the future. Many sought her advice, even 'The Liberator', Daniel O'Connell. Some 70 years after Biddy's death, Lady Augusta Gregory collected together her tales of folklore and medicine and made them the basis of a book, *Visions and*

Beliefs of the West of Ireland.

Biddy's name lives on in the BIDDY EARLY BREWERY, IRELAND'S FIRST PUB BREWERY, which opened in Inagh in 1995, utilising traditional Irish methods and recipes.

Landscape painter and book illustrator WILLIAM MULREADY (1786–1863), best known for his romantically stylised rural scenes, was born in ENNIS. He also designed sets of hand-coloured papers and envelopes for use with the Penny Black and Penny Blue stamps introduced in 1840, but they were deemed too ornate and were never adopted.

Eugene O'Curry
— 1794–1862 —

Scholar EUGENE O'CURRY was born in the little fishing village of CARRIGAHOLT at the mouth of the River Moyarta on the Shannon estuary. His father, a farmer, was steeped in the traditions and lore of the Irish communities of Co. Clare and passed his knowledge and enthusiasm on to his son. When Eugene was forced by the slump in agriculture to look for work away from the farm, he found employment in 1834 alongside John O'Donovan (*see* Co. Kilkenny), in the topographical department of the first Ordnance Survey of Ireland. Entirely self-taught, O'Curry spent the rest of his life collating, reading and copying Irish manuscripts for Trinity College and the Catholic University of Ireland until, according to Douglas Hyde, his knowledge of Irish literature and Irish lore was unrivalled by any living scholar.

O'Curry's name was inextricably linked with John O'Donovan for most of his life, not just because they were considered Ireland's greatest scholars and worked together on numerous projects, including the early stages of the *Dictionary of the Irish Language*, but also because they were married to sisters, Eugene to Anne Broughton and John to Mary Anne Broughton.

Watercolour artist SIR FREDERICK WILLIAM BURTON (1816–1900) was born at Clifden House in COROFIN, the third son of a distinguished painter. He made an early reputation for himself with pencil sketches of many Irish celebrities of the period, but it is for his exquisite miniatures and delicate watercolours that he is mostly remembered. His eyesight

weakened dramatically over time, and he finally stopped painting when he was made Director of the National Gallery in London by William Gladstone in 1874. In this capacity he is credited with accumulating what is possibly the greatest art collection in the world.

MICHAEL CUSACK (1847–1906), founder of the Gaelic Athletic Association, was born in CARRAN, on the eastern fringes of the Burren. While travelling throughout Ireland as a teacher during the Great Famine he became an expert on the ancient Irish sports, many of which had been forgotten. As well as coming up with the idea for the Association, he started a weekly newspaper, the *Celtic Times*,

which focused on Irish culture and native Irish games such as hurling and Gaelic football. 'The Citizen' in James Joyce's novel *Ulysses* is based on Michael Cusack, and there is a Michael Cusack Centre in Carran that tells of his life and times, as well as the history of the sports he championed.

ABE GRADY, the great-grandfather of world heavyweight champion boxer and 'Sportsman of the 20th Century' Muhammad Ali, was born in ENNIS, and emigrated to Kentucky in the 1860s. Muhammad Ali himself was born in Louisville, Kentucky, and was christened Cassius Clay after his father, who in turn had taken his name in honour of the Kentucky anti-slavery campaigner and politician

Cassius Clay. Ali changed his own name in 1964 when he converted to Islam.

Television sports presenter DES LYNAM was born in ENNIS in 1942.

County Cork

Cosmopolitan Cork ✦ A Distinguished Cemetery
✦ Southernmost Settlement ✦ What's in a Name?
✦ Southernmost Island ✦ First Around the World
✦ Seawater Rockpool

Blackrock Castle, Cork Harbour.

◄ CORK FOLK ►

William 'Guillermo' Bowles ✦ James Roche Verling ✦ Robert Forde
✦ Patrick and Tim Keohane ✦ Percy Ludgate

As well as being IRELAND'S LARGEST COUNTY, County Cork can also claim to have in Cork Harbour THE SECOND LARGEST NATURAL HARBOUR IN THE WORLD, after Sydney in Australia – although there are other contenders for the title including Halifax harbour in Nova Scotia, Canada, and Poole harbour in England.

Co. Cork can boast IRELAND'S ONLY PLANETARIUM, which was built in 1989 at the little town of SCHULL, near Skibbereen, with help from German industrialist Josef Menke, who spent many happy holidays in Schull with his family.

Cork

CORK was always a vibrant and innovative place, open to new cultures and ideas, and in 1784 the city became home to a Bengali entrepreneur called SAKE DEAN MAHOMED, a medic in the East India Company who was THE FIRST INDIAN TO WRITE A BOOK IN THE ENGLISH LANGUAGE, *The Travels of Dean Mahomet, A Native of Patna in Bengal, Through Several Parts of India, While in the Service of The Honourable The East India Company Written by Himself, In a Series of Letters to a Friend*. He also introduced into the West for the first time a treatment known as shampooing, from the Hindu word *champo*, meaning massage.

Sake Dean Mahomed

In the early 20th century Cork became the European headquarters of Turkish Delight when HARUTAN BATMAZIAN, a Christian Armenian whose family had settled in London after fleeing the Turkish pogroms of the mid 19th century, exhibited his exotic sticky sweet at the 1902 Cork Exhibition. It proved so popular that Batmazian moved to Cork and opened a shop selling his home-made Turkish Delight under the name Hadji Bey et Cie, a tribute to the name of the Istanbul merchant Haci Bekir who had sold the first Turkish Delight to a British sailor in the 18th century. The Hadji Bey et Cie emporium closed in 1971 and the premises, with its distinctive bay window, is now incorporated into Cork's famous 'Met' hotel.

St Finbarr's Cathedral

St Finbarr's Cemetery

St Finbarr's Cemetery is Cork's largest cemetery and the last resting-place of a number of notable people including . . .

Composer SIR ARNOLD BAX (1883–1953). Born in London, Bax became fascinated by Ireland after reading the poetry of W.B. Yeats, and much of his music reflects the Celtic romanticism of the Irish Literary Revival. He also wrote poetry under the name Dermot O'Byrne. His connection with Cork began in 1929, when he was asked to become adjudicator at a music festival organised by the

Capuchin Fathers in the city. He become great friends with Aloys Fleischmann, founder of the Cork Symphony Orchestra, who conducted Bax's work on Irish Radio and helped make his music popular throughout Ireland. Bax died while visiting the Fleischmanns in 1953.

Sir Arnold Bax

Sculptor SEAMUS MURPHY (1907–75), who was born in Mallow. Amongst his most famous pieces are five bronze busts of the presidents of Ireland at Aras an Uachtarain, the Irish president's residence in Dublin, and the United Nations Monument at Glasnevin. He also wrote a book called *Stone Mad*, about the work of Irish stonemasons from medieval times to the 1950s, which has been hailed as a classic on the subject.

Architect and antiquarian RICHARD ROLT BRASH (1817–76), born in Cork. He is celebrated as the first person to accurately decipher the Ogham script.

Baltimore

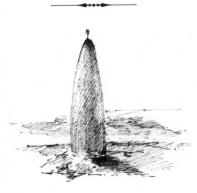

BALTIMORE, which stands near the tip of the Skibbereen peninsula, is THE SOUTHERNMOST SETTLEMENT ON THE IRISH MAINLAND. An attractive fishing village with a busy harbour, it is overlooked by a 16th-century castle that belonged to the O'Driscolls, who were the big local landowners in medieval times and before. Between the 1880s and 1920s, Baltimore was the biggest fishing port in Ireland and also an important boat-building centre.

There is some dispute as to whether or not Baltimore gives its name to the city of Baltimore in Maryland in America. The American Baltimore, which is Maryland's biggest city and the fourth largest port in the USA, was named in honour of Maryland's founding proprietor, Lord Baltimore, originally SIR GEORGE CALVERT (1579–1632), a Member of Parliament and Secretary of State to King James I.

In 1625 Calvert, born a Protestant, converted to Catholicism, which meant he was no longer allowed to work in high office in England, and so James I granted him the barony of Baltimore in Co. Longford, Ireland, so that he would have money and lands with which to support his family, and he thus became the 1st Baron Baltimore. Baltimore in Gaelic comes from *bailte* and *mora*, meaning big houses or estates, so it is quite feasible that the name Baltimore was already established in Co. Longford and Lord Baltimore took his title from the estate. It is also possible that Calvert named the estate Baltimore from the fishing village of Baltimore in Co. Cork, thus making Cork's Baltimore the original of Baltimore in the American state of Maryland. Whichever it be, the name Baltimore comes from Ireland.

Clear Island

About 45 minutes by boat from Baltimore, and only 4 miles (6.4 km) north of Fastnet Rock, Ireland's southernmost point, is CLEAR ISLAND, IRELAND'S MOST SOUTHERLY INHABITED ISLAND. Clear is a Gaeltacht island, where Irish is spoken as the first language, and the island annually hosts a number of Gaelic summer schools. Clear Island's remoteness makes it a haven for birds and Ireland's foremost centre for bird-watching, with IRELAND'S ONLY MANNED BIRD OBSERVATORY.

Saoirse (from the Irish word for freedom). While not the very first boat to fly the Irish tricolour (*see* Co. Wicklow), the *Saoirse* was the first boat to carry the new Irish flag around the world and into many of the world's ports.

Conor O'Brien
1880–1952

During the voyage, O'Brien put into Port Stanley in the Falkland Islands, and the islanders were so impressed with the *Saoirse* that they commissioned him to build a larger version for them. O'Brien returned to Baltimore and in 1926 he launched a 56 ft (17 m) ketch, AK *Ilen,* named after the river at the mouth of which the boatyard sits. He then sailed it to the Falklands, by way of Bristol and the east coast ports of South America. The *Ilen* served the Falklands Trading Company as a general service vessel for 60 years, and the fact that she remained in service for so long in the rough waters of the South Atlantic is testament to the quality of her Irish build.

In 1923 CONOR O'BRIEN became THE FIRST IRISHMAN TO SAIL AROUND THE WORLD. He achieved the feat in a boat he had designed and built himself in Baltimore, named the

Conor O'Brien was also a committed republican who several years earlier, in 1914, had used his yacht *Kelpie* to land guns from Germany at Kilcoole in Co. Wicklow, for use by the Irish Volunteers.

Lough Hyne

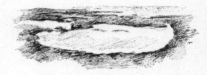

LOUGH HYNE, near Skibbereen, is EUROPE'S ONLY INLAND SALT-WATER LAKE and was designated as Ireland's first Marine Nature Reserve in 1981. It is basically a huge rock-pool, separated from the Atlantic

Ocean by a rock sill, and at high tide seawater rushes in via a narrow channel known as the 'Rapids'. The calm, warm waters of the lake support a huge variety of rare animals and plants usually found in much hotter climes, and is one of the last refuges in Europe of the purple sea urchin. Because of its unusual formation the lake experiences an asymmetrical tide, which takes four hours to rise and eight and a half hours to fall.

Well, I never knew this
about
CORK FOLK

William 'Guillermo' Bowles

—◂ 1720–80 ▸—

WILLIAM 'GUILLERMO' BOWLES, author of *An Introduction to the Natural History and Physical Geography of Spain*, the first natural history study of Spain, was born somewhere near Cork. After studying law in England and natural history, chemistry and metallurgy in Paris, he toured the Continent and gained a

reputation as a top mining consultant. In 1752 he was asked to be Spain's superintendent of mines and also to become the principal scientist at King Fernando's newly established natural history museum in Madrid. Bowles is credited with helping to build a strong and friendly relationship between the Spanish and Irish, encouraging the import of Irish wolfhounds into Spain to deal with the Spanish wolf population, and observing that the Spanish love of fiestas and dancing was similar to the Irish love of feasting and saint's day celebrations. 'Bowlesia', a Peruvian plant related to the carrot, is named after him. William 'Guillermo' Bowles is buried in the Church of San Martin in Madrid.

James Roche Verling
◂ 1787–1858 ▸

JAMES ROCHE VERLING was born in COBH and graduated in medicine from Edinburgh University, after which he served as a surgeon with the British army during the Peninsular War. In 1815 he was sent to the island of St Helena as surgeon to the Ordnance, travelling there on board HMS *Northumberland*, along with the exiled Emperor Napoleon and his party.

Verling went on to become one of a number of doctors who reluctantly attended Napoleon while he was on the island. The position as the Emperor's surgeon was fraught with danger, as the Governor of St Helena, Sir Hudson Lowe, required that the doctor report back on any interesting conversations that he overheard. The doctor, on the other hand, was bound by his oath not to breach his patient's confidence. Napoleon's first doctor on St Helena, whom Verling temporarily replaced, was an Irishman called Barry Edward O'Meara, who was dismissed by the Governor in 1818 for allegedly becoming too close to the Emperor.

O'Meara later wrote a sensational book about Napoleon's exile called *A Voice from St Helena*, in which he accused Sir Hudson Lowe of asking him to hasten the Emperor's demise.

Verling was fully aware that the position of being Napoleon's physician 'held more prospects of ultimate injury than benefit', and he was mightily relieved when finally an anatomist from Corsica was chosen for the role by Napoleon's mother and Verling was able to return safely to Cobh, where he spent the rest of his life. Verling's home, Bella Vista, is now the Bellavista Hotel.

Co. Cork's Antarctic explorers

ROBERT FORDE (1875–1959), was born in CORK, joined the Royal Navy at the age of 16 and became a member of Robert Falcon Scott's ill-fated Terra Nova Expedition. His great achievement was helping to establish Scott's 'Corner Camp' near Cape Evans in September 1912, during which time he was so severely affected by frostbite that he was sent home to Cork. The 3, 937 ft (1,200 m) high Mount Forde at the head of Hunt glacier was named in his honour.

One of Forde's companions on the Terra Nova expedition was fellow Co. Cork man PATRICK KEOHANE (1879–1950), who was born in the little fishing village of Courtmacsherry, 30 miles (48 km) south-west of Cork City. He was a member of the first group ordered by Scott to turn back from the ultimately disastrous trek to the South Pole, and during the return Keohane apparently fell down eight crevasses in 25 minutes. In October 1912 he was one of those who went to look for Scott's missing party and found their frozen bodies 11 miles (18 km) short of the supply depot at One Ton.

Keohane's father Tim was a member of the Courtmacsherry lifeboat crew who helped to rescue survivors from the *Lusitania*, torpedoed off the Old Head of Kinsale by a German submarine in May 1915.

Percy Ludgate
━━◄ 1883–1922 ►━━

PERCY LUDGATE, an accountant from SKIBBEREEN, in the far south of Co. Cork, is nowadays acknowledged as one of the most important pioneers in the history of the modern computer. Between 1903 and 1909, working entirely in his spare time, he devised an extraordinarily advanced 'analytical engine', a general-purpose, programmable, mechanical computer, that was controlled manually with a keyboard or automatically via a perforated tape.

Some 50 years earlier a Devon man called Charles Babbage had tried to assemble a huge programmable calculator based on the Jacquard loom that used punch cards to control a sequence of operations. It was so enormous that it proved impossible to build more than small sections at the time, and was also ponderously slow, relying on simple addition and subtraction. Ludgate's machine, which he began to design before he knew anything of Babbage's work, was based on multiplication, using an ingenious scheme termed 'Irish Logarithms' to transform the multiplications into additions. Also, because Ludgate used a system of rods rather than gears, his machine was much lighter and would have been portable.

Ludgate presented the details of his analytical engine to the Royal Dublin Society in 1909, and the obvious genius of his invention attracted worldwide attention. Unfortunately, although he had made some drawings of the machine, he never got round to building a prototype before the outbreak of the First World War, when he was asked to help organise food provisions for the army's horses. After the war had ended, in 1922, he went walking in the Swiss mountains to recuperate and caught pneumonia, from which he died. Sadly, the records he left do not provide enough detail for a working model of his machine to be made.

County Kerry

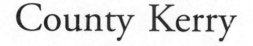

SUPERLATIVES ✦ WESTERNMOST IRELAND
✦ A FAMILY VILLAGE ✦ SCARLET PIMPERNEL
✦ THE QUEEN OF BALUCHISTAN

Dingle – Ireland's Westernmost Town.

◄ KERRY FOLK ►

Richard Cantillon ✦ Lord Kitchener ✦ William Melville
✦ Steve 'Crusher' Casey ✦ Christy Brown

Some Kerry Superlatives

——— ◆◆◆ ———

COUNTY KERRY is as far west as you can go in Europe and boasts EUROPE'S WESTERNMOST TOWN (Dingle), EUROPE'S MOST WESTERLY COMMERCIAL SHIPPING PORT (Fenit) and 'the next parish to America', the Blasket Islands.

From 1891 until 1953 EUROPE'S MOST WESTERLY RAILWAY ran from Tralee to Dingle, and early in the new millennium a 2-mile (3.2-km) section of this was reopened to link Tralee with EUROPE'S MOST WESTERLY WINDMILL at Blennerville.

The Conor Pass, which runs from Dingle northwards across the peninsula towards Brandon Bay, is THE HIGHEST ROAD IN IRELAND.

KILLARNEY NATIONAL PARK was IRELAND'S FIRST NATIONAL PARK and was created when the Muckross Estate was donated to the state in 1932.

It encompasses over 25, 000 acres (10,000 ha), includes the famed Lakes of Killarney and is home to THE ONLY NATIVE HERD OF RED DEER IN IRELAND. In 1981 the park was designated a UNESCO World Biosphere Reserve.

SHEEHAN'S THATCHED HOUSE at Finuge Cross, near Listowel, was built over 300 years ago and is THE OLDEST SURVIVING THATCHED HOUSE IN IRELAND.

The Blasket Islands

——— ◆◆◆ ———

The seven BLASKET ISLANDS lie off the south-western tip of the Dingle Peninsula, with Tearaght Island being THE WESTERNMOST PART OF IRELAND – and hence Europe. It seems almost impossible to believe these barren, inhospitable rocks were once inhabited, but they were, until 1953, and indeed they fostered some memorable books such as THOMAS O'CROHAN'S *The Islander* and MAURICE O'SULLIVAN'S *Twenty Years A-Growing*. There was one seannachie (storyteller) in particular, PEIG SAYERS, a fisherman's wife who lived on Great Blasket for 50 years, whose tales of island life became an essential contribution to the Gaelic Revival and were required reading in schools – the Irish Folklore Commission described her as 'the greatest woman storyteller in the Irish language'.

In the early 1970s tiny INISHNABRO, at the centre of the Blaskets, almost joined the Space Race when a group of scientists led by British astronomer Professor Fred Hoyle and American Dr Gary Hudson enquired about leasing the island to build a launch site for vertical take-off rockets.

The late former Taoiseach Charles Haughey owned INISHVICKILLANE and built himself a holiday home on the island, which he frequented in the summer months.

INISHTOOSKERT is home to THE LARGEST COLONY OF EUROPEAN STORM PETRELS IN THE WORLD, some 28, 000 pairs.

Sneem

SNEEM is a postcard pretty hamlet of brightly coloured houses on the south coast of the Iveragh Peninsula and a popular stopping point on the Ring of Kerry. The area retains a festive atmosphere and the locals like to say that the houses sport such vivid colours so that you can more easily recognise your own residence after a Sneem night out.

In recent times Sneem has become famous for the SNEEM FAMILY FESTIVAL, held in July, and the village was chosen in 2008 as the first Irish venue for the WORLD WIFE CARRYING CHAMPIONSHIPS.

The rules of the competition are quite strict. The wife in question need not be the competitor's own wife, but may be the wife of an understanding friend, or indeed she could be anyone's wife. She must weigh over 7½ stone (48 kg), and she must be willing to be thrown over someone's shoulder and carried over a 277-yard (253-m) course of sand, grass and asphalt that includes two dry obstacles and one water hazard, at least 3 ft (1 m) deep. A contestant who drops his wife is penalised 15 seconds – and the winner is the team that completes the course in the shortest time. The winners go on to the finals in Sonkajarvi in Finland.

The origins of the competition are said to derive from challenges set by Viking leaders when choosing their troops – in Viking days, of course, success was largely measured by the number of wives a warrior could carry off from neighbouring villages.

Monsignor Hugh O'Flaherty
1898–1962

One of the Second World War's most courageous heroes, MONSIGNOR HUGH O'FLAHERTY, the Scarlet Pimpernel of the Vatican, was born in CAHIRCIVEEN on the Iveragh Peninsula. He attended monastery schools in Killarney and Limerick and completed his theological studies in Rome. In 1928 he was appointed to the Holy Office (once known as the Inquisition) at the Vatican, and his humour and sporting prowess made him very popular on Rome's social circuit. He was Italy's amateur golfing champion and regularly played golf with Mussolini's son-in-law and King Alfonso of Spain.

In 1929 Mussolini and Cardinal Gasparri had signed the Lateran Treaty recognising the Pope's sovereignty over the Vatican City and the Vatican's independence. When war broke out in 1939 and Italy sided with Germany, O'Flaherty was sent by the Vatican to tour the prison camps where Allied soldiers were being interned, and he was able to inform worried families that their loved ones were safe.

At the same time the Fascists began to arrest and persecute many of the Jews that O'Flaherty had socialised with before the war, and he started to shelter them in his quarters in the Vatican where the Germans could not reach them. When Mussolini was toppled in 1943 and Rome was formally occupied by the Germans, O'Flaherty got together a group of diplomats and priests to form an organisation for helping and hiding Jews as well as the huge numbers of prisoners of war who were escaping from the camps and making their way to Rome. They were all lodged in various safe houses throughout Rome and sometimes within the Vatican, and supplied with food and clothing. O'Flaherty would walk around Rome in disguise, comforting and reassuring the escapees, co-ordinating the efforts of the rescuers and even, like a mother bird, sometimes leading the Germans away from the hideouts, before escaping himself back over the white line painted at the entrance to the Vatican on St Peter's Square. Between 1943 and 1944

O'Flaherty and his colleagues rescued over 5, 000 Jews and Allied prisoners from the hands of the Germans.

In 1960 Monsignor O'Flaherty suffered a stroke and returned to his beloved Ireland, dying at his sister's home in Cahirciveen in 1963. He is buried there, in the cemetery of the Daniel O'Connell Memorial Church.

His story was told in the 1983 film *The Scarlet and the Black*, with Gregory Peck playing the role of Monsignor Hugh O'Flaherty.

Jennifer Musa
1917–2008

'Mummy' JENNIFER MUSA, the 'Queen of Baluchistan', was born Bridget (Bridie) Wren, into a large Catholic farming family in Tarmons, on the banks of the River Shannon. She had a happy childhood and when she headed off to England to become a nurse, changing to her preferred name of Jennifer, everyone assumed she was destined for the life of an ordinary, middle-class Catholic girl. However, things took off in 1939 in a quite unexpected and extraordinary direction when she went to a May Ball at Exeter College, Oxford, and met handsome philosophy student Qazi Mohammad Musa. He was the ward of the British Governor-General of Baluchistan (*see* page 182) and eldest son of the Prime Minister to the Khan of Kalet, ruler of Baluchistan's dominant princedom. They fell in love and married the following year, despite the reservations of both her Catholic family and his Muslim relatives. She changed her name to Jehan Zeba, and some years later, in 1948, they went to live in the Musa family home in Pishin, some 30 miles (48 km) north of Quetta, Baluchistan's capital.

Pishin was a far cry from Co. Kerry. The land was dry, dusty and sun-baked, the temperature often exceeding 100 degrees Fahrenheit (38°C), travel was by camel, and their house was an old colonial home with thick mud walls covered in tiger skins and leopards' heads. Jennifer refused to wear the burqa, but was required to wear the traditional shalwar-kameez, and she had to live alongside Qazi's first wife, whom Qazi had been forced to marry at age 14, to prevent him from being eliminated by his father's political rivals, and their five children – they all became great friends.

It was an exotic but happy way of life and Jennifer was quickly accepted and settled, athough she never quite lost her Kerry brogue or mischievous Irish sense of humour.

Her idyllic life ended in 1956 when Qazi was killed in a car accident, and Jennifer contemplated returning to Ireland, but her in-laws begged her to stay in Pishin with her 14-year-old son Ashraf Jehangir Qazi, and apart from a brief visit in 1962 she never saw Ireland again.

Instead, she turned to politics, joining the National Awami (Freedom) Party, and in Pakistan's first free election in 1970 won a seat at the National Assembly, her fair skin, golden hair and blue eyes causing turmoil amongst her more traditional, heavily bearded colleagues.

She served for seven years, founded Pakistan's first women's association and family planning clinic, and fought tirelessly to defend Baluchistan's autonomous rights from being eroded by Pakistan's President Bhutto.

When martial law was imposed in the late 1970s, Jennifer retired to Pishin and became a local matriarch, setting up an ice factory, settling disputes, promoting education and literacy for the local women, helping Afghan refugees fleeing across the border from the Russian invasion – and serving all who visited her with afternoon tea.

Today much of Baluchistan is under the control of the Taliban, but right up until her death in January 2008, the local warlords respected and revered 'Mummy' Jennifer from Co. Kerry. Her son Ashraf Jehangir Qazi became Pakistan's ambassador to the United States.

Well, I never knew this
about
KERRY FOLK

Richard Cantillon
◄—— 1680–1734 ►——

'The land is the source or matter from whence all wealth is produced. The labour of man is the form which produces it; and the wealth in itself is nothing but the mainte-nance, conveniences and super-fluities of life.'

So begins RICHARD CANTILLON'S 'Essai sur la Nature du Commerce en Général', written in English but published in French around 1732, and first seen in England some 20 years after his death.

It is for this work that Cantillon is regarded as THE WORLD'S FIRST ECONOMIC THEORIST. His ideas greatly influenced the 'Father of Economics', Adam Smith, who quotes Cantillon in his book *An Enquiry into the Nature and Causes of the Wealth of Nations*.

Richard Cantillon was born in BALLYHEIGUE, a beautiful coastal resort north of Tralee. After working in Barcelona for James Brydges, Paymaster-General for the British army during the War of the Spanish Succession (1701–14), he moved to

Paris, where he became a banker, earning a massive fortune by specu-lating against various schemes such as John Law's Mississippi Bubble and the South Sea Bubble – so it would seem that he knew what he was talking about.

In 1734 he retired to London but died when his house was set on fire by a disgruntled employee.

LORD KITCHENER (1850–1916), the face of First World War recruitment posters, was born in BALLYLONG-FORD, near Listowel, where his father owned land.

YOUR COUNTRY NEEDS
YOU

William Melville
◄ 1850–1918 ►

A secretive but highly influential son of SNEEM was WILLIAM MELVILLE, born there in 1850, the son of a baker. As a young boy he emigrated to London to be a baker's apprentice, but soon tired of bread-making and joined the relatively new Metropolitan Police.

He turned out to have a fine brain for detective work and was one of the founders of the Special Irish Branch, set up to keep an eye on the Irish nationalists and other subversive and anarchist organisations. He was then assigned to protect the Royal Family, and from this time on the story of his career disappears into the realms of speculation and intrigue.

Melville is thought to have been involved in thwarting two celebrated plots. The Jubilee Plot of 1887 was a plan by Irish terrorists to blow up Queen Victoria and the British government in Westminster Abbey, during celebrations for the Queen's Golden Jubilee. The Walsall Plot of 1892 revolved around a group of anarchist bomb makers. Recent evidence has emerged which suggests that both of these 'plots' might actually have been instigated by government agents in order to discredit, in the first case, Charles Stewart Parnell and the Irish separatists and, in the second case, the anarchists and their ilk.

Melville was known to be a fan of the escapologist Harry Houdini, who apparently taught the detective how to pick locks, escape from rope knots and handcuffs, and how to hold his breath underwater for long periods of time – all useful tricks for Melville's next venture. This was to set up in 1904 a new, secret, counter-espionage service to monitor German intelligence in the build-up to the First World War.

This organisation, run on a tight budget out of a small office in London's Victoria Street, was the forerunner of the Secret Service Bureau, established in 1909, and later MI5 and MI6. Melville ran it as a personal fiefdom, and many of the tactics and methods still used by the secret services today were formulated and developed by Melville during this period.

William Melville was perhaps the most successful of all the early spy chiefs, partly because no one knew about him. However, it seems that James Bond's creator Ian Fleming, who himself worked for the secret services, *did* know, for it is widely believed that Fleming based Bond's boss 'M', played in the first 12 Bond films by Bernard Lee and later so memorably by Dame Judi Dench, on the baker's boy from Co. Kerry – William Melville.

Steve 'Crusher' Casey
◄ 1909–87 ►

STEVE 'CRUSHER' CASEY was born in a little white cottage buried in heather, a 3-mile row across the lough from Sneem. He grew up to be the greatest wrestler, boxer and oarsman not only in Ireland, but the world. He was one of seven brothers born to bareknuckle boxer Mike Casey and his wife, champion oarswoman Bridget Mountain, daughter of local stonemason Johnny Mountain.

Mike, who lived for a while in America, had been a sparring partner of the legendary American boxing champion John L. Sullivan (whose parents came from Co. Kerry), and had also put together American millionaire Cornelius Vanderbilt's winning rowing team, the Hibernians, made up entirely of oarsmen from Sneem. This sporting prowess was passed on in spectacular style to his sons.

The Casey brothers became known as 'the toughest family on earth', together winning every Irish rowing competition, tug-of-war, wrestling match and boxing bout they entered. As wrestlers they remained undefeated in Europe, and in 1935 they won the All-England Rowing Championships and were only prevented from going to the 1936 Olympics in Berlin because Steve and his brother Paddy had wrestled professionally. Had the Casey brothers participated in the Games, no one doubts that they would have won gold in all six rowing events.

The most remarkable of all the remarkable Caseys was Steve 'Crusher' Casey – who stood 6 ft 4 ins (1.93 m) tall and weighed 17 stone (108 kg). As a wrestler he was crowned world heavyweight champion in 1938, a title he defended successfully for the next nine years until he retired undefeated in 1947. During that time he also boxed, beating US champion Tiger

Warrentown in 1940. This win encouraged Casey to challenge Joe Louis for the world heavyweight championship, and such was Casey's reputation that Louis actually ducked the challenge – for the only time in his career.

In 1982 Steve Casey was presented with the Irish Hall of Fame award, and the following year five of the Casey brothers attended a reunion in Sneem where they proved that, even in their 70s, they could still row faster than challengers half their age.

In 1987 Steve died of cancer and he is remembered today with a statue in Sneem.

Author, poet, painter and cerebral palsy sufferer CHRISTY BROWN (1932–81) lived much of his life in BALLYHEIGUE with his wife Mary. His autobiography *My Left Foot* was turned into a film, which won Oscars for Daniel Day-Lewis playing Christy and Brenda Fricker as his mother.

County Limerick

IRELAND'S FIRST CREAMERY ✦ THE LONGEST VILLAGE
✦ LARGEST WINE CELLAR ✦ A SPORTING CHALICE
✦ IRISH BULL

Ardagh Chalice

◀ LIMERICK FOLK ▶

Sir Aubrey de Vere ✦ Aubrey Thomas Hunt de Vere
✦ Sir Stephen Edward de Vere ✦ Lord Monteagle ✦ Sir Cecil Spring-Rice
✦ William Brooke O'Shaughnessy

The lush green pastures of COUNTY LIMERICK gave rise to the first stirrings of Ireland's agricultural co-operative movement. In 1889 HORACE PLUNKETT (1854–1932), owner of a small butter factory in DRUMCOLLOGHER, launched IRELAND'S FIRST CREAMERY CO-OP, whereby local farmers got together to process and market their milk. Despite initial resistance, the idea was successfully taken up by farmers all over Ireland, at a time when Irish agriculture was in decline. In 1899 Horace Plunkett was made vice-president of the newly formed Department of Agriculture and Technical Instruction (DATI), and by 1915 his Irish Agricultural Organisation Society had swelled to 1,000 co-operatives and 100,000 members.

The pretty village of TOURNA-FULLA, which sits close to where the counties of Cork, Kerry and Limerick meet, is said to be THE LONGEST VILLAGE IN IRELAND.

Tournafulla Church

CASTLE OLIVER, birthplace of Eliza Oliver, mother of Lola Montez (*see* Co. Sligo), is now a luxurious wedding venue and is celebrated for having THE LARGEST PRIVATE WINE CELLAR IN IRELAND.

Castle Oliver

Ardagh Chalice

When PADDY FLANAGAN and JIMMY QUIN went digging for potatoes inside the ancient ring fort of Reerasta, near ARDAGH, on an autumn evening in 1868, little did they know that would come home with perhaps the finest example of 8th-century metalwork ever found, the Ardagh Chalice.

The chalice, which dates from around 790, is made from silver bronze alloy and silver gilt and is decorated with gold, semi-precious stones and enamel. A band runs around the top engraved with the names of the 12 Apostles.

Along with the chalice, Jimmy and Paddy also found a smaller bronze cup, four brooches, and a wooden cross with the date 1727 on it, suggesting that this was when the hoard was buried. In 1727 the Penal Laws were in force, and Catholics would often hold secret services in ancient places such as the ring fort at

Reerasta. On this occasion they would appear to have been surprised by enemy soldiers and had to hide the chalice in a hurry, which is why it was found buried unprotected. Whoever hid the chalice obviously had no chance to return and claim it.

Paddy Flanagan worked as a labourer for Jimmy Quin's mother, who leased the land where they found the chalice from the landowners, the Sisters of Mercy. Shortly after the discovery Paddy left the Quins' employ, apparently disgruntled at the fact that Jimmy Quin took all the glory for finding the chalice while he, Paddy, had actually been the one to discover it. Mrs Quin eventually sold the chalice to the Bishop of Limerick for £50, while Paddy died and was buried in the pauper's graveyard at Newcastlewest. The bishop later sold the chalice to the Royal Irish Academy for £500, and it now resides in the National Museum in Dublin.

Two Gaelic Athletic Association trophies are modelled on the Ardagh Chalice, the O'Duffy Cup and the Sam Maguire Cup.

The O'DUFFY CUP, named after Sean O'Duffy, the GAA administrator who donated it, is presented to the winners of the All-Ireland Camogie Championship, camogie being a women's variant of hurling.

The SAM MAGUIRE CUP, known as the Sam, is presented to the winning team in the final of the All-Ireland Senior Football Championship, the premier knockout competition of Gaelic football. Sam Maguire was an Irish republican, a Gaelic footballer and a senior official of the GAA.

Irish Bull

Limerick has, of course, long been known for the comic verse form named after it, but what is less well known is the Limerick connection with another Irish contribution to the language, IRISH BULL.

Irish bull refers to incongruous statements where the words fall between two meanings, as between the horns of a bull – such expressions are attributed particularly to the Irish, who have a reputation for theatrical rhetoric and for being especially voluble. The man credited with being the undisputed 'Father of Irish Bull' is SIR BOYLE ROCHE (1736–1807), Honourable Member for Tralee at the Irish House of Commons in the latter part of the 18th century, and great-grandson of a much-loved four times Mayor of Limerick, Toxeth Roche.

Boyle Roche was born in Co. Galway, the youngest of three sons from a colourful family. His older brother Tiger Roche became a famous adventurer and swordsman, variously described as a hero or a villain, and possibly the model for William Makepeace Thackeray's Barry Lyndon.

Boyle joined the British army and fought against the French during the Seven Years' War in America and at the siege of Quebec, before returning to Ireland and entering politics. He was an opponent of Catholic emancipation and a staunch supporter of the Union of Ireland and England – as he put it, 'Ireland and England are like two sisters; I would have them embrace one another like a brother.'

'Mr Speaker, I smell a rat; I see him forming in the air and darkening the sky; but I'll nip him in the bud!' It is for bons mots such as this that Sir Boyle Roche is chiefly remembered. His parliamentary career is littered with them, for he would memorise speeches that were written for him and then, in the heat of discussion, pepper them with mixed metaphors and malapropisms – indeed Richard Brinsley Sheridan is thought to have used Roche as the model for Mrs Malaprop in his play *The Rivals*.

When the Irish Parliament was dissolved after the Act of Union of 1801, Sir Boyle Roche, who was knighted for his services to Parliament in 1782, retired into private life with his wife Mary. He died in 1807 and was laid to rest in DUBLIN'S FIRST GALLERIED CHURCH, ST MARY'S, where Theobald Wolfe Tone and playwright Sean O'Casey were baptised and Arthur Guinness was married in 1761 – it is now a pub restaurant.

A selection of the sayings of Sir Boyle Roche – the Father of Irish bull

Why should we put ourselves out of our way to do anything for posterity? For what has posterity ever done for us?

The cup of Ireland's misery has been overflowing for centuries and is not yet half full.

All along the untrodden paths of the future, I can see the footprints of an unseen hand.

We should silence anyone who opposes the right to freedom of speech.

Half the lies our opponents tell about us are untrue.

I told you to make one longer than the other, and instead you have made one shorter than the other.

While I write this letter, I have a pistol in one hand and a sword in the other.

PS If you do not receive this letter, of course it must have been miscarried; therefore I beg you to write and let me know.

Well, I never knew this about
LIMERICK FOLK

Poetry and Rice

When CATHERINE SPRING married STEPHEN RICE, of Mount Trenchard House – which is situated on the banks of the River Shannon near Glin – and started a family, she gave rise to a political and poetical dynasty as well as a poetical name – Spring-Rice.

What ruined shapes of feudal pomp are there,
In the cold moonlight fading silently?
The castle, with its stern, baronial air,
Still frowning, as accustomed to defy;
The gate-towers, mouldering where the stream moans by,
Now, but the owl's lone haunt, and fox's lair.

From 'Kilmallock'
by Sir Aubrey de Vere

Stephen and Catherine's daughter, MARY SPRING-RICE, married a poet, SIR AUBREY DE VERE (1788–1846), from nearby CURRAGH CHASE – the

house burnt down in 1941 while the grounds, which now belong to the State, are used for woodland trails and camping. Sir Aubrey's work, romantic, enthusiastically religious in character and reflecting a love of Irish epic poetry, was an early contribution to the revival of Celtic literature and poetry.

Sir Aubrey de Vere died where he was born, in the place he loved the most, his home at Curragh Chase, Co.

Killmallock Priory

Limerick. He passed on his love of poetry to his youngest son AUBREY THOMAS HUNT DE VERE (1814–1902), who became friends with the poets Samuel Taylor Coleridge and William Wordsworth.

> I saw the Master of the Sun.
>   He stood
> High in his luminous car,
>   himself more bright;
> An Archer of immeasurable
>   might
> On his left shoulder hung
>   his quivered load
> Spurned by his Steeds the
>   eastern mountain glowed
> Forward his eager eye, and
>   brow of light
> He bent; and, while both
>   hands that arch embowed,
> Shaft after shaft pursued the
>   flying Night.
> No wings profaned that
>   godlike form: around
> His neck high held an ever-
>   moving crowd
> Of locks hung glistening:
>   while such perfect sound
> Fell from his bowstring, that
>   th'ethereal dome
> Thrilled as a dewdrop; and
>   each passing cloud
> Expanded, whitening like
>   the ocean foam.
>
> From 'The Sun God' by
>   Aubrey de Vere

Aubrey's older brother, SIR STEPHEN EDWARD DE VERE (1812–1904), also born at Curragh Chase, was a conscientious landlord who fought constantly for better conditions for the Irish people. In 1847, during the Great Famine, he booked himself passage on a 'coffin ship' to America and wrote a report of the appalling conditions that the emigrants had to suffer. It was read out in the House of Lords and resulted in the improved 'Passenger Act' of 1849, which required that strict conditions be met on all future emigrant ships. He was MP for Limerick from 1854 to 1859.

Aubrey and Stephen's uncle, Mary Spring-Rice's brother, was THOMAS SPRING-RICE, who was Chancellor of the Exchequer under Lord Melbourne and became the 1st Baron Monteagle of Brandon. Like his kinsmen, the de Veres of Curragh Chase, Thomas Spring-Rice was a popular champion of the people of Limerick, and there is a statue of him atop a tall column in Limerick's public park.

Thomas's grandson was SIR CECIL SPRING-RICE, British Ambassador to the United States during the First World War and author of the famous hymn 'I Vow to Thee My Country', set to music by Gustav Holst. The words of this hymn show something of the romance and religious fervour of the poetry of his ancestor Aubrey de Vere. Despite his English upbringing Sir Cecil was hugely proud of his Irish roots, writing

I am an Irishman you see
That is what expresses me
I am changing as the weather
You must take me altogether
Hopeless of distinguishing
Which is Rice and which is Spring.

William Brooke O'Shaughnessy
─◄ 1809–89 ►─

WILLIAM BROOKE O'SHAUGH-NESSY was born in LIMERICK and

went to study medicine at Edinburgh University, then the foremost medical school in the world. While he was there, there was an outbreak of cholera, brought to Britain by soldiers returning from India, and O'Shaughnessy began to study the blood of cholera victims. He was the first person to realise that cholera caused dehydration and that what sufferers needed was rehydrating with a saline solution – a cure he recommended in a letter to the *Lancet*, but which only slowly gained acceptance even though it was actually the equivalent of finding a cure for AIDS today. It would be nearly 20 years before Dr John Snow in London proved that cholera was caused by drinking contaminated water.

In 1833 O'Shaughnessy went to live in India to run a medical school, and here he discovered the effectiveness of the Indian drug hemp, or cannabis, for alleviating rheumatism, cholera and tetanus. He was the first doctor to introduce cannabis to Western medicine, where it was used until well into the 1950s.

While in India O'Shaughnessy was able to indulge in his other passion, telegraphy, and in 1838 he experimented by running some insulated iron wires to carry electric signals under Calcutta's River Hooghly, resulting in THE FIRST SUCCESSFUL UNDERWATER TELEGRAPHY IN THE WORLD. In 1852 he was appointed managing director of the Indian Telegraph Company, and over the next few years he laid out the first telegraph system in Asia, nearly 5, 000 miles (8, 000 km) of telegraph line linking Calcutta, Madras and Bombay, greatly aiding the British Raj. He became good friends with Samuel Morse, whom he accompanied on HMS *Agamemnon* in 1857 for the abortive attempt to lay a transatlantic telegraph cable between Newfoundland and Valentia Island, Co. Kerry.

In 1860 William Brooke O'Shaughnessy, life-saving physician and pioneer of the intercontinental communications revolution, retired to London and disappeared from the history books. He is buried in Southsea in Hampshire, England.

County Tipperary

COOLMORE STUD ✦ GAELIC ATHLETIC ASSOCIATION
✦ BIG BROTHER ✦ TEMPLEMORE OF THE MIRACLES

*Cathedral of the Assumption in Thurles –
based on the cathedral in Pisa.*

◄ TIPPERARY FOLK ►

Sir Robert Peel ✦ Lena Rice ✦ Tony Ryan ✦ Clancy Brothers
✦ Frank Patterson

Ireland's largest inland county, COUNTY TIPPERARY, was divided in 1838 into two administrative areas, the North Riding and the South Riding – intriguing names since a 'riding' actually means a third. The lush, fertile centre of the county, irrigated by the River Suir, is known as the Golden Vale and is home to THE WORLD'S LARGEST STUD FOR THOROUGHBRED RACEHORSES, THE COOLMORE STUD, which began life as a small farm.

Coolmore Stud

The Vigors family established a training organisation at the Coolmore farm near Fethard in 1945, which was inherited in 1968 by Battle of Britain fighter pilot and bloodstock agent Tim Vigors, DFC. He later teamed up with leading trainer Vincent O'Brien and the Vernon Pools magnate Robert Sangster before selling out to his son-in-law John Magnier, who built Coolmore into an international stud, consisting of the original farm, Coolmore Ireland, Coolmore America in Kentucky and Coolmore Australia in the Hunter Valley of New South Wales.

Thurles

The Semple Stadium in THURLES is the second largest sports stadium in Ireland, which is fitting since Thurles was the birthplace of the GAELIC ATHLETIC ASSOCIATION. (The only stadium larger is Croke Park in Dublin, now the headquarters of the GAA and named in honour of Thomas Croke, Archbishop of Cashel and Emly, one of the first patrons of the GAA.)

Fethard

On 1 November 1884, Tipperary farmer MAURICE DAVIN (1842–1927), who had been one of the finest athletes of his day, setting numerous world records for running, jumping and hurdling, called together six friends for a meeting at the Hayes Hotel in Thurles to establish 'a Gaelic athletic association for the preservation and cultivation of national pastimes'. At the time, athletics in Ireland was organised by an English association, and Davin was worried that Irish sports were being ignored and ordinary Irish people dissuaded from participating. Hence the aims of the association set up that day were to promote the native Irish sports, to open up athletics to all Irishmen, and to establish county competitions for hurling and Gaelic football.

Davin, who was born in Carrick-on-Suir, was elected as the first president of the GAA, and for many years afterwards top games were played on the fields of his farm, culminating in the 1904 All-Ireland Hurling Championship between Kilkenny and Cork.

Amongst the other six people at that inaugural meeting were Michael Cusack (*see* Co. Clare) and a builder and stonemason named Joseph Bracken, a noted Fenian from nearby Templemore.

Holycross Abbey, Thurles

Templemore

TEMPLEMORE is a small market town that grew up around a castle and monastery of the Knights Templar. It is reputed to have THE BIGGEST TOWN SQUARE IN IRELAND, and housed in the former army barracks is the training college of the Irish Garda.

Brendan Bracken
1901–58

Joseph Bracken lived in a big house in the main street, where his son BRENDAN was born in 1901. Joseph died when Brendan was three years old and the family moved eventually to Dublin, where Brendan proved to be an impossible child, running wild and getting into endless trouble. He was finally shipped off to Australia, returning to Ireland in 1919 to discover that his mother had remarried and moved to the countryside.

These were troubled times in Ireland, and Brendan's new stepfather was deeply involved with the Irish nationalists, so Brendan took himself off to Liverpool, where he got a teaching job by pretending to be an orphaned Australian scholar. He later blagged his way into Sedbergh School in Lancashire, pretending to be 15 when he was really 19, stayed there for one term, winning a history prize and achieving entry to the 'old boy' network.

After a number of further teaching jobs, Bracken made it to London and got himself a job in the newspaper world, commissioning articles from the rich and powerful for a revamped magazine called *English Life*. He persuaded the company he was working for to acquire a number of financial newspapers, including the *Financial News* and the *Economist*. Later, in 1945, Bracken bought the *Financial Times* and is credited with turning the *FT* into the world's premier financial newspaper. The pink-clad headquarters of the *FT* from 1959 until 1989, near St Paul's Cathedral in London, was called Bracken House in his honour.

In the 1930s Bracken set himself up in a huge Georgian house with ten bedrooms and a ballroom in Lord North Street, near the Houses of Parliament. Here he held regular dinner parties at which his butler Costello was primed to announce loudly that Bracken was wanted on the phone by the Prime Minister or some other notable figure. He became a great friend and loyal supporter of Winston Churchill, being one of the few people who stood by Churchill during his 'wilderness years', and Bracken is credited with persuading Churchill that he should fight Lord Halifax to replace Neville Chamberlain as Prime Minister in 1940.

Brendan Bracken was tall and loud, with a huge mop of red hair, and he never corrected his earlier pretence of being Australian, nor refuted the rumour that he was Winston Churchill's illegitimate son, although not everyone took him at his word. 'Everything about you is phoney,' someone once told him. 'Even your hair, which looks like a wig, isn't.' He is generally accepted to be the model for the social-climbing colonial cad Rex Mottram in Evelyn Waugh's *Brideshead Revisited*. It was Bracken who invented the term 'champagne socialist', when he tore into the young Nye Bevan at a party given by Lord Beaverbrook, haranguing him as 'you Bollinger Bolshevik, there you sit swilling Max's champagne and calling yourself a socialist!' He was quite happy to be

called BB, and when he became the rather sinister-sounding Minister for Information during the War, that nickname inspired George Orwell with the idea for Big Brother.

Brendan Bracken from Co. Tipperary, Big Brother, father of the *Financial Times*, right hand of Winston Churchill, died of cancer in 1958. In accordance with his last wishes his ashes were scattered on Romney Marsh and his papers burned.

'Templemore of the Miracles'

In 1920, in the run-up to the Irish Civil War, and just about the time that Brendan Bracken was settling in Liverpool, his home town of Templemore, for a brief but extraordinary moment, became 'Templemore of the Miracles'. Shortly after the funeral of a police inspector who had been murdered in the town, a young farm labourer called James Welsh announced that he had received messages from, and seen apparitions of, the Virgin Mary, who was disturbed by the evil happenings in Ireland. She had instructed him to dig a hole in the earth floor of his tiny farm cottage at Curraheen, in the hills above the town, and when he did so a clear spring began to bubble up –

and his three statues of the Virgin Mary began to bleed.

Welsh filled up some containers with the spring water, gathered up the statues and took them to his employer's house in the main street in Templemore, where they were set out on a table beside the open window of the front room. People couldn't resist coming to have a look, and when a local man, who had long been known as a cripple, drank some of the spring water, threw away his crutches and started dancing in the street, word got out. The local paper reported the story, and pilgrims began to converge on Templemore from all over Ireland, despite the imposition of travel restrictions designed to hamper the movements of the IRA. There were stories of further cures, and more people arrived: mothers with sick babies, the deformed and disabled, stretcher cases, invalids in wheelchairs, the elderly, until the main street in Templemore resembled a mob scene – and then, as suddenly as it had started, the phenomenon ceased. The crowds melted away, the newspapers lost interest and it was as if James Welsh and his apparitions had never existed. A mystery indeed.

Well, I never knew this
about
TIPPERARY FOLK

'Orange Peel'

CASHEL may have suffered a violent history, but in more recent times it played a small part in the struggle for Irish freedoms and self-determination. For it was as MP for Cashel that SIR ROBERT PEEL (1788–1850), the man responsible for establishing the police forces of both Ireland and Britain, and for overseeing the emancipation of Catholics in Ireland, began his political career, when he was just 21. Cashel was a rotten borough with just 24 voters, and as Peel was sponsored both by his wealthy father and the Chief Secretary for Ireland Sir Arthur Wellesley, he was elected unopposed.

In 1812 Peel was appointed Chief Secretary for Ireland himself, and became involved in a long-running struggle with Daniel O'Connell over Catholic emancipation – Peel was not opposed to it, but thought that the laws should be relaxed little by little, while O'Connell demanded change immediately. In 1814 Peel suppressed the Catholic Board, bringing down derision from O'donnell, who labelled him 'Orange Peel'.

Such was the ferocity of O'Connell's language that Peel challenged him to a duel on neutral territory in Ostend and travelled there ready to fight, but O'Connell was mysteriously detained by police on his way to the encounter.

Peel retired from his post in Ireland in 1817 but, ironically, it was he who finally made it possible for his archenemy O'Connell to take up his seat at Westminster as Catholic MP for County Clare. In 1829, as Home Secretary, and in order to avoid bloodshed in Ireland, Peel brought in the Catholic Relief Act, which repealed the last of the Penal Laws.

Lena Rice
◄ 1866–1907 ►

LENA RICE, THE ONLY FEMALE IRISH TENNIS PLAYER TO WIN THE LADIES' SINGLES TITLE AT WIMBLEDON, was born in MARL-HILL, near the village of New Inn. She was one of seven children and she learnt tennis by playing against her siblings in their large back garden, before moving on to competing against the men at the Cahir Lawn Tennis Club. She was 24 when she won her Wimbledon title in 1890, beating May Jacks 6–4, 6–1.

In that year Irish players also won the Men's Singles, with Willoughby Hamilton, and Men's Doubles titles. During her final Lena Rice is credited with inventing the forehand smash, when she leapt into the air to return a ball that had bounced above head height. After her Wimbledon victory she never played another competitive match but returned to Ireland to look after her sick and impoverished mother. Lena Rice died of tuberculosis, aged just 41.

TONY RYAN (1936–2007), founder of Ryanair, one of Europe's most successful airlines, was born in THURLES.

Patrick, Tom, Bobby and Liam Clancy, who together made up the Irish folk music group THE CLANCY BROTHERS, were all born in CARRICK-ON-SUIR between 1922 and 1935. During the 1960s the boisterous and melodious Clancy Brothers, dressed in identical Aran sweaters sent from Ireland by their mother to protect them from the cold North American winters, rode the wave of folk music's popularity in the US and for a while became 'the most famous Irishmen in the world'.

musicals, film songs and modern 'pop' favourites. He was the first Irish artist to have his own show in New York's Radio City Music Hall, selling out for six consecutive years. In 1979 he sang in front of Pope John Paul II at a papal mass in Phoenix Park, Dublin, and in 1982 he was asked to the White House to sing for PRESIDENT RONALD REAGAN (whose own family hailed from Co. Tipperary).

Ireland's Golden Tenor, FRANK PATTERSON (1938–2000), was born in CLONMEL. In his career he recorded more than 40 albums in six languages, featuring Irish ballads, hits from

County Waterford

IRELAND'S FIRST PARISH ✦ A MODEL VILLAGE
✦ IRELAND'S FIRST GARAGE ✦ FILM TYCOON

*William Peare, owner of Ireland's first garage,
in one of his cars.*

◄ WATERFORD FOLK ►

Mrs Jordan ✦ Captain William Hobson ✦ Tyrone Power
✦ Val Doonican ✦ Gilbert O'Sullivan

Ardmore

———◆◆◆———

COUNTY WATERFORD can boast IRELAND'S FIRST PARISH, THE EARLIEST CHRISTIAN SETTLEMENT IN NORTHERN EUROPE, at ARDMORE, now a pretty fishing village with one of the country's finest beaches. St Declan settled here around 410 after returning from a trip to Rome, and founded a monastery on Aird Mhór, meaning 'the great height' – a small hill beside the present village. St Declan's monastery has gone, but the remains of the 12th-century St Declan's Cathedral survive, including some exquisite carved arcading on the exterior of the west wall that is unique in Ireland. Beside the wall is Ireland's best-preserved round tower, dating from the 11th century and thought to mark the site of St Declan's burial place. Inside the ruined church are a number of Ogham stones, one of

which bears THE LONGEST OGHAM INSCRIPTION IN THE COUNTRY.

The bestselling American author NORA ROBERTS, the first author to be inducted into the Romance Writers of America Hall of Fame, set three of her novels in Ardmore – her Irish ancestors came from the area.

Portlaw

———◆◆◆———

The now quiet village of PORTLAW, lying on the River Clodagh in beautiful countryside 10 miles (16 km) west of Waterford, was amongst the first and finest of the industrial model villages of Britain and Ireland. It was planned and built by the MALCOMSONS, a Quaker family who had come to Waterford from Scotland via Lurgan in Co. Armagh.

In 1825 David Malcomson, who had already made a fortune in corn but wanted to diversify, leased the land around Portlaw, demolished the small mills already there and began to build a huge cotton factory. When it was completed in 1826 the MAYFIELD MILL, named after Sir Algernon May who had lived at Portlaw in the days of Queen Elizabeth I, measured 240 ft (73 m) long by 40 ft

(12 m) wide, and was THE LARGEST SINGLE-SPAN STRUCTURE IN THE WORLD.

Mayfield Mill

A church, shops and homes were built to serve the factory workers, the houses all finished with a distinctive architectural feature, a gently curving, timber-framed roof structure that became known as a PORTLAW ROOF. The design of Portlaw was so imaginative and effective that several similar enterprises were modelled along the same lines, including Bessbrook village, in Co. Armagh, and Bourneville, created by the Cadbury Brothers outside Birmingham in England.

The mill and the village lay at the centre of a complex industrial web that included a canal linking the River Clodagh to the River Suir, so that materials could be brought in from Waterford by boat and the finished product transported back out to be loaded on to ships for export.

In 1844 David Malcomson's son Joseph founded the Neptune Ironworks at Waterford, originally as a repair yard for the company's vessels, but later for building their own ships. Between 1846 and 1882, over 60 ships were constructed at the Neptune shipyard, including several transatlantic liners. For some of this time the Malcomsons were THE LARGEST STEAMSHIP OWNERS IN THE WORLD. The first ship out of the yard in 1846 was the *Neptune*, built to operate between London and St Petersburg for Joseph's own St Petersburg Steam Company. On its arrival in the Neva River at St Petersburg the *Neptune* was greeted by Tsar Nicholas in his state barge.

Throughout the famine years, the Malcomsons were able to offer employment to some 1,600 workers at Portlaw, and their empire continued to grow as they invested further afield, even helping to finance the development of Germany's Ruhr valley by backing William Mulvany, who opened the first deep coal-mine in the area in 1856 (*see* Co. Leitrim).

Mayfield House

The Malcomson success story began to wobble with the outbreak of the American Civil War in 1861, which disrupted the cotton trade with the southern Confederate states and landed the Malcomsons with huge debts. High tariffs levied by the new American government added to their problems, and the Malcomsons finally went bankrupt in the 1880s. The cotton mill was taken over but closed in 1904.

Between 1932 and 1985 Portlaw was home to Ireland's last shoe tannery, and the pioneering model town is now being regenerated with the establishing of numerous small businesses and enterprises.

Birthplace of Irish Motoring

The city of Waterford became the birthplace of Irish motoring when THE COUNTRY'S FIRST MOTOR

GARAGE was opened there in 1900 by WILLIAM PEARE (1868–1948) and SIR WILLIAM GOFF (c.1859–1917).

William Peare originally set up shop as a bicycle dealer, but became interested in motor cars when he assembled a four-wheeled vehicle out of a motorised De Dion tricycle – in 1899 he was appointed De Dion's official service engineer in south-east Ireland. The following year he was asked to build THE FIRST IRISH MOTOR TRICYCLE, for a Captain Langrishe of Co. Kilkenny, and quickly realised that he was going to need a proper workshop and larger premises. He went into partnership with motoring enthusiast Sir William Goff, and together they took over an old coachbuilding works in Waterford's Catherine Street, which they demolished and replaced with a brand new, two-storey, state-of-the-art 'motor works' – the first in Ireland. Upstairs were offices and accommodation for a caretaker, while downstairs there was the workshop at the back and the car showroom in front.

In 1902 Peare began to sell Gladiator cars and over the next few years became the agent for Daimler, Olds-mobile, Napier, Buick and Cadillac, amongst others. Ireland's first garage finally closed in 1917 after Peare went off to fight in the army during the First World War.

Sir William Goff was one of Ireland's first motorists, proud owner of an early Daimler, and founding chairman of the Irish Automobile Club. His Napier was THE FIRST REGISTERED CAR IN WATERFORD, and bore the registration number W1-1. In 1903 he won the four-cylinder class in Ireland's first ever hill climb at Glendu in the Wicklow mountains.

smaller companies, to become Universal Pictures, with Pat Powers as its first treasurer.

Pat Powers
1870–1948

PATRICK ANTHONY POWERS, film producer, co-founder of Universal Pictures, and the man who gave Mickey Mouse a voice, was born in Waterford. As a teenager he emigrated with his sister to Buffalo, New York, and established a business selling phonographs, an early type of record player invented in 1877 by Thomas Edison. He then set up the Buffalo Film Exchange, buying films from producers and renting them to the neighbourhood nickelodeons. In 1910 he moved to New York City, and the Buffalo Film Exchange became the Powers Motion Picture Company. In 1912 Powers's film distribution company merged with Carl Laemmle's film production company, the Independent Moving Picture Company (IMP) and four other

In 1915 Universal Pictures moved west to California and opened the world's largest film production facility, Universal City Studios, just over the hills from Hollywood itself. Universal is now the second oldest surviving film production company in Hollywood, after Paramount.

Pat Powers stayed behind in New York and in 1927 tried to take over the DeForest Phonofilm Company. Lee DeForest had invented a kind of amplifier called an audion tube and a system for putting synchronised sound directly on to film which he called Phonofilm. DeForest was a better inventor than businessman, however, and went bankrupt, but he refused to sell out to Powers, who instead hired DeForest's chief technician William Garrity and paid him to recreate a cloned version of the Phonofilm system, which he called Powers Cinephone.

Powers then persuaded Walt Disney to use the Powers Cinephone system to put sound on to his cartoons, and in 1928 Disney's first sound cartoon, *Mickey Mouse's Steamboat Willie,* was released and distributed through Powers's company Celebrity Pictures. For two successful years Powers remained Disney's sales agent, but the two then fell out over money and Powers reacted by signing up Disney's best friend, Ub Iwerks, the animator who had designed Mickey Mouse, and setting him up in his own animation studio.

The Iwerks studio was not a success and closed in 1936, while Walt Disney hired new animators and went on to build an empire.

Pat Powers remained in the film business in New York for the rest of his life, but never quite matched the glory days of those early years as a pioneering mogul. He is buried in Rochester, New York.

Well, I never   *knew this*
about
WATERFORD FOLK

Waterford Royalty

The actress MRS JORDAN (1761–1816) was born Dorothy Bland in WATERFORD. She became one of the most celebrated actresses of her day and although she never married she assumed the name Mrs Jordan, since it was considered slightly less shocking for a married woman to be on the stage. The name Jordan was a reference to her leaving Ireland across the Irish Sea, likened by some to the sacred River Jordan. In 1788 she became the mistress to William IV, by whom she had ten children, all of whom took the name FitzClarence.

Their 3rd daughter Elizabeth, born in 1801, married William George Hay, 18th Earl of Erroll, and amongst their descendants are the Conservative

politician David Cameron, and author and politician Duff Cooper, father of historian John Julius Norwich and uncle of publisher Rupert Hart-Davis, himself father of the television presenter Adam Hart-Davis.

The first governor of New Zealand, CAPTAIN WILLIAM HOBSON, RN (1792–1842), was born in Waterford.

Tyrone Power
——◄ 1795–PRESENT ►——

Actor-manager WILLIAM GRATTAN TYRONE POWER (1795–1841), first of four actors to bear the name Tyrone Power, was born in KILMACTHOMAS, home of IRELAND'S OLDEST PRIVATELY OWNED FAMILY COMPANY, FLAHAVAN'S, which has been milling oats by the River Mahon since the early 18th century. Power ran away to join some strolling players when he was 14, took Drury Lane in London by storm as a comic turn, and then conquered Broadway. In 1841, having made his fortune and purchased some land in New York that would one day become Madison Square Garden, he sailed for London in the SS *President*. The ship, the first Tyrone Power and the deeds of the land were all lost at sea.

Power and his wife Anne had six children, and the name Tyrone Power descended through his youngest son

Harold, who married an actress called Ethel Lavenu. Their youngest son was born Frederick Power (1869–1931) but acted under the name Tyrone Power. He had a highly successful career as a stage actor and silent movie star. One of his last performances was in a talking film, *The Big Trail*, in which John Wayne had his first starring role.

Frederick Power is now referred to as Tyrone Power Senior. His only son, Tyrone Power (1914–58), became a major Hollywood star and matinee idol, appearing, usually as a swash-buckling hero figure, in dozens of films, such as *The Mark of Zorro, The Black Swan* and *Captain from Castile*. He died of a heart attack aged 44.

Tyrone Power

By his second marriage to Linda he had two daughters, Romina and Taryn, who both became actors, and by his third wife Deborah he had the fourth Tyrone Power, now known as

Junior, who was born after his father's death in 1959. Tyrone Power Junior is still enjoying a successful Hollywood career, 200 years after his great-great-grandfather took to the acting life in Ireland.

Crooner VAL DOONICAN was born Michael Valentine Doonican in WATERFORD in 1927, the youngest of eight children. All his family were musical, and Val began to perform at a young age largely to help support his mother after their father died. He appeared in the first-ever television broadcast from Waterford, although it is mainly for his Saturday night show on BBC television, which ran for 20 years, that he is best remembered – as well as his cardigan and rocking chair. His hit songs included 'Walk Tall' in 1964 and 'Elusive Butterfly' in 1966, and he sang the theme song for the film *Ring of Bright Water*.

Singer GILBERT O'SULLIVAN was born Raymond Edward O'Sullivan in WATERFORD in 1946. His 1972 No. 1 hit song 'Alone Again (Naturally)' has featured in numerous films and television programmes such as *The Virgin Suicides, Ally McBeal, Stuart Little 2,*

Love Actually and *Life on Mars.* During the 1970s he had ten top ten singles on both sides of the Atlantic, including 'Clair' and 'Get Down'.

ULSTER

Belfast

---•◆•---

Belfast Castle

◄ BELFAST FOLK ►

Dame Margaret Guilfoyle ✦ Mary McAleese ✦ Tim Collins
✦ William Drennan ✦ Sir John Lavery ✦ Paul Henry ✦ Benjamin Glazer
✦ Moyna Macgill ✦ C.S. Lewis ✦ Jackie Wright ✦ Sam Kydd
✦ James Ellis ✦ Ronnie Carroll ✦ Ruby Murray ✦ Sir James Galway
✦ Van Morrison ✦ Eric Bell ✦ Kenneth Branagh ✦ Vivian Campbell
✦ Kiera Chaplin

BELFAST is Ireland's second largest city after Dublin and the only city in Ireland to owe its growth almost entirely to the Industrial Revolution.

Belfast's life as a town began with the Ulster Plantations of Protestants during the reign of James I in the early 17th century. In 1611 Sir Arthur Chichester built himself a castle on the site of a previous 12th-century motte and bailey, and a small community flourished beneath its walls.

The first industrial expansion came with the arrival of the hard-working Huguenots in the 18th century, who boosted the small linen industry that already existed. Soon there were water-mills and factories making steam engines and machines to service the linen mills, and when the mudflats were drained and docks constructed, shipbuilding kick-started the city's heavy engineering output.

By 1914 Belfast was the largest city in Ireland (a title since retaken by Dublin) and boasted THE WORLD'S LARGEST SHIPYARD, LINEN MILL, TOBACCO FACTORY AND ROPE-WORKS.

Princess Takabuti

PRINCESS TAKABUTI, THE FIRST MUMMY EVER TO BE UNRAVELLED OUTSIDE EGYPT was revealed to a wide-eyed Belfast crowd in 1835, and now occupies pride of place at the centre of the Egyptian collection in the Ulster Museum. Her bleached hair has led to her being named 'Belfast's oldest bleached blonde'.

The Palm House

The Palm House in Belfast's Botanic Gardens was completed in 1840 and is one of the earliest curvilinear glass and iron structures ever built. It was designed by Belfast's pre-eminent architect, Charles Lanyon, and constructed by Richard Turner, who went on to build the glasshouse in Kew Gardens four years later.

Chambers Cars

Between 1904 and 1924 the Chambers Brothers manufactured up to 500 cars per year in Belfast – they were Northern Ireland's only car manufacturer save for the short-lived DeLorean cars of the 1980s. One of the brothers, Jack Chambers, designed the first Vauxhall car in 1903.

William Mulholland
1855–1935

Belfast's flair for industrial innovation and enterprise has contributed some hugely influential characters to the world, including the man who transformed Los Angeles and gave his name to one of the most famous roads in Hollywood, WILLIAM MULHOLLAND, who was born in Belfast in 1855. He ran away to sea when he was in his teens and after sailing into New York harbour in 1874, decided that America was where he wanted to stay. Over the next few years he worked as a lumberjack, travelling mechanic, store assistant and gold miner in Arizona, before moving to the city where he would find immortality, Los Angeles. He began work with the Los Angeles Department of Water and Power digging ditches, but taught

himself engineering and eventually rose to become the head of the agency.

It was a time of rapid expansion for Los Angeles, with more and more people coming to settle in the west, and the city simply did not have enough water to service its growing population. In 1908 Mulholland proposed, designed and began work on THE LONGEST AQUEDUCT IN THE WORLD, for bringing water 233 miles (375 km) to Los Angeles from the Owens Valley, a deep rift valley fed by the Owens River in the Sierra Nevada mountains in south-east California.

One of the biggest engineering projects ever undertaken in America up to that time, the aqueduct took five years and 5, 000 men to build and, when completed in 1913, it enabled the semi-arid Los Angeles to become the second largest city in the United States.

In March 1928, Mulholland made an inspection of the St Francis Dam, which he had built as part of the Los

Angeles aqueduct system near the city of Santa Clarita, 40 miles north of Los Angeles, and declared it sound. Twelve hours later, at three minutes before midnight, the dam burst and flooded the San Francisquito valley and the town of Santa Paula, killing over 450 people in the largest loss of life in California's history, after the San Francisco earthquake of 1906. Although Mulholland was not personally blamed, the disaster ended his career and he retired to his home in Los Angeles where he died in 1935.

William Mulholland is commemorated by the famous Mulholland Drive, which runs along the spine of the Hollywood Hills above the Hollywood sign and has featured in numerous films and songs. Those who have lived on Mulholland Drive include Jack Nicholson, Bruce Willis, Tom Hanks, Warren Beatty, Errol Flynn, Marlon Brando and Madonna. The plot of the 1974 film *Chinatown*, directed by Roman Polanski and starring Jack Nicholson and Faye Dunaway, revolved around a character based on William Mulholland.

James Graham Fair
1831–94

James Graham Fair was a prospector who became a multimillionaire

overnight after he discovered THE LARGEST SINGLE DEPOSIT OF GOLD AND SILVER EVER FOUND, the fabled COMSTOCK LODE in Nevada. It was also the first major silver strike in America and gave Nevada its nickname of the 'Silver State'.

Belfast Celtic

Belfast can also boast a fine sporting heritage. Between 1891 and 1948 the city was home to Ireland's most successful professional football team, Belfast Celtic. They played at Celtic Park, now buried beneath a shopping complex at the foot of Donegal Road, and took their name from Glasgow Celtic, the Scottish football club founded three years previously by an Irish Marian brother from Co. Sligo. The aim of Belfast Celtic was to 'imitate our Scottish counterparts in style, play and charity'. They won their first league title in 1900 and went on to win a further 13 league titles and eight Irish cups.

Belfast Celtic drew their support largely from the Irish Nationalist population of West Belfast. During the Irish Civil War of the early 1920s they had to withdraw from playing, but returned even stronger in the inter-war years, winning four consecutive titles from 1926 to 1929.

In 1948, after a pitch invasion during an away game at arch-rivals Linfield, resulting in a number of serious injuries to Celtic players, the club withdrew once again from professional football, concerned that protection for their players could not be guaranteed. They never played another professional match.

Alexander McDonnell
1789–1835

Chess master and unofficial world champion ALEXANDER MCDONNELL

was born in Belfast in 1798, the son of a surgeon. In 1834 he took part in what is regarded as the first chess world championship, against the world's leading player, Frenchman Louis-Charles Mahe de La Bourdonnais.

McDonnell worked for some time as a merchant in the West Indies and made enough money to be able to indulge in his passion for chess. For a while he was a student of the leading player in London, William Lewis, but quickly became so good that Lewis, and others, refused to play him, and the only man to answer his challenge was the Frenchman. La Bourdonnais didn't speak any English, and McDonnell spoke no French, so the only word they exchanged during the series of six matches and 85 games, played at the Westminster Chess Club in London between June and October 1834, was 'Check!' Both players introduced new moves that are still used today, and many observers trace the birth of modern chess back to this contest.

La Bourdonnais won the first match, McDonnell the second, making him, for a brief period, unofficial world champion. The Frenchman then went on to win the next three matches, but the final match, which the Irishman was winning, was abandoned when La Bourdonnais had to return to France to deal with his creditors. The two champions agreed to resume the match at a later date, but McDonnell died the following year of Bright's disease. La Bourdonnais, who had lost his fortune in a series of bad land deals, was forced to earn his living at chess, but there were not enough players who could challenge him and he died penniless in 1840. He was buried in Kensal Green cemetery in London – just yards away from his only peer, Alexander McDonnell.

Some Distinguished Sportsmen Born in Belfast

RINTY MONAGHAN (1920–84), undisputed world flyweight boxing champion from 1947 until 1949. He endeared himself to his supporters by singing 'When Irish Eyes are Smiling' after his fights.

DANNY BLANCHFLOWER (1926–93), captain of the Tottenham Hotspur football team that in the 1960–61 season won their first 11 games, a record, and in the same season were the first English league team to win the league and cup double. In 1961 Blanchflower became the first person to refuse an invitation to appear on *This Is Your Life*, turning down Eamonn Andrews live on air.

DEREK DOUGAN (1938–2007), Wolverhampton Wanderers footballer who scored more goals in the English league than any other Irishman.

GEORGE BEST (1946–2005), the world's first celebrity footballer, and Ireland's greatest ever. 'Maradona good; Pelé better; George Best' is how the people of Belfast remember him.

Formula One motor racing drivers JOHN WATSON, born 1946, and MARTIN DONNELLY, born 1964. Watson won five Grands Prix, one for Penske and four for McLaren. Donnelly's career was ended by a horrendous crash while driving for Arrows at Jerez in Spain in 1990.

ALEX 'HURRICANE' HIGGINS, snooker player, who won the world championship in 1972 and 1982, born 1949.

RICHARD DUNWOODY, the most successful jump jockey in history, born in 1964. Three times champion jockey, he rode a record 1,699 winners and won two Grand Nationals, in 1986 and 1994. Dunwoody is best remembered for his partnership with the legendary Desert Orchid, who bore him to victory in the King George VI Chase in 1989 and 1990. In 2001 he was voted Champion of Champions. In January 2008, Dunwoody and American Doug

Stoop became the first people to conquer the South Pole along a route previously attempted only once before, unsuccessfully, by Ernest Shackleton in 1914.

Footballer NORMAN WHITESIDE, born in 1965, the youngest player ever to appear in a World Cup finals tournament, at 17 years and 42 days, for Northern Ireland against Yugoslavia in the 1982 World Cup finals in Spain.

Well, I never knew this about
BELFAST FOLK

Belfast is the birthplace of some remarkable characters including . . .

DAME MARGARET GUILFOYLE, the first woman cabinet member in Australian politics, born in Belfast in 1926.

MARY MCALEESE the eighth president of Ireland, born in Ardoyne, North Belfast, in 1951. She is the second female president of Ireland and the first woman in the world to succeed another woman as an elected head of state.

TIM COLLINS, the army colonel who during the Iraq War in 2003 galvanised his troops with an inspirational eve-of-battle speech, the text of which now hangs in the Oval Office

of the White House, was born in Belfast in 1960. His speech has been compared to that of King Henry before Agincourt in Shakespeare's *Henry V.*

A pantheon of musicians, writers and artists were also born in Belfast, including . . .

Poet DR WILLIAM DRENNAN (1754–1820), who coined the phrase 'The Emerald Isle'.

Portrait painter SIR JOHN LAVERY (1856–1941), whose portrait of his wife appeared on Irish banknotes until the 1970s.

Post-impressionist landscape artist PAUL HENRY (1876–1958), whose paintings contributed greatly to the modern romantic image of the west of Ireland.

Film director BENJAMIN GLAZER (1887–1956), one of the 36 founders, in 1927, of the Academy of Motion Picture Arts and Sciences, the body which awards the Oscars. Trained as a lawyer, he became a director and writer and won two writing Oscars himself, for Best Adaptation with *Seventh Heaven* in 1929, and for Best Original Story with *Arise My Love* in 1940.

MOYNA MACGILL (1895–1975), actress and mother of one-time highest paid actress in Hollywood, Angela Lansbury.

C.S. LEWIS (1898–1963), author of the *Chronicles of Narnia.*

Comedian JACKIE WRIGHT (1905–89), who performed for 30 years as Benny Hill's bald-headed sidekick on television in the 1960s, 70s and 80s.

Actor SAM KYDD (1915–82), best remembered for his roles as a perky working-class character in war films such as *The Cruel Sea*, *Sink the Bismarck* and *Reach for the Sky*. He spent most of the Second World War as a prisoner of war in Poland.

Actor JAMES ELLIS, who played Bert Lynch, the only character to appear in every episode of the BBC series *Z Cars* during its 16-year run from 1962 until 1978, born 1931.

RONNIE CARROLL, the only singer to have represented the UK in the Eurovision Song Contest for two years in a row, born 1934. In 1962 he reached fourth place with 'Ring-A-Ding Girl', and in 1963 he again achieved fourth place with 'Say Wonderful Things'. His first wife was actress Millicent Martin, who recently played the role of Daphne Moon's mother in the American situation comedy *Frasier.*

Singer RUBY MURRAY (1935–96), whose achievement of having five songs in the top 20 in the same week, in 1955, has never been equalled. Her name lives on as cockney rhyming slang for curry, which is known as a 'Ruby'.

The 'Man with the Golden Flute', SIR JAMES GALWAY OBE, the first flute player to establish an international solo career, born 1939.

VAN MORRISON, Grammy award-winning singer, songwriter and musician, voted No. 42 in *Rolling Stone* magazine's 100 Greatest Artists of All Time, born 1945.

ERIC BELL, original lead guitarist for rock band Thin Lizzy, born 1947.

KENNETH BRANAGH, actor and youngest ever recipient of the 'Golden Quill' Gielgud award as 'greatest Shakespearian of our day', born 1960.

VIVIAN CAMPBELL, lead guitarist with Def Leppard, born 1962.

Actress and model KIERA CHAPLIN, granddaughter of comic actor Charlie Chaplin and great-granddaughter of playwright Eugene O'Neill, born 1982. O'Neill's only daughter Oona, married Charlie Chaplin when Charlie was 54 and she was 18.

County Antrim

Market Town ✦ Secretary of War ✦ Indian Trader
✦ Police Commissioner ✦ The Hostess of Fairbanks
✦ Last of the League of Nations

Dunluce Castle

◄ ANTRIM FOLK ►

John Ballance ✦ Coslett Herbert Waddell ✦ Fred Daly
✦ Valerie Hobson ✦ James Young ✦ Jackie Woodburne

COUNTY ANTRIM has one of the most beautiful coastlines in the world, and its glories can be experienced from a remarkable coast road built between 1832 and 1842 by Scottish engineer William Bald. The road winds for over 20 miles (32 km) along the water's edge from Larne to Cushenden, and then another 13 miles (21 km) through the mountains to Ballycastle, where C.S. Lewis holidayed while writing *The Chronicles of Narnia.*

On the way it takes the traveller past IRELAND'S ONLY SALT MINE at Kilroot, a hotel once owned by Sir Winston Churchill, the Londonderry Arms at Carnlough, and THE BIGGEST EXPANSE OF CLIMBABLE ROCK IN IRELAND AND BRITAIN, Fair Head.

Fair Head

FAIR HEAD rises 643 ft (196 m) out of the sea and is considered to be the finest climbing crag in Ireland. The views from the top are sensational, across the water to Rathlin Island and beyond to the islands of Islay and Jura and to the Mull of Kintyre in Scotland, 13 miles (21 km) away. On the plateau are some freshwater lakes, the largest of which, Lough na Crannagh, has an exceptional example of a crannog, or man-made defensive island, in the middle.

Ballymena

Lying not far to the west of Slemish Mountain, where St Patrick was brought by pirates to tend swine as a young slave, Ballymena sits at the heart of rich farming country and at one time hosted the biggest agricultural show in Ireland. Today, while retaining a flourishing traditional Saturday market, Ballymena is also home to a thriving manufacturing industry and to THE UK's LARGEST INDEPENDENT

COACH-BUILDER, WRIGHTBUS, pioneers of the low-floor bus, whose vehicles can be seen in cities all over the world.

James McHenry
1753–1816

The third and most influential US Secretary of War, JAMES MCHENRY was born in Ballymena and educated in Dublin. In 1771 he emigrated to Philadelphia, where he studied medicine, and then became a military surgeon for the Americans during the War of Independence. After being captured by the British at Fort Washington he was paroled and appointed as George Washington's secretary, before joining Lafayette's staff at the Battle of Yorktown. After the war he entered the Maryland Senate and served on the Continental Congress, America's first national government. In 1787 McHenry was one of four Irish-born delegates at the Constitutional Convention in Philadelphia, which resulted in the signing of the American Constitution. Representing Maryland, he was one of the signatories.

In 1796 President Washington appointed McHenry as Secretary of War, a position he held under both Washington and John Adams. During his time in office McHenry oversaw the establishment of a professional army, and also laid down the system followed today whereby the professional soldiers organise and run the military while ultimate control remains in the hands of a democratically appointed civilian Secretary of War.

McHenry retired in 1800 and spent his final years on his Maryland estate Fayetteville. After the War of Independence the Americans constructed a brick-built, star-shaped fort to defend the entrance to Baltimore harbour, which they named after McHenry who, as Secretary of War, had supported its construction. In the 1812 war, McHenry's son took part in the defence of the fort when it was being bombarded by the British in 1814. It was during this siege that Francis Scott Key was inspired to write the words for what became the American national anthem, 'The Star Spangled Banner'.

Miss Northern Ireland 2005, LUCY EVANGELISTA, was born in Bally-mena in 1986. In 2005 she also became the first Miss Northern Ireland to be placed in the top ten at a Miss World competition.

and French colonists. He also took several Indian wives, by whom he had a number of children – one of his descendants is said to be William Penn Adair Rogers, better known as Will Rogers, the much-loved Hollywood star of the 1920s and 30s.

Adair lived with the Indians, more or less cut off from the outside world, for nearly 40 years, and used his experiences to write *A History of the American Indians*, which was published in London on the recommendation of Benjamin Franklin. It is perhaps the most insightful and authentic picture of 18th-century Native American life and culture, during a time of transition and invasion, that exists.

James Adair
1709–83

◆•◆•◆

American-Indian trader JAMES ADAIR was born in Antrim and left Ireland to make his fortune in the New World in 1735. He arrived in Charleston in South Carolina and started trading with the local Indian tribes, the Catawbas and the Cherokees. Having earned their respect and trust, he later went to live among the Chickasaws in Mississippi and spent many years trading amongst the different tribes, while endeavouring to keep the peace between the Indians and the British

Will Rogers

Possibly less authoritative is Adair's argument that the Indians were descended from one of the Lost Tribes of Israel, although this theory was accepted by Elias Boudinot, president of the Continental Congress, in his book *A Star in the West.* It has also been suggested that Adair's book might be one of the sources of the *Book of Mormon,* a sacred text of the Mormon Church.

Sir Charles Rowan
1782–1852

The joint first commissioner of the world's first professional police force, the Metropolitan Police, Lieutenant-Colonel SIR CHARLES ROWAN was born near Carrickfergus. He joined the army at the age of 16 and fought in many of the conflicts of the Napoleonic Wars, including the Battles of Corunna and Waterloo.

It was the memory of Rowan's courage and leadership at Waterloo that led the Duke of Wellington later to recommend him to the Home Secretary, when Sir Robert Peel was looking for a commander for his new Metropolitan Police Force in 1829. Rowan was made the senior commissioner in charge of organisation and discipline, while barrister Richard Mayne was made junior commissioner in charge of legal matters. Between them the two men spent the next 20 years developing the new police force, recruiting, training and organising over 1,000 men, drawing up regulations and pay, designing uniforms and equipment and setting up police stations across London.

Modern police forces all over the world owe their existence and organisation to Irishman Charles Rowan, to the extent that many historians think that 'Bobbies' should really be 'Charlies'.

Eva McGown
1883–1972

The 'Hostess of Fairbanks', EVA MCGOWN was born Eva Montgomery in the town of Antrim. In 1914 she travelled to Fairbanks, Alaska, to marry the owner of the Model Café, Arthur McGown, but not long after their marriage Eva's husband became ill and finally died in 1930 of a bone tumour.

Eva had fallen in love with Alaska and decided to stay, even though she

was penniless. She moved into Room 207 of the Nordale Hotel in Fairbanks and lived there for the rest of her life, supporting herself by doing odd jobs. At the outbreak of the Second World War, thousands of soldiers and construction workers arrived in Fairbanks, taking over the hotels and university campus for accommodation. When their wives arrived to be with their menfolk there was nowhere left for them to stay and Eva, having experienced the acute loneliness of losing her husband, set herself up to look after the new arrivals and settle them in. Dressed up to the nines she would welcome a newcomer to her office in the hotel lobby with a cheery 'Come in, Dearie!', give her a cup of tea and then provide her with an address where she could go and stay – and as the newcomer left the hotel she would ring up the owner of the address and say, 'I've sent over the sweetest lass to stay with you,' and then put the phone down.

The Fairbanks authorities put Eva on the payroll as official greeter, and her reputation spread far and wide. She arranged church marriages, found places for people to stay with their pets, commandeered church halls, school rooms and even prison cells as dormitories – no one was ever turned away. Her story featured in *Reader's Digest*, she appeared on television in *This Is Your Life*, and in 1953 was proclaimed by the Governor as Alaska's Honorary Hostess. When she became the first woman to win the Fairbanks Chamber of Commerce distinguished service award she accepted it with the words '. . . now the only thing left is Heaven.'

On the night of 22 February 1972 Eva McGown died when the Nordale Hotel caught fire and she was trapped in her room. She was 88. Found under her bed was a small box. When it was opened up it was found to contain a small clump of dried moss – a little bit of Ireland that Eva McGown had brought to Alaska with her nearly 60 years earlier and kept close by.

Sean Lester
1888–1959

The last secretary-general of the League of Nations, SEAN LESTER, was born in Carrickfergus. Growing up in a strongly Unionist town, but attracted to the principles of the Gaelic League, Lester was an unusual combination of Ulster Protestant and Irish Nationalist, a dichotomy that would serve him well when negotiating his way through the diplomatic world in later life.

Having worked as a journalist, after the War of Independence he was asked to become Director of Publicity for the newly formed government of the Irish Free State, and in 1929 he was sent to Geneva as Ireland's representative at the League of Nations, forerunner of the United Nations. He

so impressed the League that in 1933 he was seconded to the organisation's secretariat and sent to Gdansk as High Commissioner, a position that put him right at the heart of events leading up to the Second World War – and he put himself at considerable risk by objecting loudly to Adolf Hitler's persecution of the Jews. In 1940, with the League of Nations rendered ineffective, he was made Secretary-General with responsibility for eventually overseeing the transfer of the League's functions to the United Nations.

Well, I never knew this
about
ANTRIM FOLK

John Ballance
◂——— 1839–93 ———▸

JOHN BALLANCE, founder of New Zealand's first organised political party, the Liberal Party, and New Zealand's first Liberal Prime Minister, was born in Glenavy, the son of a farmer. He was 27 when he emigrated to New Zealand and started up a newspaper, the *Wanganui Gazette*, in Wanganui on the south-west coast of the North Island. In 1875 he entered the New Zealand parliament and in

1890 gathered together a coalition of liberal-minded politicians and forged them into the Liberal Party, which then won that year's general election. Ballance died in office at the height of his powers in 1893, but the government he formed stayed in office until 1911 and went on to establish women's suffrage, an old age pension and the Department of Health.

In foreign policy they introduced the New Zealand national flag, formally ended the country's status as a colony by declaring the Dominion

FRED DALY (1911–90), THE FIRST IRISH GOLFER TO WIN THE OPEN CHAMPIONSHIP, was born in Portrush. He won at the Royal Liverpool Golf Club, Hoylake, in 1947, and it would be 60 years before another Irish golfer took the title, Padraig Harrington winning in 2007.

Valerie Hobson
—◄ 1917–98 ►—

of New Zealand, and committed the country's troops to their first overseas conflict, the Boer War.

Church of Ireland clergyman and leading botanist COSLETT HERBERT WADDELL (1858–1919) was born in Drumcro. His mother Maria was the niece of Edward Langtry, husband of 'The Jersey Lily', actress Lillie Langtry, mistress of the Prince of Wales, later Edward VII. While Vicar of Saintfield and Rector of Greyabbey, Waddell was able to indulge his great interest in botany, writing numerous books and papers for naturalist journals. His speciality was bryophytes, moss-like plants that reproduce via spores, and he was a founder of the British Bryological Society. His unrivalled collection of specimens was donated by his widow to Queen's University of Belfast and is now in the Ulster Museum Herbarium.

VALERIE HOBSON, the actress who would find herself at the heart of the greatest political scandal of 20th-century Britain, was born in Larne, the daughter of an impoverished naval officer. She grew up haunted by poverty and put herself on to the stage at 16, where her extraordinary beauty attracted the attention of Hollywood's Universal Studios. Her first starring film role was as Baroness Frankenstein opposite Boris Karloff in the 1935 film *Bride of Frankenstein*. In 1939 she married film producer Sir Anthony Havelock-Allan, who produced David Lean's *Great Expectations* in 1946, in which Valerie played the grown-up Estella. She is also remembered for her performance as Edith D'Ascoyne in the classic film *Kind Hearts and Coronets*, with Alec Guinness. She had two children with Havelock-Allan, the eldest being born in 1944 with Down's syndrome.

In 1951 she had a second son, who would become a judge, but in 1952 she divorced her husband over his affair with actress Kay Kendal, and a year later married the vastly wealthy, aristocratic junior minister John Profumo. In 1963, when he was forced to resign from Harold Macmillan's government after lying to the House of Commons about having an affair with call-girl Christine Keeler, who was also sleeping with the Soviet military attaché, Valerie earned huge praise and admiration for standing by her husband, and together they devoted the rest of their lives to charity work. Valerie Hobson died of a heart attack at the age of 81.

James Young
◄ 1918–74 ►

Comedian JAMES YOUNG was born in Ballymoney, and his family moved into Belfast when he was five months old. As a youngster he trod the streets of the city collecting rent for an agency, meeting the wonderful assortment of characters that he would later portray in his act. 'Cherryvalley Lady', 'Orange Lil', 'Derek the Window Cleaner' and 'Mrs O'Condriac' were among the comic characters who reflected the essence of Belfast and were recognisable to people from both sides of the religious divide. James sold over a quarter of a million records and appeared many times on television, but he was at his best live on stage. His sketch show became one of the longest-running shows of all time, performed mostly at the Group Theatre in the Ulster Hall (where Led Zeppelin first performed 'Stairway to Heaven', on 5 March 1971). James Young never stopped performing and was 56 when he died, it is said, of working too hard.

Actress JACKIE WOODBURNE, best known for playing teacher Susan Kinski in the Australian daytime soap opera *Neighbours,* was born in Carrickfergus in 1956.

County Armagh

✦◄◆◆◆►✦

Killevy Churches ✦ Tandragee Tayto
✦ Irish Robin Hood ✦ The Sintons
✦ The Man Who Gave Us the Penalty Kick

Armagh Observatory

◄ ARMAGH FOLK ►

Joe Coburn ✦ Sir John Greer Dill ✦ Patrick Magee ✦ Ian Paisley
✦ Tommy Makem ✦ Gloria Hunniford

COUNTY ARMAGH may be Ulster's smallest county, but its capital town is the centre of Christianity in Ireland, home to both the Roman Catholic and Protestant Primates and the only city in the world to boast two cathedrals of the same name – St Patrick's. Armagh Friary, founded by Archbishop Patrick O'Scanail in 1263 is now in ruins but, at 163 ft (50 m) in length, is THE LONGEST FRIARY CHURCH IN IRELAND. Meanwhile Dan Winter's house at Loughgall is IRELAND'S LONGEST THATCHED COTTAGE.

Armagh is also the orchard of Ireland, rich in fruit-growing country and bright with blossom in springtime.

site of one of Ireland's earliest nunneries, founded in the 5th century by St Blinne. The substantial ruins appear to be of one long stone church but are, in fact, two conjoined churches sharing a common gable. The west church is one of Ireland's most important pre-Norman churches and has a massive lintel over the west doorway, while the east church is 13th century and has a simple pointed east window.

Killevy Churches

The unique KILLEVY CHURCHES lie at the foot of Slieve Gullion, Co. Armagh's highest mountain, on the

Tandragee

TANDRAGEE is a small town on the River Cusher, with some fine Georgian buildings, and a main street that winds up a steep hill to a grand baronial castle built by the Duke of Manchester in 1837. The castle was originally a stronghold of the O'Hanlons, one of the most powerful of the Gaelic clans of Ulster before the 17th century. They were also Lords of Orier,

Tandragee Castle

an area which covered much of the east of present-day Co. Armagh and some of Co. Louth. After the Plantation of Ulster in 1609, O'Hanlon Castle, as Tandragee was then known, was handed over to the Lord Lieutenant of Ireland, Oliver St John, but in the Ulster Rebellion of 1641 it was burnt down when the O'Hanlons attempted to regain their property. The castle was then abandoned and remained empty until it passed by marriage to the Montague family and was eventually restored as the Irish seat of the Duke of Manchester.

TANDRAGEE CASTLE is now the home of the Tayto potato crisp company, founded by businessman Thomas Hutchinson, who bought the castle in 1955 and started manufacturing Ulster's bestselling crisps there in the following year. Tours of the crisp factory and castle can be booked in advance.

Redmond O'Hanlon
c.1620–81

The 'Irish Robin Hood', REDMOND O'HANLON, was born at POYNTZ-PASS, a small village near Portadown sometime in the 1620s. His father was Loughlin O'Hanlon, the rightful heir to O'Hanlon Castle. Although robbed of his castle, Loughlin O'Hanlon was allowed to keep much of his land and was still a considerable figure in Armagh, and so his son Redmond was sent to England for a proper education, and then employed as a footman by Sir George Acheson of nearby Markethill.

Redmond was not satisfied with this lowly position. He wanted his inheritance back, and in 1641 he joined the Irish Rebellion, determined to regain O'Hanlon Castle. The enterprise was a failure and the castle was lost to the flames. Even worse, when

Cromwell invaded Ireland in 1649 all the O'Hanlon lands were confiscated as well, and Redmond was forced to flee to France, where he fought bravely for the French army and was made a Count of the French Empire.

He returned to Ireland in 1660 at the Restoration of Charles II, but his hopes of reclaiming his lands were dashed and he took to the hills around Slieve Gullion, and became an outlaw. Others in a similar situation joined him and the legend was born. Just as Robin Hood, the dispossessed Earl of Huntingdon, robbed his Norman persecutors and gave back to the honest Saxon poor, so Redmond O'Hanlon harried the English and Scottish settlers and became a hero to the native Irish. Priests, both Anglican and Catholic, villagers, and even the local militia aided O'Hanlon's cause, providing him with information and tipping him off to the best places to rob. He demanded protection money from the local landlords, and such was his power and reputation that no one under his protection was ever robbed or harmed. Redmond became the uncrowned King of Armagh, with a far greater income than the King's revenue men could recover, and eventually the Lord Deputy of Ireland, James Butler, the Duke of Ormonde, put a price his head.

Redmond was duly murdered in his bed by one of his own gang, his foster brother, McCall O'Hanlon, who collected 200 pounds and a full pardon for his treachery. Redmond's head was raised on a spike over the gaol in Downpatrick, and his remains were taken to Letterkenny for burial in the Church of Ireland cemetery.

Poyntzpass Gaelic football team are nicknamed the Redmond O'Hanlons in his memory.

MARKETHILL is home each summer to the biggest Lambeg drumming competition in the world. A Lambeg is a large drum, beaten with malacca canes, of a type that was brought over to Ireland by the Duke of Schomberg, commander of William of Orange's army at the Battle of the Boyne. Used today in Orange Order parades, the drum is thought to be THE LOUDEST ACOUSTIC INSTRUMENT IN THE WORLD.

Laurelvale and the Sintons

Taking its name from the proliferation of laurel bushes in the area, LAURELVALE is a small model village, northeast of Armagh, that was built in 1850 to serve Thomas Sinton's new linen

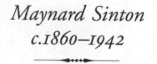

mill. THOMAS SINTON (1826–87) was born in Tandragee from a Quaker family that had lived in Co. Armagh for several hundred years. He was keen to provide employment for local people during the famine years, and linen was a key industry in Ulster, particularly around Belfast, as it had been since the 16th century, when it was encouraged in an effort to dissuade the Irish from competing with the English wool and cotton trades. By the 1880s over 1,000 people worked at the mill, and Sinton had opened further mills in Tandragee, Portadown and Killyleagh in Co. Down.

In 1859 Thomas Sinton married Elizabeth Buckby, daughter of another Tandragee family, and they went on to have eight children. For himself and his family Sinton built a large house, also called Laurelvale, and it was here that he died in 1887.

Laurelvale House remained in the Sinton family until after the Second World War. It then became home to the Lord Lieutenant of County Armagh, Michael Torrence-Spence, who had flown a Swordfish for the Fleet Air Arm during the war and achieved the unique distinction of having held commissions in the Royal Navy, the Royal Air Force, the British Army and the Royal Ulster Constabulary.

Both Laurelvale House and the mill complex have since been demolished to allow the land to be developed for housing.

Maynard Sinton
c.1860–1942

After Thomas Sinton died, Laurelvale and the family firm were taken over by his oldest son MAYNARD SINTON,

David Sinton
1808–1900

who became High Sheriff of County Armagh in 1892. In 1908 Maynard bought BALLYARDS HOUSE, not far from Armagh, near the linen village of Milford (*see* below), and doubled the size of the house, renaming it Ballyards Castle. Maynard Sinton was the first person in Co. Armagh to own a motor car, a Clement-Talbot with the registration number IB 1.

Ballyards Castle is now a retreat for those with alcohol and drugs problems.

The 27th President of the United States, William Howard Taft, owed his presidency to DAVID SINTON, born in Co. Armagh in 1808. A cousin of Thomas Sinton, David was taken by his parents John Sinton and Mary McDonnell, to settle in Pittsburgh, Pennsylvania, when he was three. At 16, David took himself off to Cincinnati, Ohio, and made a fortune in the iron trade, starting as a furnace stoker and eventually buying the furnace company and profiting greatly from demand for

William Howard Taft

iron during the American Civil War.

He lived in what has been described as America's finest Palladian-style house, built in 1820 by Cincinnati's first millionaire and mayor, industrialist Martin Baum. Sinton's daughter Anna married Charles Taft, brother of the future President William Taft, whose presidential campaign was financed, through Anna, by David Sinton's fortune, estimated at $200 million at today's values. William Taft accepted the presidential nomination

in the house in 1908. It is now the Taft Museum of Art.

David Sinton was commemorated in Cincinnati by the Hotel Sinton, demolished in 1964, and is still remembered in Texas by the town of Sinton, where he owned a cattle company.

William McCrum
c.1865–1932

WILLIAM MCCRUM, the man who gave the penalty kick to the world, was born in Milford, a red-brick Victorian model village lying in apple tree country not far from Armagh. Milford was built by William's father, linen manufacturer Robert Garmany McCrum, to house the workers from his mill. McCrum's own residence, Milford House, was an extraordinary place, full of innovative gadgets and, it is claimed, was THE FIRST HOUSE IN IRELAND TO HAVE ELECTRICITY.

While Robert Garmany McCrum was a stern and rockbound Victorian entrepreneur, authoritarian, responsible and driven by duty, his son William

McCrum was not. He was approachable, fun-loving and, as soon became apparent, hopeless at business. Shunned by his father, denied a place in the family firm and divorced by his disappointed wife, he found fulfilment on the football field, where he excelled in his role as goalkeeper for Milford Everton FC.

In 1890, the first season of the Irish Football League, McCrum submitted a revolutionary proposal to the Irish Football Association, of which he was a leading member. He was keen to find a way of stopping large, clumsy defenders from using underhand means such as tripping, holding or causing grievous bodily harm to stop attackers from scoring, means that quite often resulted in serious injury or even deaths. To this end he had developed a procedure during matches at Milford that cast the goalkeeper, until then a peripheral figure, in a heroic role.

The world of Victorian football was incensed. Amateur footballers rose up as one to condemn what they referred to as this 'Irishman's motion', since it was inconceivable that the gentlemen who played football – it was, after all, a game for gentlemen – could possibly cheat. C.B. Fry, captain of the Corinthians, considered it beyond the pale that anyone might assume that sportsmen could behave like 'cads of the most unscrupulous kidney'.

Nonetheless, in 1891, after a pause for reflection and another couple of fatalities, McCrum's penalty kick, perhaps the most dramatic and far-reaching sporting rule ever devised, was adopted as rule number 13 in the Laws of Football. Today the dreaded penalty kick, once derided as the 'Irishman's motion', is even used to decide World Cup matches, and it can break the toughest of professionals, as many an England international can testify.

The footloose playboy William McCrum ended up having a far more electrifying effect on the world than his worthy father – but alas, his gambling and wild ways did for him, for he had to sell the mill to pay his debts and eventually died, alone, forgotten and penniless, in a cheap Armagh boarding house.

The football pitch in Milford, where William McCrum invented the penalty kick, was threatened with development, but after a hard-fought battle the centre of the pitch was preserved and houses were put up

Gate Lodge

around the edge. The green space was named the William McCrum Memorial Park and is dominated by a bust of the man himself.

In 2008 a museum opened in the Gate Lodge to Milford House, tracing the story of Milford and the McCrum family.

Well, I never knew this
about
ARMAGH FOLK

Joe Coburn

————◄ 1835–90 ►————

Heavyweight boxing champion JOE COBURN was born in MIDDLE-TOWN. He emigrated to New York in his teens and in 1856 fought Ned Price in a bareknuckle fight that gained him the middleweight championship of America. Coburn was quite small, only 5 ft 9 ins (1.75 m) and his success in the ring was down to his agility rather than his strength. He appears

to have been an early version of Muhammad Ali, in that he would deliver a sharp blow and then leap back out of reach or, to paraphrase Ali, 'float like a butterfly, sting like a bee'.

In 1862 Coburn challenged John Heenan for the heavyweight championship, but Heenan refused the challenge and Coburn took the title by default. He remained champion until 1865 when he retired, but he returned to the ring in 1871 to fight Jem Mace for the world heavyweight championship. Both fights ended in a draw. In 1877 Coburn was sentenced to ten years in prison for assaulting a policeman, a crime he denied. He was released early in 1882 for good behaviour and ended his career with a number of exhibition fights against greats such as John L. Sullivan and 'Nonpareil' Jack Dempsey.

Field Marshall SIR JOHN GREER DILL (1881–1944), architect of the 'special relationship' between Britain and America and described by President Roosevelt as 'the most important figure in the remarkable accord which has been developed in the combined operations of our two countries', was born in LURGAN.

Actor PATRICK MAGEE (1924–82), best remembered for his roles in the Stanley Kubrick films *A Clockwork Orange* and *Barry Lyndon*, was born in ARMAGH. He was a favourite of the playwright Samuel Beckett, who wrote *Krapp's Last Tape* specifically for him.

The booming REVD AND RT. HON. IAN PAISLEY, former First Minister of Northern Ireland, was born in ARMAGH in 1926.

The 'Godfather of Irish Music' and 'Bard of Armagh' TOMMY MAKEM (1932–2007), who performed with the Clancy Brothers, was born in KEADY.

Television and radio presenter GLORIA HUNNIFORD was born in PORTADOWN in 1940.

County Cavan

Irish Rivers ✦ A Flavour of Ireland ✦ Sheridans
✦ Cradle of a Dynasty

Cavan Cathedral

◄ CAVAN FOLK ►

William Dawson ✦ Father Matthew Gibney ✦ Ned Kelly
✦ Eric Dorman-Smith ✦ Reginald Dorman-Smith ✦ Paddy Smith
✦ Brían F. O'Byrne ✦ T.P. McKenna

COUNTY CAVAN may be small and unpretentious, but this beautiful, quiet, unassuming place is the source of two of Ireland's great rivers, the Shannon and the Erne. Shannon Pot, the mystical source of Ireland's longest river, is found on the slopes of Cuilcagh Mountain in the north of the county, while the first settlement on the river, the tiny village of Dowra, marks the Shannon's uppermost navigable point.

The River Erne, which takes its name from the mythical Princess Eirne and is notable for its rich fish stocks, particularly trout, begins its 75-mile (120-km) journey northwards from Lough Gowna in the south. The lough is considered one of the finest lakes for fishing in the world.

Virginia

The small Ulster plantation town of VIRGINIA named, like the American state, in honour of the Virgin Queen Elizabeth I, has more than played its part in exporting a flavour of Ireland around the world. The lush green meadows of Co. Cavan feed the cows that provide the cream for that seminal Irish liqueur, Bailey's Irish Cream, and furthermore a number of prominent world figures can trace their origins to the area too – particularly Sheridans.

The REVD THOMAS SHERIDAN (1687–1738), father of the actor-manager THOMAS SHERIDAN (1719–88) and grandfather of the playwright RICHARD BRINSLEY SHERIDAN (1751–1816), owned a house near Virginia called Cuilcagh, where the Dean of St Patrick's, Jonathan Swift, is believed to have written his best-selling novel *Gulliver's Travels*.

General Philip Sheridan
1831–88

According to local parish records, and a stone marker on the remains of the cottage where his parents lived, the American general PHILIP HENRY SHERIDAN was born at GEAGH, between Balieborough and Virginia, in 1831. When he later began to develop ambitions to run for the US Presidency, Sheridan claimed that he had in fact been born in Albany, New York, since only those born in the United States are eligible.

Sheridan enjoyed a colourful military career and played a significant role in the Union's defeat of the Confederate army in the American Civil War, being described by Abraham Lincoln as 'a little Irishman, but a big fighter'. Sheridan gave credit for some of his success to his redoubtable warhorse Rienzi (named after the town in Mississippi where he was found). Rienzi was given to Sheridan by his fellow officers and proved brave and strong, carrying Sheridan through many battles, despite being wounded four times. In 1864 Rienzi galloped 12 miles (19 km) to get Sheridan to the Battle of Cedar Creek in time to rally the Union forces on to victory – a decisive victory that got Lincoln re-elected and turned the war in favour of the Union. There is a famous statue of General Philip Sheridan on Rienzi in Washington, DC, created by Gutzon Borglum, who sculpted the four presidents on Mount Rushmore. Rienzi is preserved in a glass cage in the Smithsonian Museum.

As a mark of honour, just before his death in 1888, Sheridan was promoted to General of the Army of the United States. He was one of the first national figures to be buried in the grounds of Arlington House, the former home of Confederate General

Robert E. Lee outside Washington, and his presence there led to the rise of Arlington as the nation's most prestigious National Cemetery.

Ballyjamesduff

BALLYJAMESDUFF, a small plantation town near Virginia, is featured in Percy French's popular ballad 'Come Back, Paddy Reilly, to Ballyjamesduff'.

Ballyjamesduff was also the cradle of a remarkable dynasty. In 1789 WILLIAM JAMES emigrated to America from Ballyjamesduff, where he was born in 1771. He made a considerable fortune in upstate New York, with property dealings in

Albany and an interest in the construction of the Erie Canal. He also fathered 12 children and his wealth allowed his descendants to indulge in intellectual and philo-sophical pursuits free from money worries – although many of them were stricken by physical ailments.

One of those 12 children was Henry James (1811–82), a theologian, follower of the Swedish Christian philosopher Emanuel Swedenborg, and friend of many well-known writers and thinkers such as Walt Whitman, Henry Thoreau, William Makepeace Thack-eray, Thomas Carlyle and Ralph Waldo Emerson, who was godfather to Henry's oldest son William.

WILLIAM JAMES (1842–1910) trained as a doctor but took a greater interest in studies of the mind, becoming one of the first psychologists and giving one of the first ever lectures on psychology. He suffered from frequent depression, an ailment that also afflicted his younger brother, the much admired and groundbreaking novelist HENRY JAMES (1843–1916), who is credited with introducing realism into the art of novel writing. Much of Henry's work deals with relationships between the Old World Europeans and New World Americans, and many of his novels have been turned into films and television dramas, such as *The Europeans, Washington Square* (where James was born), *Portrait of a Lady, The Bostonians, The Wings of the Dove* and *The Ambassadors.*

Well, I never knew this
about
CAVAN FOLK

Banker WILLIAM DAWSON (1825–1901) was born in CAVAN and emigrated to America in 1846. In 1878 he became the first Irish mayor of St Paul, the capital city of the state of Minnesota.

FATHER MATTHEW GIBNEY (1835–1925), the priest who gave the last rites to Australia's most celebrated bushranger, Ned Kelly, was born in KILLESHANDRA, a few miles west of Cavan.

Ned Kelly

Ned Kelly was the son of Irishman John 'Red' Kelly who was transported from Ireland to Van Diemen's Land (Tasmania) in 1843 for stealing pigs. Ned, the oldest of eight children, was born in Beveridge, Victoria, just north of Melbourne.

As the son of a convict, Ned and his brothers were treated as suspects in any crimes perpetrated in the area, and when a local policeman was injured while attempting to molest one of Kelly's sisters, Ned was accused of shooting him and had to flee into the bush. He thus become a bushranger, or outlaw, who had to rely on his wits to survive out in the Australian bush with his gang.

Kelly's gang, consisting of Ned, his brother Dan and friends Joe Byrne and Steve Hart, were involved in a number of stand-offs with the police, as well as some fatal shootings and two bank robberies, and were declared outlaws. In June 1880 the gang took 70 guests hostage in the Glenrowan Inn after ripping up the rail tracks so that the train bringing police reinforcements would be derailed. The police were tipped off, however, and laid siege to the inn. The most intriguing aspect of the story was the extraordinary home-made armour worn by the Kelly gang, thought to have been made for them by sympathetic local blacksmiths. All the gang members except Ned Kelly died in the hotel. Ned himself walked out of the building toward the police lines, the bullets rebounding off his body armour, until he was brought down by shots to his unprotected legs. As Ned lay seemingly dying, Father Gibney, who had been travelling on a train halted by the siege, ran forward to hear Ned's confession and administer the last rites. Ned survived however and in an all-Irish affair, was put on trial and sentenced to death by the Irish judge Sir Redmond Barry. Twelve days after Ned Kelly was executed, Barry himself died, of a carbuncle on his neck.

Opinion remains divided, to this day, on whether Ned Kelly was a hero or a villain.

The Dorman-Smiths of Cootehill

COLONEL ERIC DORMAN-SMITH (1895–1969), known as 'Chink', was born in

Cootehill. He joined the British army and served in the North African desert at the start of the Second World War, and is credited with having planned Operation Compass, which led ultimately to the defeat of Rommel's forces in Libya. A brilliant military tactician, regarded by some as 'the outstanding soldier of his generation', Dorman-Smith was considered by others to be 'a menace', with his unorthodox approach. He later fell out with the British high command and returned to Co. Cavan. Disillusioned with the British, he changed his name to Dorman O'Gowan and became a military advisor to the IRA. (O'Gowan or MacGowan is the Irish equivalent of the English name Smith or Smyth. It comes from Mac an Ghabhainn, meaning 'son of the smith'.)

The writer Ernest Hemingway was an admirer and friend of Dorman-Smith and used him as the model for Colonel Cantwell, the hero of his novel *Across the River and into the Trees*. He also asked Dorman-Smith to be godfather to one of his sons.

Eric Dorman-Smith's youngest brother, Reginald Dorman-Smith, was also born in Cootehill. Interested in agriculture, he became President of the National Farmers Union and then entered politics and became Minister for Agriculture in Neville Chamberlain's government. Like his brother Eric, Reginald fell foul of Winston Churchill and was dropped from the

government in 1940, becoming Governor of Burma in 1941. He was expelled by the Japanese after their invasion in 1942.

Cabra Castle, Cootehill

PADDY SMITH (1901–82), THE LONGEST SERVING MEMBER OF THE DAIL, was born in COOTEHILL. He was a founder member of Fianna Fail and served in the Dail for a record 54 years.

Tony award-winning actor BRÍAN F. O'BYRNE, who starred in the

Oscar-winning film *Million Dollar Baby*, was born in MULLAGH in 1967.

Character actor T.P. MCKENNA was born Thomas Patrick McKenna in MULLAGH in 1929. He has appeared in countless film and television programmes, amongst them *Straw Dogs, All Creatures Great and Small, Morse, Heartbeat* and *Ballykissangel.*

County Derry

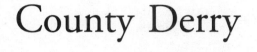

SCENIC SPLENDOURS ✦ LONGEST BEACH
✦ ST AIDAN'S GRAVE ✦ OLDEST HARPIST
✦ THE MAN WHO INVENTED THE DOLLAR SIGN
✦ NELSON'S SURGEON

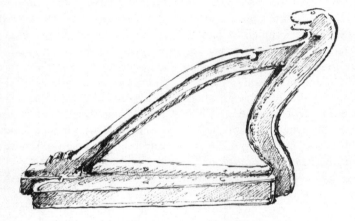

Denis O'Hempsey's Harp

◄ DERRY FOLK ►

Knipe Brothers ✦ Robert Sands ✦ James Campbell
✦ Charles Donagh Maginnis ✦ Martin McGuinness ✦ Roma Downey

COUNTY DERRY was established in 1613 by the Irish Society and the London livery companies (hence the original Londonderry) at the behest of James I, and was carved out of the old county of Coleraine and parts of counties Antrim, Donegal and Tyrone. Although it is a relatively new county, the area is one of the longest continuously inhabited parts of Ireland. MOUNTSANDEL FORT, by the River Bann just outside Coleraine, was occupied by hunter-gatherers around 7, 000 BC and shows the earliest signs of human activity found in Ireland.

Co. DERRY is blessed with a huge variety of scenic splendours. The south of the county is dominated by the dramatic and rugged Sperrin Mountains, while in the centre are the ancient forests of Banagher and Ness Wood, where the Burntollet River drops 30 ft (9 m) over THE HIGHEST WATERFALL IN ULSTER.

The Magilligan lowlands in the north of the county are a vast area of sand and dunes that peak at a point where the narrow mouth of Lough Foyle is marked by a martello tower, with Co. Donegal barely a mile (1.6 km) across the water. Stretching for 6 miles (9.6 km) to the south-east is MAGILLIGAN STRAND, IRELAND'S LONGEST BEACH, backed by the distinctive basalt cliffs of Binevenagh Mountain, reminiscent of the formations of the Giant's Causeway, rising

over 300 ft (90 m) above the flats.

Tucked away down country lanes near Magilligan is the ruined church and grave of ST AIDAN (600–51), an Irish-born monk from Iona who founded the monastery on Lindisfarne off the Northumberland coast. In one corner of the grave, which lies beside an old gable wall, there is a curious hole. Legend has it that any pilgrim who withdraws a handful of sand from the hole will receive good luck.

There must be something in the soil here, for buried in the churchyard is SARAH SWEENEY, who lived most of her life in Magilligan, in a sod-house made from mounds of soil. She died in 1963, aged 110. She was a mere youngster, however, compared with the legendary 'Last of the Bards', Denis O'Hempsey, who also lies here.

Denis O'Hempsey
1695–1807

The oldest harper who ever lived, DENIS O'HEMPSEY was born at CRAIGNORE, near Garvagh. Blinded by smallpox when he was three, he took up learning the harp almost as soon as he was old enough to hold it. At the age of 18 he was donated a fine harp by the people of Garvagh and turned professional, touring Ireland and Scotland for ten years. As well as learning new tunes and songs he gathered anecdotes and gossip to complement his music, as harpists needed to be all-round entertainers, storytellers as well as simply musicians.

O'Hempsey played the harp like the harpists of old, with his fingernails rather than the actual finger, a technique which gave him remarkable dexterity and range, and he could play the most intricate pieces using staccato and legato passages that left his audiences amazed. In addition to his musical skill O'Hempsey's witty conversation and humorous observations made him a consummate entertainer, and he was invited to perform in all the big cities and noble houses of Ireland.

A friend in his youth of Turlough O'Carolan, 'last of the traditional Irish harpist composers', O'Hempsey stuck to playing the old Irish tunes such as 'The Coolin' and 'The Dawning of the Day'. One of his favourites was 'Eileen a Roon' which he took to Scotland and made popular there. The tune was spread across the Highlands and was played so often that it came to be thought of as a Scottish air, and was eventually put to words as the popular Scottish folk song 'Robin Adair'. When he was 50, O'Hempsey was summoned to Edinburgh to play for Bonnie Prince Charlie – for an encore, on that occasion, he played 'The King Shall Enjoy His Own Again'.

Denis O'Hempsey was finally married at the age of 86, to a woman from Magilligan, and fathered a daughter who cared for him in his declining years. In 1792, aged 97, he was the oldest of the ten harpists who were invited to attend the Belfast Harp Festival, organised for the purpose of preserving traditional Irish harp music. This festival is credited with saving many Irish songs from being lost, including 'Deirdre's Lament for the Sons of Usneach', the oldest of all the known Irish songs.

On his deathbed, O'Hempsey asked for his harp to be placed in his hands so that he could pluck out a few notes of his favourite tune. Satisfied, he sank back into the pillows and passed away. He was 112 years old.

Denis O'Hempsey's harp, the only one he ever played, is on show at the Guinness Museum in Dublin.

Oliver Pollock
1737–1823

*Statue in Louisiana of Oliver Pollock
sculpted by Frank Hayden*

The man who invented the dollar sign ($), OLIVER POLLOCK, was born in COLERAINE. After emigrating to Philadelphia with his family in 1760, Pollock based himself in Havana, Cuba, and became a merchant, trading with the Spanish in the West Indies. During this time he got to know the Governor-General of Cuba, Dublin-born Alejandro O'Reilly, one of the 'Wild Geese' who had left Ireland in the 18th century. In 1769 O'Reilly was appointed by the King of Spain as Governor of Louisiana, which had been ceded to Spain by the French in 1763, and Pollock went along with him, settling in New Orleans and establishing a lucrative business as a plantation owner and land agent.

In 1777 Pollock was appointed commercial agent for the colonies in New Orleans, and during the American War of Independence he was instrumental in obtaining, through his Spanish connections, scarce supplies and finance for the Americans. He more or less single-handedly financed the American Revolution, donating over $300 million for the cause, and since his business was conducted mostly with the Spanish and hence in Spanish pesos, Pollock used the standard abbreviation for pesos which was a large 'P' with a small 's' above it and to the right, which over time became simplified by using just the upward stroke of the 'P' running through the 's' – hence $.

By the time the US dollar was created in 1785 this sign was being widely used, and was first seen in print in an accountancy text for students, *American Accomptant* by Chauncey Lee, published in 1797.

Sir William Beatty
1773–1842

The surgeon who tended Lord Nelson at the Battle of Trafalgar, SIR WILLIAM BEATTY, was born in DERRY. He joined the Royal Navy as a teenager in 1791, and experienced all the normal perils of naval life – shipwreck, court martial, yellow fever,

and the capture of a Spanish treasure ship – before being appointed ship's surgeon on Nelson's flagship HMS *Victory* before Trafalgar, in 1805.

At the height of the battle, as Nelson lay dying in the cockpit, having been shot in the chest by a sniper perched in the rigging of the French ship *Redoutable*, Beatty knelt next to him and cleansed the wound while trying to keep the Admiral comfortable. Both knew it was hopeless. 'Ah, Mr Beatty, you can do nothing for me. I have but a short

time to live,' said Nelson and sent Beatty off to help others who might yet still live.

Nelson had asked Beatty not to have his body thrown overboard, and the surgeon had to come up with a way to preserve it until *Victory* reached port. He decided to put it in a barrel full of brandy and placed a sentry to watch over it to dissuade thirsty sailors from drinking the barrel dry. It would be over three months and two changes of brandy before Nelson's corpse was finally removed from the cask – and found to be in a state of almost perfect preservation.

After Trafalgar, Beatty became something of a hero himself and was made Physician of the Channel Fleet, and later of Greenwich Hospital.

Perhaps the most lasting contribution he made to history was the eyewitness account he wrote of his admiral's courageous death. This firmly established the legend of Nelson as Britain's greatest hero in the public consciousness – amongst the last words he recorded of Nelson were 'God bless you, Hardy' and 'Thank God I have done my duty . . .'

Well, I never   knew this
about
DERRY FOLK

THE TALLEST IDENTICAL TWINS WHO
EVER LIVED, THE KNIPE BROTHERS,
were born in MAGHERAFELT in 1761.
Described as 'singular and appealing
in appearance, their persons truly
shaped and proportionate to their
height . . .', at the age of 24 they stood
7 ft 2 ins (2.18 m) in height in their
stockinged feet.

ROBERT SANDS (1828–92), the
conductor of the Mormon Tabernacle
Choir for its first performance in the
new Salt Lake Tabernacle in Salt Lake
City, Utah, in October 1867, was
born in BANAGHER.

Irish patriarch of America's only royal
family, JAMES CAMPBELL (1826–
1900), was born in DERRY. Trained
by his father as a carpenter, he
emigrated to New York by himself at
the age of 13, and after two years
joined the crew of a whaling ship
heading for the South Pacific. After a
series of adventures, including being

shipwrecked on a desert island and
held prisoner by natives, he ended up
in Hawaii in around 1850. His first
wife Hannah died in 1858 and Campbell put the land he inherited from
her to good use, building up a sugar
business and buying up more land
around the Hawaiian islands. In 1877
he retired from the sugar business a
wealthy man and married a Hawaiian
girl Abigail Maipinepine, by whom
he had four children. The oldest,
another Abigail, married Prince
David Kawananakoa of the reigning
House of Kalakaua. Their descendants, as members of the House of
Kawananakoa, are now heirs to the
throne of the Kingdom of Hawaii.

Charles Donagh Maginnis
◄ 1897–1955 ►

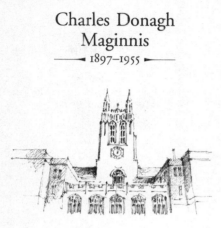

The 'Father of Gothic Revival Architecture in America', CHARLES DONAGH MAGINNIS, was born in DERRY. Educated in Dublin, he emigrated to Boston when he was 18 and began working as a draftsman for a Boston architect, eventually becoming a full member of the Boston Society of Architects in 1900. Always a fan of Gothic architecture, Maginnis got his chance to champion the style when he won a competition to build the new campus for Boston College, and his 'Oxford in America' collegiate Gothic complex, for which he won an American Institute of Architects Gold Medal, was declared 'the most beautiful campus in America'. Gasson Tower, the most prominent feature of the Boston campus, was the first of the dominating towers that are so iconic of American university campuses and inspired, amongst others, the Harkness Tower at Yale.

Maginnis was also well known for his eclectic ecclesiastical architecture, which included churches in the Spanish and Lombard styles, as well as 'primitively simple' buildings that reminded him of the village churches of his native Ireland. One of his most celebrated churches was St Aidan's Church in Brookline, Massachusetts, which opened in 1911. John F. Kennedy was baptised here in 1917 and his brother Robert in 1925.

St Aidan's, Brookline

Former IRA activist and Deputy First Minister of Northern Ireland MARTIN MCGUINNESS was born in DERRY in 1950.

Actress ROMA DOWNEY, who starred as Monica, lead character in the American television series *Touched by an Angel*, which ran from 1994 to 2003, was born in DERRY in 1960. She is also known for her portrayal of Jackie Kennedy Onassis in *A Woman Named Jackie* and for playing Hippolyta, Queen of the Amazons, in the television movie *Hercules and the Amazon Women*.

County Donegal

---•◦•◦•---

IRELAND'S OLDEST PLACE ✦ IRELAND'S OLDEST CROSS
✦ IRELAND'S OLDEST TOWN
✦ THE BARD OF BALLYSHANNON ✦ LEPRECHAUNS
✦ A GUITAR LEGEND
✦ A BRITISH PRIME MINISTER'S MOTHER
✦ A FAMOUS ALL BLACK
✦ FOUNDER OF AMERICAN PRESBYTERIANISM

The Donagh Cross, Ireland's Oldest Cross.

---◄ DONEGAL FOLK ►---

Richard Montgomery ✦ Thomas Nesbit ✦ Father Leonard Eugene Boyle
✦ Ray McAnally

Inishtrahull Island

INISHTRAHULL ISLAND, lying 5 miles (8 km) north-east of Ireland's most northerly mainland point, Malin Head, is not only THE MOST NORTHERLY ISLAND OF IRELAND, and home to IRELAND'S MOST NORTHERLY LIGHTHOUSE, but it is also THE OLDEST PLACE IN IRELAND. About one mile (1.6 km) long and half a mile (0.8 km) wide, the island is formed of an ancient gnarled metamorphic rock known as gneiss and is estimated to be some 1,780 million years old. There are no other rocks like it in Ireland and this is because, like the Scottish island of Islay, Inishtrahull is actually a part of Greenland which broke away from its motherland quite a long time ago.

The island was inhabited until 1928 by up to 100 people, who survived by fishing, growing oats and potatoes, and trading with ships out of the ports on the west coast of Scotland – Inishtrahul was the first or last landfall for transatlantic ships sailing between Scotland and America.

Carndonagh

Standing in the Church of Ireland graveyard in CARNDONAGH, a flourishing little town on the Inishowen peninsula, are two short decorated pillars, a cross slab known as the Marigold Stone (because of the flower carved on one face), and THE OLDEST STANDING CROSS IN IRELAND, THE DONAGH CROSS, which dates from about AD 650. The cross is decorated with a mix of Celtic interlacing patterns and Christian references, reflecting the transition from druidical worship to Christianity.

Ballyshannon

BALLYSHANNON, which received its Royal Charter in 1613, is IRELAND'S OLDEST TOWN. According to the *Annals of the Four Masters*, around 2700 BC a chieftain from Scythia called Parthalon landed on Inis Saimer, a little island in the Erne estuary near where the Mall Quay is now, with his wife and three sons and three fellow chieftains and their families. It was here that they established the first permanent settlement in Ireland.

William Allingham
1824–89

The Bard of Ballyshannon, WILLIAM ALLINGHAM, was born in the town in 1824, the son of the local bank

manager. He went to school in Killeshandra, Co. Cavan, and then joined the customs service and worked in various places in Ireland and England before retiring in 1870 to write full time. His poetry was colourful and descriptive, full of the wildness and folk flavour of his native Donegal, and he became something of an authority on mythical creatures such as fairies and leprechauns (*see* page 262). He was also an important figure in the Pre-Raphaelite movement, with Rossetti and Millais contributing illustrations to his *Day and Night Songs*, published in 1854.

In 1874 he married the painter Helen Paterson, who was half his age. She did the illustrations for many of Thomas Hardy's novels and was the first woman to become a full member of the Royal Watercolour Society. She is best remembered for her idyllic rural scenes, and her romantic pictures of Irish cottages and landscape beautifully complemented the spirit of her husband's poetry.

William Allingham died in London, but he was brought back to be buried in his beloved Ballyshannon and lies in the graveyard of St Anne's Church beneath a stone slab inscribed with the word 'Poet'.

The Allingham Literary Festival is held in his memory every autumn, and writers and poets from all over Ireland descend on Ballyshannon to compete for various Allingham prizes, awarded for poetry and other forms of writing,

The blues and rock guitarist RORY GALLAGHER (1948–95) was born in Ballyshannon. Although he sold over 30 million albums worldwide, it is for his marathon live performances that Gallagher is best remembered. His favourite guitar was a STRATOCASTER, THE FIRST EVER TO BE SEEN IN IRELAND. He was considered by his peers to be one of the finest guitarists who ever performed and was an inspiration to many of the legends of today.

'I owe Rory Gallagher my sound' – Brian May, of Queen

'The man who got me back into the blues' – Eric Clapton

Gallagher's music and memory are commemorated in Ballyshannon by a permanent exhibition and by an

Leprechauns

Up the airy mountain
Down the rushy glen,
We dare not go a-hunting,
For fear of little men.
        from 'The Faeries',
        by William Allingham

Little men, faeries, leprechauns, call them what you will, they are all part of Irish folklore and frequently appear in William Allingham's lyrical poetry. Leprechauns in particular are exclusively associated with Ireland, and are small mischievous sprites said to have inhabited Ireland before the arrival of the Celts. They generally have a crock of gold hidden at the end of the rainbow and, if you are lucky enough to spot one, you must keep your eye on him or he will vanish. The word leprechaun is thought to be derived from the old Irish *leath bhrogan*, meaning shoemaker, and leprechauns are indeed traditionally portrayed as shoemakers. William Allingham describes a leprechaun thus:

. . .A wrinkled, wizen'd, and bearded Elf,
Spectacles stuck on his pointed nose,
Silver buckles to his hose,
Leather apron – shoe in his lap . . .

annual weekend music festival in May. HAZEL CORSCADDEN, mother of Tony Blair, the 51st prime minister of Britain, and the first British Prime Minister to address the Dail, was born in a room above her family's hardware shop in Ballyshannon's main street. Her father, George Corscadden, was a butcher from a family of Scots-Irish Protestant farmers from nearby Cashelard; her mother, Sarah Lipsett, was descended from a German Jew who had immigrated to Donegal in the 18th century. As a boy, Tony Blair spent holidays in Rossnowlagh. In 1998 he told the Dail, 'We would travel in the beautiful countryside of Donegal. It was there in the seas off the Irish coast that I learned to swim, there that my father took me to my first pub, a remote little house in the country, for a Guinness.' The pub, the Traveller's Rest in Cashelard, is still there.

Dave Gallaher
1873–1917

DAVE GALLAHER, founding father and first captain of the New Zealand All Blacks rugby team, was born in RAMELTON. His family emigrated to New Zealand when he was five, settling first in the area of the Bay of Plenty on the North Island and later in Auckland. Gallaher grew to be over 6 ft (1.8 m) tall and 13 stone (82 kg) in weight, and in 1896 was chosen to play rugby for Auckland's famous Ponsonby Club.

After fighting with the New Zealand Army in the Boer War in South Africa, he was nominated for the national team and played in the first-ever Test match between New Zealand and Australia.

As well as being a good tactician, Gallaher was a great motivator, and in 1905 he was appointed captain for the national side's first tour of Britain.

It was on this tour that New Zealand first attracted the name All Blacks, from the colour of their strip, and Gallaher's team became known as the Original All Blacks.

These legendary 'Originals' tore through the world of rugby like a tornado, winning 34 out of 35 matches, only losing 3–0 to Wales thanks to a controversial refereeing decision. One of their most impressive victories was a 33–0 win over Munster, at Limerick, in that province's first international match. Nearly 70 years later, in 1973, Munster gained revenge by becoming the first Irish team ever to beat the All Blacks, again at Limerick.

The Originals' success was partly due to new tactics promoted by Dave Gallaher, including the use of a wing forward, a position he invented and developed. He also introduced dummy runs and code words to signal certain moves, he was the first to get the hooker to throw the ball into the line-out and, in particular, he ordered the forwards to push forward en masse to support the line in attack – all of which helped to shape the game we know today.

The Originals, and Gallaher in particular, returned to New Zealand as heroes, and their exploits established rugby as the country's national game.

Gallaher retired at the height of his game and became a member of the All Blacks selection committee until the outbreak of the First World War in 1914, when he joined up again even though by now he was over 40. After fighting at Ypres he was killed leading his men over the top at Passchendaele and is buried in the Nine Elms Military Cemetery at Poperinge in Belgium.

In 2005 the All Blacks visited Letterkenny Rugby Club, the nearest rugby club to Gallaher's birthplace of Ramelton, to attend the unveiling of a plaque honouring Dave Gallaher and the renaming of their ground as the Dave Gallaher Memorial Park.

Francis Makemie
1658–1708

FRANCIS MAKEMIE, the founder of Presbyterianism in America, was born in RAMELTON. Ordained in 1682 by the Presbytery of Laggan, he was sent to the New World as a missionary and established the first Presbyterian congregation in America at Snow Hill in Maryland. In 1706 he gathered together Presbyterians from different parts of the colonies to establish America's first Presbytery in Philadelphia, of which he was elected the first moderator. He also established a Presbyterian congregation in Rehobeth, Maryland, which is still in existence and can boast the oldest Presbyterian church still in use in the United States.

In January 1707, Makemie was arrested by the governor of New York,

Edward Hyde, for preaching without a licence, but after spending six weeks in jail he was acquitted, having based his defence on the English Toleration Act of 1689. This case is considered a landmark ruling in favour of the cause of religious tolerance in America.

The Naomi Makemie Presbyterian Church in Onancach, Virginia — the first Presbyterian church to be named after a woman

Well, I never knew this about
DONEGAL FOLK

Richard Montgomery
◄── 1738–75 ──►

America's first national hero, RICHARD MONTGOMERY, was born in CONVOY HOUSE, NEAR RAPHOE, the son of Thomas Montgomery, MP, from Lifford. He served with distinction in the British army during the Seven Years' War until, fed up with being passed over for promotion by those with money and social connections, he resigned his commission and bought some land in Westchester County in New York, where he settled down to be a gentleman farmer. In 1773 he married Janet Livingston, the sister of Robert Livingston, who was on the committee that drafted the Declaration of Independence, administered the first oath of office to George Washington, and negotiated the Louisiana Purchase in 1803.

In 1775, at the start of the Revolution, Montgomery was commissioned into the Continental Army as a brigadier general and led the invasion of Canada, capturing two forts and the city of Montreal. In December 1775, while leading an assault on Canada's capital, Quebec, during a fierce snowstorm, he was cut down by musket fire along with 11 of his men, the first American general to die in the American Revolution. Congress arranged for a monument to be raised to Montgomery's memory in New York. It was erected in 1789 as America's first Revolutionary War Monument and stands today across the street from the former site of the World Trade Center.

The harpoon gun was invented by a Donegal man called THOMAS NESBITT, who set up a whaling business in Donegal Bay with his brother

Andrew in 1759. The harpoon was mounted on a swivel, and with it Nesbitt could achieve great accuracy and power. His success was witnessed by the writer Arthur Young, who toured Ireland in 1776–9 and noted, 'From many experiments he brought the operation to such perfection that, for some years, he never missed a whale, nor failed of holding her by the harpoon.'

FATHER LEONARD EUGENE BOYLE (1923–99), the first Irish prefect of the Vatican Library in Rome – from 1984 to 1997 – was born in BALLINTRA. Renowned for his quick wit and his vast knowledge of antiquities and history, he began the task of putting the library's many thousands of manuscripts, some dating from hundreds of years BC, on to a digital database, to widen access to the material for scholars anywhere in the world. He

also employed women in the library for the first time.

Actor RAY MCANALLY (1926–89), known for his roles in films such as *The Mission* and *My Left Foot*, was born in BUNCRANA on the Inishowen Peninsula.

County Down

DOWN FACTS ✦ A CELEBRATED PORT ✦ OYSTERS
✦ A LIFE SAVER ✦ WORLD'S FIRST UNDERPASS
✦ A POLAR HERO ✦ WORDS OF COMFORT

Donaghadee Harbour

◄ DOWN FOLK ►

William Clanny ✦ Francis Rawdon Chesney ✦ George Hunn Nobbs
✦ Arthur Edward Kennedy ✦ John Butler Yeats ✦ Greer Garson
✦ Pat Jennings ✦ Colin Bateman

COUNTY DOWN is much blessed with rich farmland, the mystical Mountains of Mourne and possibly the sunniest climate in Ireland.

Ireland's first Gothic architecture can be found in the beautiful ruins of GREYABBEY, founded in 1193 by Affrica, daughter of the King of Man. ST PATRICK'S CHURCH in NEWRY, founded in 1578, was IRELAND'S FIRST PROTESTANT CHURCH.

In 2001 THE WORLD'S LARGEST HEDGE MAZE, THE PEACE MAZE, was opened in CASTLEWELLAN FOREST PARK in the foothills of the Mountains of Mourne.

Donaghadee

During the 19th century, the little seaside town of DONAGHADEE was one of the principal cross-channel ports between Ireland and Britain. It boasts a famous lighthouse designed by Sir John Rennie, the walls of which were painted by writer Brendan Behan when he was employed by the Irish Lights Commission.

The American privateer John Paul Jones is said to have stayed at Grace Neill's pub in Donaghadee's high street, which opened in 1611 as the King's Arms and vies with the Old Inn at nearby Crawfordsburn for the title of Ulster's oldest inn. Many celebrities of the day stayed at both establishments on their way to and from Britain, including Jonathan Swift, Charles Dickens, Anthony Trollope, Alfred Lord Tennyson and William Makepeace Thackeray. In 1958 Belfast-born C.S. Lewis spent a belated honeymoon at the Old Inn with his wife Joy.

In 1853 THE FIRST TELEGRAPH CABLE BETWEEN IRELAND AND BRITAIN was laid from Donaghadee to Portpatrick in Scotland.

Hillsborough

In early September HILLSBOROUGH, Ulster's most English village and home to the official residence of the Secretary of State for Northern Ireland, hosts

Greyabbey

the Northern Ireland heats of the annual WORLD OYSTER EATING CHAMPIONSHIP, attracting visitors from as far afield as Russia, Japan and New Zealand. The competition is open to all and in 2008 the record stood at 233 oysters in three minutes.

Frank Pantridge
1916–2004

The 'Father of Emergency Medicine', FRANK PANTRIDGE, whose pioneering techniques for treating heart patients before they get to hospital have saved millions of lives, was born in Hillsborough. While working at the Royal Victoria Hospital in Belfast in 1965, he invented a portable defibrillator, a machine that gives a controlled electric shock to heart attack victims to restore their normal heart rhythm. Pantridge's machine could be operated from a car battery, enabling paramedics to administer emergency treatment while in the ambulance on the way to hospital. Thanks to this invention, Belfast in the 1960s was known as 'the safest place in the world to have a heart attack'. It took until 1990 for all ambulances in Ireland and Britain to be equipped with portable defibrillators.

Banbridge

BANBRIDGE owes its existence to the bridge, first built in 1712, that carries the Belfast to Dublin road across the River Bann. The town sits on a steep hill, which was difficult for a horse and carriage to negotiate and so, in 1834, at the request of the postal services, the main street was run through by means of a sunken cutting, with slip roads on both sides and a bridge across the top. This curious construction is claimed to be THE WORLD'S FIRST UNDERPASS.

Banbridge sits at the heart of what was Ireland's principal linen-producing district and was once an important linen market town. It is still home to THE ONLY REMAINING IRISH LINEN DAMASK WEAVER IN IRELAND, THOMAS FERGUSON & CO. LTD.

Across the road from the Protestant church, four stone polar bears guard a statue of one of Banbridge's most famous sons, Captain Francis Crozier.

Captain Francis Crozier
1796–1848

One of the greatest polar explorers of them all, FRANCIS CROZIER was born into a wealthy Banbridge family, 11th of 13 children of a solicitor. He joined the Royal Navy in 1810, when he was just short of his 14th birthday, and fought through the last years of the Napoleonic Wars. On one of his voyages, to the South Pacific, he visited Pitcairn Island and met the last surviving mutineer from the *Bounty*, John Adams.

After the Battle of Waterloo and the defeat of Napoleon, Britain found itself possessed of a huge navy with not much to do, and so ships were sent out on great voyages of exploration, to the North and South Poles and to find the fabled North-West

Passage around the top of North America. Crozier went on two expeditions to look for the North-West Passage and in 1839 he set off on an epic four-year journey with James Clark Ross to map Antarctica, donating his name to the celebrated Cape Crozier on Ross Island, which would later feature prominently in the tragic story of Robert Falcon Scott.

On his way south to Antarctica, Crozier stopped for supplies in Tasmania and fell in love with Sophy Cracroft, niece of the island's governor, Sir John Franklin. He even proposed marriage, several times, but was turned down because Sophy did not want to be the wife of a sea captain.

On his return to Britain, driven on by heartbreak, or perhaps in a further bid to impress Sophy, Crozier agreed to sail on another search for the North-West Passage, as second-in-command under none other than Sir John Franklin, his lost love's uncle.

In the summer of 1845 the expedition's two ships, the *Erebus*, commanded by Franklin, and the *Terror*, under Crozier's command, disappeared into the treacherous waters of the Arctic and were never seen again. Some 50 ships were sent to look for the lost expedition over the next few years but their fate remained a mystery until 1859, when Captain Francis McLintock (*see* Co. Louth) discovered a diary written by

Crozier hidden near some graves on King William Island. It told how the *Erebus* and *Terror* had been trapped in the ice for two years, how Franklin had died in 1847, and how Crozier had taken command, leading the survivors across the ice in a vain but heroic attempt to walk to the Canadian mainland.

As a final irony, it turned out that they had unknowingly achieved their original goal, for the bodies of Crozier and his men were found at Simpson's Strait, which is the final leg of the North-West Passage.

Joseph Scriven
1819–86

What a Friend we have in Jesus
All our sins and griefs to bear

Author of the beautiful lyrics to one of the world's best-loved hymns, JOSEPH SCRIVEN was born at BALLY-MONEY LODGE just outside Banbridge. When he was asked how he came to write such beautiful words, he replied, 'The Lord and I did it between us.' The words were born out of much grief and sadness.

After obtaining a degree at Trinity College Dublin, Joseph fell in love with a beautiful girl from Banbridge and they became engaged. On the eve

of their wedding day Joseph was standing beside the River Bann waiting for his bride-to-be to ride across the bridge towards him, when her horse reared up and she was hurled into the water and drowned before his very eyes, while he looked on help-lessly.

The tragedy devastated Joseph, and in order to forget, he took himself away to Canada, finally settling down in Ontario, at Rice Lake, and later Port Hope, and becoming a tutor. A devoutly religious man, he spent much of his time helping those in need, giving away much of his money, doing menial tasks, cutting wood for those who couldn't pay for it and even selling his own watch to help a couple who had lost their cow.

In 1854 it seemed he had found happiness again when he became engaged to a Canadian girl, but once more tragedy struck. After going for a swim in Rice Lake his fiancée caught pneumonia, weakened, and three years later she died, as before, on the eve of their wedding. Around the same time, Joseph's mother back in Ireland became ill and Joseph wrote his poem, which he called 'Pray without ceasing', to give her comfort.

Although composed in 1857, the poem wasn't discovered until just before Joseph himself died, ironically by drowning, in 1886.

It was put to a piece of music called 'Erie', written by Charles Crozat

Converse, and renamed 'What a Friend We Have in Jesus'. With its comforting and moving words, and a tune that was easy to sing and simple to play, 'What a Friend We Have in Jesus' quickly became a favourite across America and around the world. During the First World War soldiers in the trenches would sing it to lift their spirits. It is sung at memorial services and recited quietly at moments of great bereavement or sorrow. Strangely, in Japan, it is sung at western-style wedding ceremonies. How proud the saintly Irishman would be to know that the words he wrote to bring comfort to his mother have brought comfort to countless millions too.

Joseph Scrivens is buried beneath a white granite obelisk in the Pengelly Cemetery, beside Rice Lake in Ontario. The little cottage where he lived in Port Hope still stands, and there is a plaque on his birthplace at Ballymoney Lodge in Co. Down.

Well, I never knew this about
DOWN FOLK

William Clanny
1776–1850

Inventor of a miner's safety lamp two years before Humphry Davy, WILLIAM CLANNY was born in BANGOR. Working as a doctor in Sunderland, Clanny had to deal on a regular basis with the many victims of mine explosions from the Durham coal-mines, and he determined to do something about making their lives safer. In 1813 he presented a paper to the Royal Philosophical Society entitled 'On the means of procuring a steady light in coal-mines without danger of explosion', which intro-duced his safety lamp – an oil-soaked wick within a glass shield, isolated from the air by water seals. The only drawback was that it needed someone to pump air into it continuously with a pair of bellows, and this made the lamp somewhat ungainly and imprac-tical in the narrow confines of a mine.

Clanny continued to improve on his design, however, and by 1840 had perfected his invention with a lamp known as a 'Clanny', where the flame was surrounded by glass and the air was fed in through a wire gauze. Clanny worked closely with Humphry Davy, and the two men regularly swapped ideas – between them they must have saved many thousands of miners' lives.

FRANCIS RAWDON CHESNEY (1789–1872), hailed as the 'Father of the Suez Canal' by Ferdinand de Lesseps, the canal's French builder, was born in ANNALONG. For part of his duties as an officer in the Royal Artillery he made a survey of Egypt and wrote a report in 1830 that convinced the French, if not the British, of the feasibility of constructing a canal linking the Mediterranean and the Red Sea.

Francis Rawdon Chesney

George Hunn Nobbs
—◄ 1799–1884 ►—

Pitcairn Island missionary and Pacific patriarch GEORGE HUNN NOBBS was born in MOIRA, the illegitimate son of the 1st Marquess of Hastings, who refused to acknowledge the boy.

George was fostered by the Nobbs family and spent his youth travelling the world in a succession of merchant ships. In 1828 he visited Pitcairn Island, inhabited by the descendants of the *Bounty* mutineers, and decided to stay on as schoolmaster to continue the Christian education introduced by the last of the mutineers, John Adams. In 1829 George married Sarah Christian, the granddaughter of Fletcher Christian, leader of the mutineers, who had been murdered on the island 35 years earlier. Together they had 12 children, most of whom married descendants of the other mutineers. Today, many progeny of the man from Moira can be found living in Australasia – a long way from County Down.

Colonial administrator ARTHUR EDWARD KENNEDY (1809–83), known as the 'Governor', was born in CULTRA. During his career he served as governor of The Gambia, Sierra Leone, Western Australia, Vancouver Island, the West African Settlements, Hong Kong and Queensland. He died in Aden and was buried at sea.

Artist JOHN BUTLER YEATS (1839–1922), father of Nobel Prize-winning poet William Butler Yeats and artist Jack Butler Yeats, was born at Vicarage Farm, LAWRENCETOWN. He spent the last 15 years of his life in New York, where he is buried.
.

The family of Oscar-winning actor JEREMY IRONS (Best Actor Oscar for his portrayal of Claus von Bulow in *Reversal of Fortune* in 1990) originated from nearby GILFORD village.

Greer Garson
——◄ 1904–96 ►——

The flame-haired actress who made THE LONGEST EVER OSCAR ACCEPTANCE SPEECH, GREER GARSON, liked to claim that she was born in CASTLEWELLAN. In fact she was born in East London but she preferred to stress her Irish roots. Her mother Nancy Greer was Irish, and Greer herself did spend much of her childhood at her grandfather's house in Castlewellan. Her Oscar speech came when she was awarded the Best Actress Oscar for *Mrs Miniver* in 1943

and she spoke for five and a half minutes. Along with Bette Davis, Greer Garson holds the record for the highest number of consecutive Oscar nominations, being nominated five years in a row from 1941 to 1945.

International goalkeeper PAT JENNINGS was born in NEWRY in 1945. One of the few goalkeepers to score in a competitive match (for Tottenham Hotspur against Manchester United in the 1967 Charity Shield), he played a world record 119 games in goal for Northern Ireland.

Novelist and screenwriter COLIN BATEMAN, whose novel *Murphy's Law* was adapted in 2001 for a BBC television series starring Co. Derry-born James Nesbitt, was born in BANGOR in 1962.

County Fermanagh

---◆◆◆◆---

FAIRYTALE TURRETS ✦ FINE FOSSILS
✦ A RAILWAY PIONEER ✦ BESTSELLING SONG
✦ EAT MORE FIBRE ✦ OLDEST ROBIN

Enniskillen Castle

◀ FERMANAGH FOLK ▶

Andrew Graham ✦ Father Brian D'Arcy ✦ Sean Quinn
✦ Adrian Dunbar ✦ Laurena Lacey

COUNTY FERMANAGH is the only county of Northern Ireland that does not border Lough Neagh, the largest lake in both Ireland and Britain, but then it doesn't need to – almost a third of the county already lies underwater, most of it beneath Upper and Lower Erne.

Enniskillen

————— ❖❖❖❖ —————

ENNISKILLEN, Co. Fermanagh's county town, is supremely situated in glorious lacustrine countryside, on an island between Upper and Lower Lough Erne. The skyline of the town is dominated by the fairytale, twin-turreted watergate tower belonging to its castle, built between the 15th and 17th centuries.

Overlooking the town from the summit of Forthill Park is SIR GALBRAITH LOWRY-COLE (1772–1842), second son of the 1st Earl of Enniskillen, who fought as a prominent general under Wellington in the Peninsula War. The statue of Sir Galbraith, sculpted by the Irish sculptor Terence Farrell, sits on a 100-ft (30-m) high column that provides sensational views from the top for those willing to tackle the 108-step climb.

Sir Galbraith Lowry-Cole

Sir Galbraith Lowry-Cole was the uncle of WILLIAM WILLOUGHBY COLE, 3rd Earl of Enniskillen (1807–86) who, as well as being Fermanagh's MP before he succeeded to his title, amassed the world's finest collection of fossil fish at his palatial home, Florence Court, 8 miles (13 km) south-west of Enniskillen. Experts from all over the world, including Swiss geologist Louis Agassiz, the first person to float the idea of an Ice Age, came to gaze at what Cole's father, the 2nd Earl, called 'this damned nonsense'. The collection is now in the Natural History Museum in London. William Willoughby Cole was also an Imperial Grandmaster of the Orange Order.

James Beatty
1820–56

JAMES BEATTY, chief engineer of the Grand Crimean Central Railway, was born in ENNISKILLEN, the son of a doctor. His first job, in 1842, was as part of the team building the Norwich to Lowestoft railway in East Anglia. In 1853 he was sent to Nova Scotia to survey the European and North American Railway, which was designed to link Portland, Maine, the eastern terminus of the US rail network, with an Atlantic port, probably Halifax, in Nova Scotia.

The following year he was appointed as chief engineer for the Grand Crimean Central Railway, which was to be built to carry supplies from Balaclava to the Allied soldiers engaged in the siege of Sevastopol, during the Crimean War. Seven miles

long and including a stretch with a gradient of 1 in 14, the line was completed in seven weeks, a testament to the talent and energy of James Beatty. It played a major part in the success of the siege – and will also be remembered for carrying THE WORLD'S FIRST HOSPITAL TRAIN. After the war ended in 1856, the track was taken up.

In April 1855, Beatty was badly injured when a train on the Grand Crimean Central Railway ran out of control and he was hit. His work more or less completed, Beatty returned to England for treatment, but died in March 1856 from an aortic aneurysm.

If you ever go across the sea to
  Ireland,
Then maybe at the closing of your
  day
You will sit and watch the moonrise
  over Claddagh,
And see the sun go down on
  Galway Bay.

DR ARTHUR COLOHAN (1884–1952), born in ENNISKILLEN, wrote these lyrics in 1947, pining for his home country while living in Leicester, where he was practising as a neurological specialist. They are the first words of a song he composed called 'Galway Bay', which was made popular by Bing Crosby and, for a long while, was the bestselling record of all time.

Denis Parson Burkitt
1911–93

DENIS PARSON BURKITT, the medical scientist who first championed the high-fibre diet, was born in ENNISKILLEN. He lost his right eye in an accident when he was 11, an event that turned his thoughts to becoming a doctor, and although he entered Trinity College Dublin to study engineering, he soon changed to medicine. He served with the Royal Army Medical Corps during the Second World War, and afterwards moved to Africa to practise as a 'simple bush surgeon' in the developing world. He settled in Kampala, in Uganda, and identified a new type of cancer, which now bears his name, Burkitt's lymphoma, and which it has recently been recognised can be the initial manifestation of AIDS. In 1961 he embarked on a famous 10,000-mile safari to track the geographical distribution of the tumour, and became the first person to identify a link between a cancer and the victim's environment. He also found that the cancer could be cured by chemotherapy – the only cancer that could be at that time. His discoveries were a major breakthrough in cancer treatment.

In 1966 Burkitt moved to London to work for the Medical Research Council and, using what he had learnt in Africa, began studying the link between diet and cancer. In 1979 he published a bestselling book, *Don't Forget Fibre in Your Diet*, in which he suggests for the first time that a high-fibre diet can help prevent bowel cancer.

Denis Burkitt's father JAMES BURKITT (1870–1959) was County Surveyor for Co. Fermanagh and also an enthusiastic bird-watcher. He made a particular study of the robins in his garden, near Enniskillen, and pioneered the use of leg rings to identify individual birds and see where they roamed. One female robin he ringed in 1927 appeared again in 1938, making it, at 11 years of age, the oldest known robin in the world.

Well, I never knew this
about
FERMANAGH FOLK

THE FIRST AND ONLY IRISH ASTRONOMER TO DISCOVER AN ASTEROID WHILE OBSERVING FROM IRELAND, ANDREW GRAHAM (1815–1908), was born in ENNISKILLEN. In 1848, while working at the Markree Observatory in Co. Sligo, he discovered asteroid 9 Metis, one of the largest asteroids from the main belt.

Passionist priest FATHER BRIAN D'ARCY, Rector of St Gabriel's Retreat, the Graan in ENNISKILLEN, and presenter of BBC Radio 2's *Sunday Half-Hour*, was born in BELLANALECK in 1945. As a young priest in Dublin he worked amongst the city's show-

business community, and became the inspiration for the character Father Ted Crilly played by Dermot Morgan in the sitcom *Father Ted*.

Arguably the richest man in Ireland, SEAN QUINN, was born on his father's farm in DERRYLIN in 1947. Always an enthusiastic sportsman, he left school at 14 and became an active member of the Gaelic Athletic Association, a move that would pay off spectacularly later on in his career. In 1973 Quinn borrowed £100 from friends, formed Sean Quinn Quarries Ltd, and began to dig up the gravel beneath his 23-acre (9.3-ha) family farm. He graded it, washed it and then sold it to local builders. The gravel was top grade, and Quinn's reputation spread both north and south, partly thanks to his contacts within the GAA, who gave him an entrée into the market south of the border. Quinn progressed on to Quinn Cement, then concrete, glass, plastics, financial services, BUPA Ireland and hotels – including one of Dublin's oldest, Buswells Hotel, and the Belfry Golf Resort, near Birmingham, a Ryder Cup venue.

The group now has interests in countries as diverse as Germany, the Czech Republic, Russia and Wales – where Quinn Radiators owns the largest radiator plant in the world. However, the core-business world headquarters of the Quinn Group, one of the largest multinational companies in the world, is located in the quiet Irish county where it all began – Co. Fermanagh.

Actor ADRIAN DUNBAR was born in ENNISKILLEN in 1958. Amongst the many films he has appeared in are *My Left Foot*, the story of Christy Brown, *The Crying Game* and *Hear My Song*, which he co-wrote and is based on the story of Irish tenor Josef Locke.

The first Irish girl to become a *Playboy* 'playmate', LAURENA LACEY, was born Laurena Coffey, in ENNISKILLEN, in 1986.

County Monaghan

A Great Poet ✦ An Actor's Retreat ✦ Clones
✦ God's Own Country
✦ The Cyclone and the Colossus

St Tiernach's Church, Clones

◀ MONAGHAN FOLK ▶

Sir Charles Gavan Duffy ✦ Eoin O'Duffy ✦ Ardal O'Hanlon

According to *The Annals of the Four Masters*, the name Monaghan comes from the Irish Muineachain, meaning 'place of small hills'. The landscape of the county is dotted with gently moulded drumlin hills resembling, in the words of one observer, 'a basket of eggs', and certainly in COUNTY MONAGHAN the modern world treads lightly.

> *Monaghan Hills*
> *You have made me the sort of man*
>   *I am*
> *A fellow who can never care a*
>   *damn*
> *For Everistic thrills*

These are the words of Co. Monaghan's most famous son, the writer and poet PATRICK KAVANAGH (1904–67), born in INNISKEEN, whose greatest work, the long poem *The Great Hunger*, was originally banned for all too openly and accurately portraying the hardship and oppression imposed on Ireland's rural communities

(such as those of Co. Monaghan) by both government and the Catholic Church. When it was published in 1942, *The Great Hunger* was considered obscene; today it is celebrated as a work of genius. In 1948 Kavanhagh published what he called 'the only authentic account of life as it was lived in Ireland this century', a novel called *Tarry Flynn*. This was banned, too, before being made into a play performed at the Abbey Theatre in Dublin in 1966.

This independent mindset, forged in adversity, has been exported wherever the people of Monaghan have settled across the globe – in Canada there is an expression 'Never say Boo to a Monaghan!' Between 1830 and 1850 over 3, 000 people left Co. Monaghan and emigrated to Prince Edward Island, Canada's smallest province, and it is estimated that at least one-fifth of the population of the island can trace their ancestry to Co. Monaghan.

Tyrone Guthrie Centre

'. . . my said dwelling-house, furniture, pictures and chattels and the income of my residuary estate to be used for the purpose of providing a retreat for artists and other like persons . . . so as to enable them to do or facilitate them in doing creative work.'

dance with his wishes, a committee was formed from the Arts Councils of Ireland and Northern Ireland to establish the Tyrone Guthrie Centre in the house, and Annaghmakerrig has since become one of Ireland's most sought-after artistic retreats. Each artist has their own room and work-space, and looks after their own catering, except in the evening – another stipulation of the will was that all residents should sit down to dinner together each evening. Over the years various outbuildings have been converted to create more studios, and the grounds have been further landscaped to provide an attractive setting for exercise and inspiration.

So reads the will of the theatrical producer and director SIR TYRONE GUTHRIE (1900–71), great-grandson of the actor-manager Tyrone Power (*see* Co. Waterford). The said dwelling-house is Guthrie's family home ANNAGHMAKERRIG HOUSE, set in beautiful grounds near Newbliss, where he spent his happiest days, surrounded by the peace and tranquillity of Co. Monaghan. After Guthrie's death in 1971, and in accor-

Clones

Set in glorious countryside, CLONES is a small agricultural centre which was originally a monastic settlement founded in the 6th century by St Tighearnach and can boast the remains of

Arraghmakerrig House

a 9th-century round tower, a marvellous high cross and the ruins of a 12th-century abbey. For somewhere so quiet, the town has given birth to a remarkable number of Clones who have made their presence felt across the world.

General Joseph Finegan

JOSEPH FINEGAN (1814–85) emigrated to Florida in 1830 and built up a large business practice which included construction of the Florida Railway connecting the east and west coasts. At the outbreak of the American Civil War he was put in command of Florida's Confederate forces and inflicted a crushing defeat on the Union forces at the Battle of Olustee in 1864, a rare Confederate victory which persuaded the Union commanders to leave Florida alone for the rest of the campaign.

Thomas Bracken

THOMAS BRACKEN (1843–98) was born of Protestant parents. His mother died a few days after he was born and his father when he was nine. Thomas was looked after by an aunt for three years and then packed off to Australia to live with his uncle in Victoria. He eventually found work as a gold fossicker (someone who looks for gold) and began writing stories about the gold rush and life amongst the gold diggers. At age 25 he moved to New Zealand and became a journalist, becoming editor of the *Saturday Advertiser*, a newspaper set up to encourage native New Zealanders to develop their own literature and writing style. Bracken contributed some of his own work, including a poem called 'God Defend New Zealand', which was put to music by the winner of a competition, John Joseph Woods, and adopted by the New Zealand government as a national hymn for the country's centennial celebrations in 1940. In 1977 'God Defend New Zealand' officially became New Zealand's second national anthem, with equal status to 'God Save the Queen'.

In 1889 Bracken wrote a poem entitled 'God's Own Country', and this phrase was picked up by New Zealanders to describe New Zealand. Since then the phrase has been borrowed by other countries around the world, but thanks to an Irishman, Thomas Bracken, New Zealand remains the original 'God's Own Country'.

Patrick McCabe

Playwright and novelist PATRICK MCCABE was born in 1955. He is the author of five novels so far, darkly comedic tales of small-town life in contemporary Ireland. Two of his books, *The Butcher Boy* and *Breakfast on Pluto*, were shortlisted for the Booker Prize, and in 1996 *The Butcher Boy* was made into a film, directed by Neil Jordan.

Barry McGuigan

Born in 1961, world featherweight champion boxer BARRY McGUIGAN, the 'Clones Cyclone', is considered by some to be the best Irish boxer of all time. In 1985, the year he won his title by beating Panama's Eusebio Pedroza, McGuigan became the first person born outside the United Kingdom to win the BBC Sports

Personality of the Year award. His greatest inspiration was his father, singer Pat McGuigan, who competed for Ireland in the Eurovision Song Contest in 1968 and used to sing 'Danny Boy' before his son's boxing matches. Barry briefly retired from boxing after his father's death in 1987, returning to fight for two further years in 1988 and then leaving the ring permanently. Today he works in the administration of boxing and appears regularly on television light entertainment shows.

Kevin McBride

The 'Clones Colossus', the 6 ft 8-in (2.03-m) All-Ireland heavyweight and IBC Americas heavyweight champion KEVIN McBRIDE, was born in 1973. Now living in Boston, Massachusetts, McBride's greatest claim to fame is his defeat of former world heavyweight champion Mike Tyson in 2005.

Well, I never knew this
about
MONAGHAN FOLK

Sir Charles Gavan Duffy
—◄ 1816–1903 ►—

SIR CHARLES GAVAN DUFFY, founder of *The Nation* newspaper and premier of Victoria, Australia, was born in Dublin Street in the county

town of MONAGHAN and educated at Ulster's oldest Catholic grammar school, St Malachy's College in Belfast. In 1839 he was appointed editor of *The Vindicator* in Belfast. In 1842 he met two young barristers in Dublin, Thomas Davis and John

Blake Dillon, and the three of them decided to start a newspaper reflecting their desire 'to make Ireland a nation'. They called it *The Nation*, and Duffy was the first editor. *The Nation* was an immediate success, greatly helping to promote Daniel O'Connell's Repeal Association, of which all three were members; but from 1844 they split with O'Connell over his refusal to consider violent protest, and became Young Irelanders.

In 1850 Duffy founded the Tenant League and in the election of 1852 was returned to Westminster as member for New Ross, Co. Wexford. Eventually, despairing of any hope for Irish independence, he emigrated to Melbourne in Australia, where he was persuaded by the large Irish population to make use of his political experience and enter the Victorian parliament. In 1871 he became premier of Victoria and later became Speaker of the House of Assembly, receiving a knighthood. In 1880 he retired to France and devoted the rest of his life to writing.

He was married three times, having one child by his first marriage, four by his second marriage and four more, when he was well into his 70s, by his third marriage in Paris.

Eoin O'Duffy
◄ 1892–1944 ►

EOIN O'DUFFY, controversial politician, Irish fascist and key figure in the creation of modern Ireland, was born in LOUGH EGISH, a rural community near Castleblaney. After training as an engineer he worked as an architect in Monaghan and also took a great interest in local sports, becoming a member of the Ulster Gaelic Athletics Association. In 1917, after the Easter Uprising, O'Duffy joined the IRA and was very active in the War of Independence, becoming director of the Monaghan Brigade and effecting the IRA's first capture of a Royal Irish Constabulary barracks, at Ballytrain in Co. Monaghan. A friend and supporter of Michael Collins, in 1922 he became the IRA Chief of Staff and served as a general (at 29, the youngest in Europe) in the Free State Army, set up by the pro-Treaty wing of the IRA during the Irish Civil War.

When the Irish Free State was established in 1922, O'Duffy was appointed as the second Commissioner of the Garda Siochana (Civic Guard), which the Provisional government had formed out of the Royal Irish Constabulary and the Irish Republican Police to police the Irish Free State. He remained in this position for 11 years and is credited with the early development of the modern Garda, before being dismissed by Eamon de Valera in 1933 for encouraging a military coup. O'Duffy then became leader of the Army Comrades Association, a pro-Fascist organisation intended to defend former members of the Free State Army and oppose the rise of left-wing and Communist elements in Ireland. O'Duffy renamed the group National Guard and began running the association along the same paramilitary lines as Hitler's Brownshirts and Mussolini's Blackshirts – the National Guard became the Blueshirts. It was perhaps at this point that O'Duffy began to lose his grip on reality. He proclaimed himself 'the third most important man in Europe after Adolf Hitler and Benito Mussolini', and at rallies would exhort his followers to give the straight-arm Roman salute while crying out 'Hail O'Duffy!'

When the Blueshirts were prevented from marching on Dublin and declared illegal, O'Duffy merged them in 1933 with two smaller political parties, Cumann na nGaedhael (founded by Arthur Griffith in 1900) and the Centre Party, to form Fina Gael, with himself as the first president. Today Fina Gael is the second largest political party in the Republic of Ireland. Because of his strong fascist sympathies O'Duffy was forced to resign in 1934, and in 1936 he led the 700-strong Irish Brigade to fight for General Franco in the Spanish Civil War. They returned to Ireland after six months, having seen little fighting but having suffered heavy casualties when accidently fired upon by Spanish Nationalist Troops.

After this Eoin O'Duffy retired from active politics. He died in 1944, was given a state funeral and is buried in Glasnevin Cemetery.

Ardal O'Hanlon

Actor and comedian ARDAL O'HANLON was born in CARRICK-MACROSS in 1965. After graduating from Dublin City University he helped to set up Ireland's first alternative comedy club, the Comedy Cellar, in Dublin. He 1994 he was voted Comedy Newcomer of the Year, an accolade that brought him to the attention of writer and director Graham Linehan, who cast O'Hanlon in his new TV sitcom *Father Ted*, as Dougal Maguire.

Father Ted became a cult classic,

and O'Hanlon went on to appear in a number of television shows before being cast as the mild-mannered shopkeeper George Sunday, alias Thermoman, in the BBC sitcom *My Hero*, about a superhero struggling to cope with suburban life on earth, while finding the time to save the world. He reprised the role from 2000 until 2005.

O'Hanlon also played a small role in Neil Jordan's film *The Butcher Boy*, adapted from the novel by a fellow son of Co. Monaghan, Patrick McCabe.

County Tyrone

Omagh Cathedral of the Sacred Heart

◄ TYRONE FOLK ►

COUNTY TYRONE is the least populated county of Northern Ireland but was once at the heart of a thriving neolithic farming community, as evidenced by the huge complex of stone circles and cairns at Breaghmore in the Sperrin Hills in the north of the county.

Omagh

OMAGH, the county capital, sits where the Camowen and Drumragh rivers join to form the River Strule. The classic view of the town from the river, with the two irregular spires of the Catholic Cathedral of the Sacred Heart rising above the stone road bridge, is tremendous. The cathedral was built on the highest point of the town in 1899 and has been called 'the poor man's Chartres'.

Omagh possesses THE SHORTEST STREET IN IRELAND, MICHAEL STREET, which is occupied by just one house, belonging to local publican Michael McGlinchey.

Tony award-winning playwright BRIAN FRIEL was born in Omagh in 1929. The play for which he is best known internationally is *Dancing at Lughnasa*, which won three Tony awards when it opened on Broadway in 1992. Set in the fictional village of Ballybeg in Co. Donegal, it is thought to be based on the lives of Friel's mother and aunts, who lived in the central Donegal village of Glenties. *Dancing at Lughnasa* was made into a film starring Meryl Streep in 1998.

Actor SAM NEILL was born Nigel John Dermot Neill in Omagh in 1947, the son of a third-generation New Zealander and Irish Guards officer stationed in Northern Ireland. The family owned Neill and Co., once New Zealand's largest liquor retailers, and when Neill was seven years old they returned to New Zealand's South Island. Called Sam at school to avoid confusion with another Nigel in his class, Neill found international fame playing Dr Alan Grant in the Steven Spielberg *Jurassic Park* film series.

Jimmy Kennedy
1902–84

❦

Award-winning songwriter and lyricist JIMMY KENNEDY was born in Omagh, the son of a policeman in the Royal Irish Constabulary. His birthplace on the Brookmount Road is marked by a plaque.

Educated at Trinity College, Dublin, he was about to be posted to Nigeria for a job with the Colonial Service when he got an offer to join a music publisher in the heart of London's own Tin Pan Alley, Denmark Street. Over the next 50 years he wrote more than 2, 000 songs and, prior to Lennon and McCartney, had achieved more hit songs in the United States and across the world than any previous Irish or British songwriter.

In 1931 he had his first hit with 'The Barmaid's Song', performed by Gracie Fields, and in 1935 he wrote a song about a summer evening in the seaside town where he grew up, Portstewart in Co. Derry, called 'Red Sails in the Sunset', which was taken to No. 24 in the US charts by Nat King Cole in 1951.

Kennedy served in the Royal Artillery during the Second World War and wrote both the words and the music for one of the most famous and popular of wartime songs, 'We're Going to Hang out the Washing on the Siegfried Line', which he dedicated to the British Expeditionary Force.

Jimmy Kennedy's other hit songs included 'The Teddy Bears' Picnic', which he put to a tune written in 1907 by American composer John Walter Bratton, and the dance favourite 'Hokey Cokey'. He won two Ivor Novello awards and in 1997 was posthumously inducted into the Songwriters Hall of Fame.

Clogher

❦

The tiny village of CLOGHER is rather unexpectedly, THE OLDEST BISHOPRIC IN IRELAND and boasts a fine cathedral, dedicated to ST MACARTAN, uncle of St Brigid, and a companion of St Patrick, who was made bishop of Clogher by St Patrick himself in 454. The name Clogher is derived from the Cloch Oir, or 'golden stone', that used to sit in the cathedral churchyard. It was once the throne of a gold-covered pagan idol called Cermand Cestach, which was worshipped as an oracle by the northern druids, and came to St Macartan through a druid chief converted to Christianity by the bishop. The last mention of the stone being seen in the churchyard was in 1837.

Clogher is one of the three villages erroneously said to be five miles distant from Fivemiletown, giving that village its unusual name.

Brackenridge's Folly

Not far from Clogher is a square, three-tiered hilltop tower called BRACKENRIDGE'S FOLLY. Brackenridge was actually a local barrister and landlord called George Charles Trimble

(1814–79), who referred to himself as Lord Brackenridge, a title appropriated from his grandmother's name. He apparently carried something of a chip on his shoulder and built the tower as a mausoleum – so that 'the squirearchy who had looked down on him during his lifetime were compelled to look up to him after his death'.

Castlederg

CASTLEDERG, the most westerly town in Co. Tyrone, suffered greatly during the Troubles in the 1970s and has the dubious distinction of being the most bombed small town in Ireland. The family of the 'King of the Wild Frontier', DAVY CROCKETT, who died at the siege of the Alamo in Texas in 1836, emigrated to New York from Castlederg in the 18th century.

Dungannon

————◆◆◆◆————

Once the stronghold from which the O'Neills ruled Ulster, and today home of Tyrone Crystal, DUNGANNON is also the proud possessor of an Afghan fort. Situated in the town centre, the extraordinary castle-like structure, with its projecting apertures from which to hurl missiles at rampaging tribesmen, is actually the police station. It was built to guard the Khyber Pass but because of a bureaucratic mix-up was sent to Dungannon instead. No doubt somewhere in Afghanistan a group of warlords are enjoying tea and toast in the welcome comfort of a cosy Irish police station . . .

Lawyer and politician THOMAS WILSON (1827–1910) was born in Dungannon. He emigrated to America and set up a law practice in Winona, Minnesota, the township where film star Winona Ryder was born and got her name.

Well, I never   *knew this*
about
TYRONE FOLK

Body snatcher WILLIAM BURKE (1792–1829), who along with his colleague William Hare from Newry, Co. Down, found gainful employment supplying cadavers to the Edinburgh medical establishment, was born in URNEY. The two men emigrated to Scotland initially to work as navvies on the Union Canal, but quickly discovered that the doctors in Edinburgh paid good money for dead bodies on which to experiment. They began by digging up corpses from graveyards, but decent specimens were hard to find and they soon moved on to providing their own fresh produce by murdering their tenants and an assortment of local street characters. They were finally caught when the medical students recognised one of the bodies on the dissecting slab, a well-known and much-loved simpleton called 'daft Jamie'.

Astronomer SIR THOMAS MACLEAR (1794–1879) was born in NEWTOWN-STEWART. Although trained as a doctor, and with a thriving medical practice in Bedfordshire in England, Maclear was an enthusiastic amateur astronomer, and in 1833 he was appointed as Her Majesty's Astronomer at the Royal Observatory of the Cape of Good Hope in South Africa. Here he worked closely with John Herschel, son of Sir William Herschel, on a detailed survey of the southern sky. The calculations from their examination of the earth's curvature in the southern hemisphere, which proved invaluable in the later mapping of Southern Africa, were also of immense help to Maclear's great friend, David Livingstone, on the explorer's expeditions to the African interior.

Maclear was married to one of the great beauties of the age, and together they had five children. A crater on the moon is named after him.

Lieutenant-Colonel Latham Valentine Blacker

◄ 1887–1964 ►

Aviator and weapons inventor LATHAM VALENTINE BLACKER was born in LISNAHANNA, near Omagh. In 1933, along with the Marquess of Douglas and Clydesdale and Air Commodore Peregrine Forbes Morant Fellowes, great-uncle of the Oscar-winning writer and actor Julian Fellowes, Lt.-Col. Blacker was part of the expedition that completed the first aeroplane flight over Mt Everest, in an open-cockpit Westland Wallace aircraft.

An enthusiastic inventor since boyhood, when he blew up his

teacher's conservatory at Cheltenham College with a home-made mortar, Blacker devised several effective weapons that were used in the Second World War. These included the Blacker Bombard, a cheap anti-tank mortar that was widely used by the Home Guard, a more substantial Infantry Anti-Tank Projector, modified from the Bombard, that fired explosive projectiles without smoke or a back blast to give away the operator's position, and the Blacker 'Hedgehog', a kind of depth charge that showered the target with mortar bombs and was particularly useful against submarines.

Boxing promoter and bookmaker BARNEY EASTWOOD was born in COOKSTOWN in 1932. After running a local boxing club behind a pub in Carrickfergus, Eastwood opened a show club in Belfast and never looked back. Five boxers won world titles under his management, and among those he promoted were the flyweight from Larne, Dave 'Boy' McAuley, and the 'Clones Cyclone', Barry McGuigan (*see* Co. Monaghan), with whom Eastwood fell out after McGuigan was defeated in Las Vegas by an unknown, Steve Cruz. In his autobiography McGuigan blamed Eastwood for the defeat and this led to a bitter high-profile court case from which Eastwood won substantial damages. *Father Ted* actor Dermot

Morgan composed a comic song based on their relationship called 'Thank You Very Much, Mr Eastwood', which reached No. 1 in the Irish charts.

In 2008 Barney Eastwood sold his betting shop business Eastwood Bookmakers, the largest bookies in Northern Ireland, to Ladbrokes for an estimated £117 million.

World champion snooker player DENNIS TAYLOR was born in COAL-ISLAND in 1949 and became local champion there at the age of 14. Taylor is fondly remembered for his huge trademark spectacles, and for his 1985 world championship final against Steve Davis, when he came back from 8–0 down to win THE FIRST CHAMPIONSHIP EVER TO BE DECIDED ON THE BLACK BALL.

Ryder Cup golfer DARREN CLARKE was born in DUNGANNON in 1968. Between 2000 and 2002 he was ranked in the world top ten.

Gazetteer

Connacht

COUNTY GALWAY

Aughnanure Castle
  Oughterard
  Tel: +353 91 552214
  Email: aughnanurecastle@opw.ie

Galway City Museum
  Spanish Parade, Co. Galway
  Tel: +353 91 532 460
  www.galwaycity.ie

Galway Races
  Galway Race Course, Ballybrit
  Co. Galway
  Tel: +353 91-753870
  www.galwayraces.com

Galway Oyster Festival
  Áras Failte, Co. Galway
  Tel: +353 91 522066
  Fax: +353 91 527282
  www.galwayoysterfest.com

Cregg Castle
  Corandulla, Co. Galway
  Tel: +353 91 791434
  www.creggcastle.com

Dan O'Hara's Cottage
  Lettershea, Clifden, Co. Galway
  Tel +353 95-21808/21246
  Fax: +353 95-22098
  www.connemaraheritage.com

St Cleran's Hotel
  Craughwell
  Tel: +353 91 846555
  Fax: +353 91 846600
  www.stclerans.com

Kylemore Abbey
  Kylemore, Connemara
  Tel: +353 (0) 9541146

COUNTY LEITRIM

Lough Rynn Castle
  Mohill
  Tel: +353 (0)71 9632700
  Fax: +353 (0)71 9632710
  www.loughrynn.ie

COUNTY MAYO

Ballintubber Abbey
  Ballintubber, 7 miles south of
  Castlebar
  Tel: +353 (0)94 9030934
  Fax: +353 (0)94 9030018
  www.ballintubberabbey.ie

Turlough Park House
  Turlough, Castlebar
  Tel: +353 94 24444
  Fax: +353 94 904 7690

Grainne ni Mhaille Centre, (Grace
  O'Malley Centre)
  Church Street, Louisburgh
  Tel: + 353 (0)98 66341

Westport House & Country Park
  Westport
  Tel +353 (0)98 27766 / 25430
  Fax +353 (0)98 25206
  www.westporthouse.ie

COUNTY ROSCOMMON

Boyle Abbey
  Boyle
  Tel: +353 71 9662604
  Fax: +353 71 9664817
  Email: roscreaheritage@opw.ie

Cruachan
  Cruachan Aí Heritage Centre
  Tulsk
  Tel. +353 (0)71 9639268
  www.cruachanai.com

Hells Kitchen Railway Museum
  Main Street
  Castlerea, Co. Roscommon
  Tel: +353 (0)94 96 20181
  www.hellskitchenmuseum.com

Elphin Windmill
  Windmill Road, Elphin,
  Co. Roscommon
  Tel: +353 (0)71 963 5181
  www.discoverireland.com

King House Interpretive Galleries &
  Museum

Main Street, Boyle
  Tel: +353 71 966 3242
  Fax: +353 71 966 3243
  www.kinghouse.ie

O'Carolan Harp Festival
  Keadue, Co. Roscommon
  Tel: +353 (0)71 9647247
  Fax: +353 (0)71 9647511
  www.ocarolanharpfestival.ie

Matt Molloy's
  Bridge Street, Westport
  Tel: +353 (0)98 26655
  www.mattmolloy.com

COUNTY SLIGO

The Model Arts and Niland Gallery
  Sligo
  Tel: 071 914 1405
  www.modelart.ie

Leinster

DUBLIN CITY

Dublin Castle
  Dublin 2
  Tel: +353 1 677 7129
  Fax: +353 679 7831
  www.thedublincastle.com

St James's Gate Brewery
  St James's Gate
  Dublin
  Tel: +353 1 408 4800
  Fax: +353 1 408 4965
  www.guinness-storehouse.com

COUNTY CARLOW

St Laserian's Cathedral
Old Leighlin
Open daily

Mount Wolseley Hotel, Golf and Spa
Resort
Tullow
Tel: +353 59 91 80100
Fax: +353 59 91 52123
www.MountWolseley.ie

COUNTY DUBLIN

Dunsink Observatory
Castleknock, Dublin 15
Tel: +353 1 8387911
Fax: +353 1 8387090
www.science.ie

Luttrellstown Castle
Castleknock Dublin 15
Tel: +353 1 8609500
Fax: +353 1 8609501
www.luttrellstowncastleresort.com

Rathfarnham Castle
Rathfarnham, Dublin 14
Tel: +353 (0)1 4939462
www.rathfarnham.com

COUNTY KILDARE

Larchill Arcadian Gardens
Larchill, Kilcock
Tel: +353 1 628 7354
Fax: +353 1 628 4580
www.larchill.ie

COUNTY KILKENNY

Kilkenny Castle
The Parade, Kilkenny City
Tel: +353 (0)56 772 1450

Fax: +353 (0)56 776 3488
www.kilkenny.ie

Shee Almshouse
Rose Inn Street, Kilkenny
Tel: +353 56 775 1500
www.kilkenny.ie

Rothe House Museum
Kilkenny
Tel: +353 56 7722893
www.kilkenny.ie

St Francis Abbey Brewery
Parliament St, Kilkenny
www.kilkennytourist.com

Kells Priory
Kells
Tel: 056 772 8255 or 056 772 1450

Edmund Ignatius Rice Birthplace
Callan, Kilkenny
Tel: +353 (0)56 772 5141
www.callan800.com

COUNTY LAOIS

Stradbally Steam Museum
Tel: 057 8641878
www.irishsteam.ie

Mountmellick Embroidery
www.mountmellick.net

Castle Durrow Country House
Hotel
Durrow
Tel: +353 (0)57 8736555
Fax: +353 (0)57 8736559
www.castledurrow.com

COUNTY LONGFORD

Tel: +353 (0)43 86643/86086/86721
Fax: +353 (0)43 86922
www.granard.harp.net

COUNTY LOUTH

Cooley Distillery
  Riverstown, Cooley
  Tel: +353 (0)42 937 6102
  Fax: +353 (0)42 937 6484
  www.cooleywhiskey.com

Beaulieu House, Gardens & Car
  Museum
  Beaulieu, Drogheda
  Tel: +353 (0)41 983 8557
  Fax: +353 (0)41 984 5051
  www.beaulieu.ie

COUNTY MEATH

Sonairte, The Ninch
  Laytown
  Tel: 041 982 7572
  www.sonairte.org

Slane Castle
  Tel: 041 988 4400
  www.slanecastle.ie

COUNTY OFFALY

Charleville Forest Castle
  Tullamore
  Undergoing Refurbishment

Cloghan Castle
  Lusmagh, near Banagher
  Open for guided tours in summer
  Tel: +353 (0)509 51650

Leap Castle
  Clareen
  Open Daily

COUNTY WESTMEATH

Old Kilbeggan Distillery
  Kilbeggan
  Tel: +353 (0)57 933 2183
  Fax: +353 (0)57 933 2139
  www.cooleywhiskey.com

COUNTY WEXFORD

Browne Clayton Monument
  Carrigbyrne, Wexford
  Open Daily

Dunbrody Abbey
  Visitor Centre, Campile
  Tel: +353 (0)51 38 8603
  www.dunbrodyabbey.com

COUNTY WICKLOW

Wicklow Head Lighthouse
  Tel: +353 (0)1 670 4733
  Fax: +353 (0)1 670 4887
  www.irishlandmark.com

Avondale House and Forest Park
  Rathdrum
  Tel: 0404 46111
  Fax: 0404 46333
  www.coillteoutdoors.ie

Munster

COUNTY CLARE

O'Brien Tower
  Cliffs of Moher New Visitor
  Experience
  Tel: +353 (0)65 7086141
  Fax: +353 (0)65 7086142
  www.cliffsofmoher.ie

Willie Clancy Summer School
  Miltown Malbay
  Tel: +353 65 708 4281
  www.willieclancy-
  summerschool.com

Lisdoonvarna Matchmaking Festival
  The Hydro Hotel Lisdoonvarna
  Tel: +353 65 7074005
  www.matchmakerireland.com

Dromoland Castle
  Newmarket-On-Fergus
  Tel: +353 61 368144
  Fax: +353 61 363355
  www.dromoland.ie

The Little Ark
  Our Lady, Star of the Sea Church
  Kilbaha
  Open Daily

Biddy Early Brewery
  Inagh, Ennis
  Tel: +353 65 6836742
  Fax: +353 65 6836742
  www.beb.ie

Michael Cusack Centre, Carron
  Tel : +353 (0)65 7089944
  Fax: +353 (0)65 7089942
  www.michaelcusack.ie

COUNTY CORK

Schull Planetarium
  Colla Road, Schull
  Tel: +353 2828315
  www.schull.ie

Clear Island
  Tel: +353 28 39153
  Fax: +353 28 39164
  www.capeclearisland.com

COUNTY KERRY

Sheehan's Thatched House
  Finuge Cross, Listowel
  Tel: +353 (0)68 40203
  www.finugeweekend.com/thatched-
  house

COUNTY LIMERICK

Castle Oliver
  Ballyhoura Mountains
  Tel: +353 1 6607975
  Tel: +353 87 9720602
  www.castleoliver.net

Curragh Chase Forest Park
  Kilcornan
  Tel: +353 61 337322

COUNTY TIPPERARY

Holycross Abbey, Thurles
  Tel: +353 0504/43124 or 43118
  Fax: +353 0504
  www.holycrossabbey.ie

COUNTY WATERFORD

St Declan's Cathedral, Ardmore
  www.ardmoretidytowns.ie

Peare's Motor Works
  Catherine Street, Waterford (Blue
  Plaque)

Ulster

BELFAST

Belfast Castle
  Antrim Road
  Belfast
  Tel: 028 90370133
  www.belfastcastle.co.uk

Botanic Gardens
Tel: 028 90314762
www.belfastcity.gov.uk/parks
andopenspaces

Ulster Museum
Tel: 028 9042 8428
Fax: 028 9042 8728
www.ulstermuseum.org.uk

COUNTY ANTRIM

Dunluce Castle
On A2 approximately 3 miles East
of Portrush on the road to
Bushmills
Tel: 028 207 31938
www.northantrim.com/dunluce-
castle

COUNTY ARMAGH

Armagh Observatory
College Hill, Armagh
Tel: 028 3752 2928
Fax: 028 3752 7174
www.arm.ac.uk

Tandragee Castle Factory
Main Street, Tandragee
Tel: 028 3884 0249
Fax: 028 3884 0085
www.tayto.com

Gate Lodge, Milford
3 Ballyards Road, Milford
Tel: 028 3752 5467
www.milfordhouse.org.uk

COUNTY CAVAN

Cabra Castle Hotel, Cootehill
Tel: +353 42 966 7030

COUNTY DERRY

St Aidan's and Denis O'Hempsey's
burial place
Near Magilligan
Country lanes off the Coleraine to
Limavady road
Open Daily

COUNTY DONEGAL

Donagh Cross
Carndonagh, Inishowen
Tel: +353 74 9374933/34
Fax: +353 74 9374935
www.visitinishowen.com

Allingham Literary Festival
Dicey Reilly's Bar and Office
Licence, Market Street,
Ballyshannon
Tel: +353 (0)71 9851646
www.ballyshannonfolkfestival.com

COUNTY DOWN

Greyabbey
Tel: 028 9054 6552
www.ehsni.gov.uk

COUNTY FERMANAGH

Enniskillen Castle
Castle Barracks, Enniskillen
Tel: 028 6632 5000
www.enniskillencastle.co.uk

Cole's Monument
Forthill Park, Enniskillen
Tel: 028 6632 5050
www.goireland.com/fermanagh/
cole-s-monument

COUNTY MONAGHAN

Tyrone Guthrie Centre,
Annaghmakerrig House, Newbliss
Tel: +353 (0)47 54003
Fax: +353 (0)47 54380
www.tyroneguthrie.ie

COUNTY TYRONE

St Macartan's Cathedral, Clogher
Open daily

Brackenridge's Folly
Near Clogher
Open daily

Index of People

Index of Places